BIZ-WAR
AND THE OUT-OF-POWER ELITE

The Progressive-Left Attack on the Corporation

BIZ-WAR
AND THE OUT-OF-POWER ELITE

The Progressive-Left Attack on the Corporation

Jarol B. Manheim
The George Washington University

LEA LAWRENCE ERLBAUM ASSOCIATES, PUBLISHERS
2004 Mahwah, New Jersey   London

Director, Editorial:	Lane Akers
Executive Assistant:	Bonita D'Amil
Cover Design:	Kathryn Houghtaling Lacey
Textbook Production Manager:	Paul Smolenski
Full-Service Compositor:	TechBooks
Text and Cover Printer:	Sheridan Books, Inc.

This book was typeset in 10.5/11.5 pt. Goudy Old Style, Bold, and Italic.
The heads were typeset in Goudy Old Style, Bold, and Bold Italic.

Copyright © 2004 by Jarol B. Manheim
All rights reserved. No part of this book may be reproduced in any form, by photostat, microform, retrieval system, or any other means, without prior written permission of the author and the publisher.

Lawrence Erlbaum Associates, Inc., Publishers
10 Industrial Avenue
Mahwah, New Jersey 07430
www.erlbaum.com

A summary version of the argument of the book was presented as Jarol B. Manheim, "Biz-War: Origins, Structure and Strategy of Foundation-NGO Network Warfare on Corporations in the United States," Conference on the International NGO Phenomenon, American Enterprise Institute, June, 2003. Portions of Chapter 5 are drawn from Jarol B. Manheim, *Corporate Conduct Unbecoming: Codes of Conduct and Anti-Corporate Strategy* (St. Michael's, MD: Tred Avon Institute Press, 2000). Figures 2.1, 3.1, 6.1, 8.1, 8.2, and 9.1-9.4 were prepared using Borgatti, S.P., Everett, M.G. and Freeman, L.C. *Ucinet for Windows: Software for Social Network Analysis*, Version 6.12. Harvard: Analytic Technologies, 2002.

Library of Congress Cataloging-in-Publication Data

Manheim, Jarol B., 1946–
    Biz-war and the out-of-power elite : the progressive-left attack
on the corporation / Jarol B. Manheim.
        p.   cm.
    Includes index.
    ISBN 0-8058-5068-6 (casebound : alk. paper)
    1. Industrial policy—United States.   2. Liberalism—United States.
3. Corporations—Moral and ethical aspects—United States.   4. Social responsibility of business—United States.   5. Business and politics—United States.   I. Title.

    HD3616.U46M27   2004
    338.0973—dc22   2003022775

Books published by Lawrence Erlbaum Associates are printed on acid-free paper, and their bindings are chosen for strength and durability.

Printed in the United States of America
10 9 8 7 6 5 4 3 2 1

Table of Contents

v

He was for the student of philosophy like the model skeleton who hangs on his peg in anatomy class. He is on the one hand an artificial creation; no actual skeleton hangs together like that, and he corresponds to no person we know, either living or dead. His obvious unreality makes him, despite his macabre appearance, slightly ridiculous. Students give him absurd names and wheel him out for practical jokes and pranks.

But when class begins, we realize he reveals something important, something concealed beneath the skin, muscle, and tissue. He reveals the hidden structure, the essential anatomical parts and relationships without which none of the rest could exist. He exposes to us our own essential reality, stripped of outward appearance—he shows the bones, the marrow, the core of things.

Arthur Herman, *How the Scots Invented the Modern World*

Preface

It is the argument of this book that the contemporary Progressive movement in the United States, designed to replace the Liberalism whose demise was the object and accomplishment of the Reagan Revolution, is the product of a series of strategic experiments and decisions by activists in organized labor, in the environmental and human rights movements, and elsewhere on the Left, guided by an antipathy to the business community and by an understanding of the forces that had contributed to the resurgence of the American Right in the 1970s and 1980s.

This is not an argument about competing ideologies *per se* but about the strategies and tactics by which one set of ideologues—on the Left—has chosen to contend with its competitors to the Center and Right. It is composed of five elements:

1. a guiding empirical theory of social, political, and economic organization;
2. selection of nomenclature around which, and construction of an enemy against which, to rebuild a political movement;
3. development of an institutional counterstructure;
4. development and adaptation of a strategy of attack; and
5. the waging of a social netwar against the identified enemy—the corporation as a political and economic institution.

It is this final element that gives the book—and the phenomenon around which it is built—its distinctive title: *Biz-War*.

It is, in a sense, a rather odd book for me to write, for it is a book about ideologues, and I do not regard myself as an ideological person—postmodern deconstructionists to the contrary notwithstanding. It matters not whether the ideology in question is grounded in the Left, in the Right, or in a piece of pecan pie. I have always been fascinated less by the colorful philosophical banners around which true believers rally than by the strategies and tactics employed by their leaders to attract and mobilize them.

Yet in another sense, this book is a natural. It grows directly out of my last one, *The Death of a Thousand Cuts: Corporate Campaigns and the Attack on the Corporation*, in which I examined the use of multidimensional attacks on corporations by organized labor to pressure them into meeting demands that ranged from unionization of the workforce to specific contract concessions. Labor was forced to develop this attack strategy because it was losing market share, influence, and legitimacy, and because the tried and true methods of the past—NLRB-administered elections and strikes—no longer met its needs. As a movement, labor was in a death spiral and was desperate to escape it. Corporate campaigns, which have at their center a framing of the corporation as a social outlaw, together with a collection of other recruitment and mobilization strategies, offered perhaps the only salvation. So it came to pass that unions adopted the corporate campaign as a primary mode of operation and in the process began a decades-long assault on the reputations of individual companies and on the standing of the corporation itself.

But labor was not alone in its power failure. By the 1980s, lights were going out all across the Liberal Left. The conservative onslaught that put Ronald Reagan in the White House in 1981 wrought devastation on every ideological outpost in its path. New Deal programs that had literally defined the role of government in American society for two generations were swept aside. Taxes were slashed to make sure these programs could not easily find new purchase. And by the time Newt Gingrich became Speaker of the House in 1994 with the first Republican majority in nearly half a century, the Liberals had been deprived even of their name. Who would dare speak "the dreaded L-word"?

Then, just when things were looking most hopeless, the Left found a new vision, or perhaps more accurately, rediscovered an old one. For the corporate campaign—the new strategy being employed by organized labor—had actually been developed not by the unions but by activists of the so-called New Left of the 1960s and 1970s. It was anticipated in the *Port Huron Statement*, a manifesto drafted for the Students for a Democratic Society (SDS) by Tom Hayden in 1962, and was first codified in 1970 by a coalition formed by SDS, the National Council of Churches and others. But in the early 1970s, many of these activists were consumed by the anti-war protests of the late Vietnam Era, and their anti-corporate strategies did little more than gather dust. It was at about that time that labor became aware of these strategies and began to develop them for its own purposes.

Now, life has come full circle. Because labor unions of the period, as noted, suffered from poor reputations and lack of public support, they found it expedient to build coalitions with nonlabor activists, such as environmentalists and human rights advocates, and to channel many of their attacks on targeted companies through these surrogates. Over the years, many such groups that worked with labor came to understand and appreciate the potential uses of these techniques to serve their own ends. They began to conduct their own campaigns, this time to force changes in corporate policies on environmental and other issues. And as the post-Reagan Left reconfigured itself, its numbers were joined by more inherently ideological activists who introduced a new, quasi-religious fervor into the mix. The result has been an increasing number of campaigns against companies and an increasingly philosophical attack on

the corporation itself. Where the unions had some discernible common interest in preserving the companies they targeted—because those companies
were the sources of members or potential members—as a result of which their
range of actions was self-limiting, the new activists often see the corporation
as fundamentally evil and therefore are willing to carry their attacks further.
For this reason, it makes sense to label them not corporate campaigns, but
anti-corporate campaigns.

But there is much more to contemporary activism on the Left than a new
tactical toolbox. There is a new objective—to build an alternative power
structure—and a new set of strategies to achieve it. The alternative power
structure—I call it here the Out-of-Power Elite—is based on an understanding
of the old power structure as seen from the Left. Much of the activism we see
today is designed for one of two purposes—either to undermine confidence
in the political and economic establishment or to replicate portions of the
current system but under new management and with a new purpose. The
strategy being employed to this end is to build and deploy extensive and
well-funded networks of advocates to wage what is termed a social netwar
against the same establishment. And because, from the perspective of the
Left, the corporation is the central player in, and beneficiary of, the existing
power structure, it is the corporation that becomes the essential target of their
activism. The result? *Biz-War*.

This book examines the history, theory, objectives, strategy, and tactics of
the Progressive Left in the context of its attack on the corporation as a social—
the Left would say anti-social—institution. It is intended to illuminate the
dynamics of movement building (and of corporate bashing) but not to render
a judgment on the merits of one or the other point of view. The book is based
on a wide variety of sources and methods, among them an extensive review
of media coverage of the organizations and campaigns discussed here, news
releases, publications and other materials produced by the activists, interviews
and conversations with knowledgeable individuals, correspondence, Internet
postings, case law summaries, publicly available tax and regulatory filings,
documents, and other materials.

It is not my intention, nor is it my claim, to have reinvented the wheel.
Various aspects of the argument presented here have been developed by other
researchers—John Arquilla and David Ronfeldt, Margaret Keck and Kathryn
Sikkink, and Manuel Castells, to name but a few—and their work is gratefully
acknowledged. And as long ago as 1981, William T. Poole of the Heritage
Foundation, in a report entitled "The Attack on the Corporation," produced
an analysis of the anti-corporate agenda on the Left, much of which has
proven highly predictive of events in the years since. My hope is that the
present volume will help the reader to weave together these important ideas
and observations into a coherent whole that will give new meaning to a great
many events of our own time.

Having acknowledged this scholarly grounding, let me hasten to say that
Biz-War is intended less as an exercise in basic research than as an exercise in

applying to advantage much that we already know. It is my argument here—backed with some evidence—that the activists on the Left are directly aware of the relevant theories and research and have knowingly used them to advance their cause. Indeed, as we will see, some of the very scholars who developed the theories and methods discussed here have themselves been participants in the action.

As in all such efforts, the burden for accuracy, clarity, and insight in these pages rests squarely on the author's shoulders. I accept it willingly. But that is not to say that I completed the book without a great deal of assistance and support. To Jeff and Dan, to Mike and Don and Gary, to Pat, and especially to Steve—thank you. Thanks, too, to Lane Akers, for his continuing faith in these books, and to all his colleagues at Lawrence Erlbaum Associates—Bonita D'Amil, Susan Barker, and Paul Smolenski—and to Susan Detwiler at TechBooks, who have helped to bring them into being. And thanks to everyone else who has supported—or tolerated—this effort over the last several years. I hope these pages convince you it was worthwhile.

—Jarol B. Manheim

BIZ-WAR
AND THE OUT-OF-POWER ELITE

The Progressive-Left Attack on the Corporation

1

Epiphany

Every so often in American politics there comes a point in time, a moment of pristine clarity—be it a decade, a year, a month, or even a day—when everything changes or more, correctly, when changes that have been under way for a long time are suddenly crystallized by events, by experience, or by some insight. Some portion of the political world reorganizes itself. And for those caught in the refracted light of the new era, nothing is ever the same again.

The Great Depression was such a time. It changed the way Americans thought of government and its proper role in national affairs. The Vietnam Era and Watergate were such a time. Together they wrapped a people long characterized by innocence, blind trust, and political naiveté in a new cloak of pessimism, distrust, and cynicism. September 11, 2001, was such a time. It fundamentally changed the way Americans understood the world and ended, perhaps forever, their teen-like sense of invulnerability. And for those on the political Left, the so-called Liberal Elite and their minions, the 1980s Reagan–Bush assault on their dominance of the political culture was such a time. It changed the way they thought about themselves.

Indeed, such was the breadth and intensity of the Reagan–Bush attack that, for a time, those on the Left did not know what to think. They had not a clue about how to survive politically, let alone how to respond. It would not be overstatement to describe the American Left of the 1980s as wholly in disarray.

Yet today, some 20 years later, while the forces of conservatism remain ascendant, the Left—much transformed—has been reinvigorated and, in the tradition of long cycles in American politics, may be on its way to reclaiming influence. Out of chaos has emerged a more or less unified, more or less organized, and more or less effective American Left, which, for want of a better term and taking a cue from its adherents, I label the Progressive Left or the new Progressive Movement.

The objective of this book is to tell the story of this resurgence. Or perhaps more correctly, its purpose is to tell *a* story of the rising anew of the American Left. For there are many ways to cut this cake, and this is but a slim volume, not intended as a comprehensive history. This book focuses on the ways Progressive activists have used the very tools of their own destruction—the power of language, perception management, media manipulation, control over elite and quasi-elite institutions to generate and advance a political agenda, and just plain smarts—to restake a claim to a legitimate place at the political table.

Although this is a story of the twenty-first century, its roots reach deep into the soil of the twentieth. And though, at story's end, we arrive at a manifest destination, that destination point itself is best understood not as a map dot but as the conjunction of many roads traversing a unique political landscape that has given them shape as well as direction.

If we could map this landscape—and the premise here is that we can—it would include at least the following elements:

- The rise and fall of the labor-and-working-class-based Old Left and its displacement in the 1960s and beyond by an intellectual-and-middle-class-based New Left;
- The development in the social sciences, and more particularly among students of political sociology, of a comprehensive argument about how power in America's faux democracy was, in fact, exercised by an interlocked and relatively closed network of social and economic elites;
- A demonstration on the Right, limited in scope but genuinely impressive in effect, of how this networked power structure could be replicated on a smaller scale by a highly motivated ideological cohort to achieve political power;
- A fundamental change in the language of politics that forced the Left, over time, to redefine its objectives and to recast its own image;
- A long-developing change in the structure and distribution of capital that at last began to mature and, critically, a new recognition by a few on the Left of its significance and potential utility;
- The development and rapid widespread adoption of a new technology, the Internet, that facilitated communication and organization among those for whom these had been unduly expensive and difficult to achieve; and, certainly not least,
- The emergence, partly by design and partly by serendipity, of a plan—a systematic scheme for reclaiming both legitimacy and power.

That plan was simple in concept if not in implementation: Reverse engineer the political system. Rather than overthrowing, figuratively speaking, the interlocked, networked structure by which power was effectively exercised to the disadvantage of the Left, capture that structure or, in the alternative, mimic it with a parallel network to produce what is to the Left a more salubrious set of outcomes. And, recognizing that the ideology of the Left is no more representative of majority public opinion in the United States than that of the Right, find an organizing symbol around which to frame an argument to make it more palatable to the vast political middle. In effect, find an enemy—one people are already predisposed to distrust and one whose weight can be hung like a rock around the neck of the Right.

The Left found that enemy in big business—more specifically, in the corporation, a decidedly impersonal legal construct with a serious image problem. It built its rival network of interlocked organizations and institutions. It honed its rhetoric, tactics, and strategy into a dynamic methodology of attack, the so-called anti-corporate campaign. And it began, by the 1990s, to wage a political war on the corporation and, through it, on the underlying structure of American political power that, in its view, rested on a bedrock of wealth and, more specifically, the massive business enterprises that generated wealth.

The Left began to wage Biz-War.

Although this campaign to reclaim power and redirect its purposes has yet to come to fruition, its elements are today well defined, well positioned, and increasingly well established. Biz-War is being waged on all fronts—from the forest and the field to the marketplace, from the bargaining table to the dinner table, from the banks to the churches and the local coffee shops. Corporate greed. Corporate indifference. Corporate welfare. Corporate scandal. Corporate malfeasance. Corporate corruption. Corporate crime. These are the images of battle, and they fill the nation's newspapers and television screens. The American people want reform. They want change. They want justice.

But these corporate constructs, these verbal associations, are in some measure images of convenience—a knowing and purposeful exploitation, at least by some, of the contemporary stew of events, underlying public perceptions and sheer cupidity or stupidity on the part of certain corporate leaders. For where the public sees the prospect of reform as an end in itself and a solution to the "problem" posed by antisocial corporate behaviors, some on the Left see the promise of reform as little more than a mask, a façade behind which they are free to pursue a far more fundamental restructuring of the American polity.

The early years of the current century certainly have seen their share of genuine corporate wrongdoing—at Enron, at WorldCom, at Global Crossing, at Arthur Andersen, and at a host of other companies whose executives proved to be genuine bad actors. Their deeds—and the very real harm they have done—have helped to make corporation bashing into a sport that is fun for the whole family. Indeed, they follow a well-trod path through history, a trail marked by villains such as Thomas M. Durant of the Union Pacific Railroad in the Grant-era Credit Mobilier Scandal, Harry Sinclair of Sinclair Oil in the Teapot Dome Scandal, Robert Vesco in a 1960s investment scandal, and many others. But, even as they fertilize the ground on which the battle is to be fought, these true corporate outlaws are not what Biz-War is about.

Biz-War is not about reform, it is about reformation. Biz-War is not about change, it is about transformation. Biz-War is not about justice, it is about power.

Biz-War takes many forms: anti-globalization demonstrations, but also shareholder resolutions and corporate governance initiatives; class-action lawsuits, but also legislative actions and regulatory complaints; media events, but also real pressures on Wall Street; institutional attacks, but also highly personal ones. Biz-War is being waged all around us, but in ways that are so closely integrated with our everyday routines and so closely aligned with public expectations that most people fail to notice, let alone to recognize it for what it is—a challenge to the established social order.

Biz-War is, arguably, the dominant fact of political life in the early twenty-first century. And the most overlooked.

That is, of course, a rather bald assertion. To defend it, and to convince readers of its accuracy, let me begin with a somewhat less abbreviated overview of the political cartography that I laid out a moment ago. In this way, I believe, we will begin to see that all roads do lead to that junction in time and political space where the regenerative needs of the Left, the cultural vulnerabilities of the corporation, the social technology of the anti-corporate campaign, developments in theory and research in political sociology, and the bright bulb of activist insight intersect. Or, put another way, all roads lead to Biz-War.

SOMETHING OLD, SOMETHING NEW: THE SAGA OF THE LATTER-DAY AMERICAN LEFT

If we think of the full spectrum of global political ideologies as ranging from the salad fork to the soup spoon, we can say with some assurance that the totality of American political discourse from Left to Right takes place well within the confines of the dinner plate. That is not to say that there are no far Left or far Right voices to be heard, but only that no one is listening. There is a range of potentially influential opinion on the Left, then, but it is a relatively narrow one, and somewhere between the middle of the plate and the edge there is a line of demarcation. To the right of that line—nearest the political center—there is a constituency and a grant of legitimacy; to the left there is neither. What Reagan and Bush did in the 1980s was to move that line very near to the center of the plate. This was an act of some historic significance, at least in the intermediate term. But to understand how and why it was significant, and why, in a sense, it marks the true starting point for our own story, we need a little history lesson.

At the risk of gross oversimplification, let us divide the pre-Reagan–Bush American political Left into two clusters: one that operated within the sphere of electoral politics—call them the Liberals—and one that operated without regard to such considerations—call them the Ideologues. The distinction was one of both style and substance. The Liberals were not only more centrist in their views but more willing to compromise and to follow public opinion to achieve power. The Ideologues were more radical and less compromising in their views but also tended to view power as the means to redirect public opinion rather than the reverse. Still, on matters of policy, it is probably fair to say that there was some modicum of agreement between the two groups, and each was more likely to feel more at ease politically with the other than with anyone further away from the mashed potatoes.

It was not always so. This sometimes delicate balance was itself a product of the pitch, roll, and yaw of history. The frame for understanding the American Left traces back to the October 1917 revolution in Czarist Russia, the revolution that brought the Bolsheviks, the most radical faction of the Russian Communist Party, to power. This event touched off a worldwide wave of revolutionary and terrorist activity—not so much guided by the Russian revolutionaries as inspired by them—and for a time scared the silk pants off the leading capitalists of the day.

The economic and political stability of United States was never fundamentally threatened by these events, but neither did the nation escape unaffected. In the international arena, thousands of American troops were dispatched to Siberia as components of what was known as the Allied Expeditionary Force, a substantial army of the Western alliance dispatched ostensibly to reopen an Eastern front in the war against Germany but in truth to limit the spread of anticapitalist ideology. The campaign continued into April 1920, nearly 2 years after the war's end, and it remains a source of lingering Russian distrust of American intentions to this day. But the more significant action came in the domestic arena.

The year 1919 was like no other in American history before or since, except perhaps for 1968. As I have summarized this period elsewhere[1]:

> Cities were burning across the country, and racial hatred had surfaced in North and South alike. Jobs were tight because of the large number of returning veterans, and those lucky enough to have jobs were refusing in record numbers to perform them. Industrialization and modernization were proceeding apace, but the government had just determined that the nation's supply of oil, which was becoming an increasingly vital fuel, could last only ten more years. The President of the United States (Wilson) had suffered a debilitating stroke, and it appeared that the nation was drifting for lack of leadership. American women had just been given the vote. And American boys were still fighting in an icy wasteland halfway around the world because a year and a half earlier some godless Russians had denounced everything that Americans thought they stood for and everything that the greatest war in the history of mankind had sought to establish. (pp. 215–216)

It was, to say the least, a traumatic time. And it set the stage for what was to come.

In early February 1919, some 35,000 shipyard workers in Seattle went out on strike, and, when management declined to negotiate with them—unions at the time were regarded as illegitimate and subversive organizations—the city's Central Labor Council and several local unions agreed to walk off their jobs in sympathy. This amounted to a threat of a general strike and produced a run on local stores, which sold out of everything from butter to guns. And when the local newspapers labeled the threat of a general strike as a Bolshevik and anarchist tactic, the feeding frenzy commenced. The strike itself was short-lived, but the memory lingered on. Seattle's mayor resigned his office and embarked on a nationwide speaking tour decrying the dangers of the "red menace." And as the number of strikes across the country increased to more than 300 a month—products of the war's end and the associated dislocations—newspaper after newspaper described them as Communist plots. There were also several instances of what would be described today as terrorist bombings, including, among others, an effort to seize the United States arsenal in Pittsburgh, a series of mail bombs sent to leading politicians and industrialists such as Supreme Court Justice Oliver Wendell Holmes and John D. Rockefeller, and blasts that demolished the front of the home of the Attorney General and claimed 34 lives on Wall Street. Then, in September 1919, the Communist Party of the United States was formed for the stated purpose of stimulating industrial unrest and destroying the capitalist system. Not surprisingly, these events produced a significant political backlash, not least of which was reinforcement of the already deep distrust of organized labor or any left of center political voice.[2]

Alhough things calmed down for a time after 1920, the images of the period remained fresh and may well have contributed to the contrary excesses of the decade that followed. They most certainly framed the fears that spread far and wide when the good times came crashing to an end in the Great Depression. It is, then, all the more surprising that it was the Depression, and the New Deal coalition to which it gave rise, that ultimately legitimized both organized labor and, to a point, the American Left. Returning to the dinner plate analogy, it was during the New Deal years that the line of demarcation between legitimate and illegitimate voices first moved left of center. Liberalism—more specifically, New Deal, big government, problem-solving Liberalism—became acceptable, then chic, and then the predominant chord in the political hymnal. Those who had been forever on the outside of the power structure looking in suddenly found themselves on the inside and looking out. Even organized labor gained legitimacy during this time, its rights and objectives codified in the National Labor Relations Act and other legislation.

There was, of course, no real choice in the matter. With the threat of anarchy a recent memory, with a functioning model of revolutionary change in play just an ocean away, and with their failings on display for all to plainly see, the power elite of the era were greatly at risk. It was the political genius of Franklin D. Roosevelt, himself a card-carrying member of that elite, that found a way to manage the risk and yet preserve much of the underlying structure of American capitalism. Although hardly seen as such in his own day, Roosevelt was, by historical standards, very much a conservative's Liberal.

Going into the New Deal, organized labor was viewed as anti-American syndicalism; Negroes were routinely excluded from voting and deprived of equality in many other aspects of citizenship and daily life; women were largely confined to roles as homemakers or to third-tier jobs supervised by men; the courts eschewed any role in the making of public policy; and the regulatory burden on business was, despite the initiatives of the Progressive Movement some years earlier, minimal by contemporary standards. By the 1960s, organized labor was not only accepted as a legitimate political and economic actor but as a powerful one; blacks had gained access to the system and full political rights and were advancing their economic agenda; women had redefined their roles and were on the way to establishing their economic independence; the courts were thoroughly enmeshed in the policy process; and the government's regulatory authority was vastly expanded. These changes and others associated with them were, in a sort of iterative and self-reinforcing process, at once the engines and the products of New Deal liberalism. They found their 1960s voice in John F. Kennedy's New Frontier and Lyndon B. Johnson's Great Society, programs that envisioned government as the great equalizer, the antidote to social and economic disparity.

It was, one would think, the Liberal Moment.

Think again. For at this Liberal Moment, the New Deal coalition lay in tatters, its labor members estranged from its social activists by disagreements over everything from human rights to economics, by divergent views on Vietnam, and even, in some instances, by labor's support for the reviled Richard Nixon. The Liberal agenda had run its course, its white knights having slain all the available dragons. It's leadership was tired and in some cases dishonored. And within a few short years, the nation found itself held hostage, at least figuratively, by a radical Islamic regime in Iran that was itself, arguably, a consequence of a failed American policy.

Out toward the salad fork, of course, more radical voices were emerging, voices calling for change more fundamental than anything the establishment Liberals would brook. There were the voices of the Old Left—the Left of Karl Marx, of class conflict, and of an ideology grounded in the rising up of labor. But more and more, there were the voices of the so-called *New* Left—the Left of C. Wright Mills, of campus organizing, and of an ideology grounded in the rising up of ideas. At the forefront of this movement, at least for a time, was Students for a Democratic Society (SDS). I have detailed elsewhere the nature of SDS and its central role as an incubator for the ideas and the leaders that have dominated the Left for an entire generation.[3] Let us take that as a given, though I return to it later in this narrative. For the moment, what is of particular significance in the SDS experience is the group's ideological underpinning, and specifically its grounding in the sociological theories of Professor Mills.

THE POWER ELITE

Charles Wright Mills, born in Waco, Texas, in 1916, graduated from Dallas Technical High School in 1934, intending to pursue a career in architecture or engineering. But after an unhappy year at Texas A&M, he transferred to the University of Texas, where he redirected his interests to the social sciences—philosophy, economics, and sociology. He received his B.A. and M.A. in philosophy in 1939 and then undertook his graduate work at the University of Wisconsin, completing a dissertation on pragmatism, and received his doctoral degree in 1941. He then taught at the University of Maryland before moving to Columbia University in 1945, where he remained through the balance of his brief career. He died of heart disease in 1962 at the age of 45.[4]

Always a maverick, Mills made his mark on his discipline—and became, arguably, the most influential American sociologist of his century—through a trilogy of books published between 1948 and 1956. *The New Men of Power: America's Labor Leaders* (1948) took a critical look at the "management" of the American labor movement and, in the process, offered a critical assessment of the American Left of that era—what Mills divided into the Leninist and Independent Lefts and what today would be termed the Old Left. Both, in his view, relied on claims and assumptions about the working class that were simplistic and disconnected from reality. As he summarized in describing the Leninists[5]:

> Although some of the college educated in the far left work in factories, the membership is certainly not predominantly wage workers. The main source of supply has been one or two of the New York City colleges. As people of faith, members are dedicated, rationalized, and inflexible; they always have great political will and vast energies, and sometimes a little vision. Given their inconsequential power, they often seem like bureaucrats without a bureaucracy. (p. 16)

Of the Independent Left, he observed[6]:

> In the main, the independents are upper-class and upper-middle-class people, many of them professional, some of them writers with independent incomes.... Since [World War II], the independent left has grown somewhat, having been augmented by ex-liberals...and by discouraged socialists of every brand. It is as if all bankrupt left movements...have left behind a small and stalwart residue. (p. 17)

If he saw the Left as a collection of ciphers and dilettantes relegated to the fringes of American society, what was his view of the great middle? In *White Collar: The American Middle Classes* (1951), Mills offered a perspective on the rapidly expanding post-war phenomenon of middle class life that was, in its way, equally critical. He saw the middle class, in essence, as an economic resource to be managed for the benefit of business, for which it was at once the labor force and the customer base, and as politically flat-lined. In his rather dismissive words, most Americans were[7]:

Not radical, not liberal, not conservative, not reactionary; they are inactionary; they are out of it. If we accept the Greek's definition of the idiot as the privatized man, then we must conclude that the U.S. citizenry is now largely composed of idiots. (p. 328)

These two volumes attracted attention—and, as one might expect, critics— but they were mere prelude to the main event. For it was through the third book in this series, *The Power Elite* (1956), that Mills made his true mark. Here Mills described a new and for many a compelling view of the American polity, a system with all the trappings of democracy, yet one that was in truth dominated by a relatively small cadre of economic, political, and military elites who exercised power by virtue of position. In Mills' words[8]:

The power elite is composed of men whose positions enable them to transcend the ordinary environments of ordinary men and women; they are in positions to make decisions having major consequences. . . . [T]hey are in command of the major hierarchies and organizations of modern society. They rule the big corporations. They run the machinery of the state and claim its prerogatives. They direct the military establishment. They occupy the strategic command posts of the social structure, in which are now centered the effective means of the power and the wealth and the celebrity which they enjoy. (pp. 3–4)

In a series of chapters dedicated to specific subelites, Mills then examined groups such as celebrities, the very rich, chief executives and the corporate rich, and those he termed the "warlords" and the "political directorate." In all of this, Mills rejected the simplistic class-based notions of the Old Left. He did not see the power elite as a capitalist class, per se, but instead as an organizational elite, one in which entry might be facilitated by wealth but in which the power resided not in the wealthy but in the corporations themselves.[9]

Taken together, these three volumes constitute a scathing critique of American society as one in which an elite maintains power through the control of major societal institutions and exploits a massive and relatively passive middle class both economically and—through a patina-deep set of democratic practices—politically, while those who might constitute a countervailing force—the Left by whatever label—remain smug, out of touch, and ineffective. It was not a portrait calculated to win many friends.

But it was a view that attracted a great deal of attention—even, it seems, from then-President Dwight D. Eisenhower who, in his farewell address in 1961 warned[10]:

[The] conjunction of an immense military establishment and a large arms industry is new in the American experience. The total influence—economic, political, even spiritual—is felt in every city, every State house, every office of the Federal government. We recognize the imperative need for this development. Yet we must not fail to comprehend its grave implications. Our toil, resources and livelihood are all involved; so is the very structure of our society.

In the councils of government, we must guard against the acquisition of unwarranted influence, whether sought or unsought, by the military-industrial complex. The potential for the disastrous rise of misplaced power exists and will persist. . . .

Akin to, and largely responsible for the sweeping changes in our industrial-military posture, has been the technological revolution during recent decades.

In this revolution, research has become central; it also becomes more formalized, complex, and costly. A steadily increasing share is conducted for, by, or at the direction of, the Federal government.

Today, the solitary inventor, tinkering in his shop, has been overshadowed by task forces of scientists in laboratories and testing fields. In the same fashion, the free university, historically the fountainhead of free ideas and scientific discovery, has experienced a revolution in the conduct of research. Partly because of the huge costs involved, a government contract becomes virtually a substitute for intellectual curiosity. For every old blackboard there are now hundreds of new electronic computers.

The prospect of domination of the nation's scholars by Federal employment, project allocations, and the power of money is ever present and is gravely to be regarded. Yet, in holding scientific research and discovery in respect, as we should, we must also be alert to the equal and opposite danger that public policy could itself become the captive of a scientific-technological elite. (pp. 1035–1040)

Of greater interest in the present context, however, are two other sets of ears that were attuned to the Mills message. The first were the ears of scholars who, though they did not necessarily accept Mills' argument at face value, nevertheless found much of it compelling. These scholars picked up, in effect, where Mills had left off, examining his core argument with a critical eye, offering both varied and enriched interpretations, and putting their own formulations to the test. Given his early death, had Mills' ideas not attracted this sort of scholarly interest, they likely would have proven far less influential among the second audience of interest. That second set of ears belonged to political activists in the student generation of the 1960s, who encountered Mills and his ideas in their sociology and political science classes and found them both persuasive and motivational. From this group there would arise in short order a New Left—no less intellectual in its roots than that which Mills derided, but more pragmatic in its understanding of political realities and profoundly more strategic in its actions than its ideological forbears.

Among the scholars who might be characterized as disciples of Professor Mills, two emerged as particularly influential, one a sociologist and the other a political scientist. Although they worked separately and did not agree on certain important issues, their scholarship was interactive and mutually reinforcing.

The sociologist, G. William Domhoff, believed that, in focusing so much attention on institutional elites, Mills had significantly understated the importance of class—especially of a "ruling class"—as a factor in explaining the power structure of the United States. But he nevertheless accepted Mills' core argument about the dynamics of elite influence and, in a series of books that continues to this day, has systematically delineated these elite mechanisms.

In his defining work, *Who Rules America?*, first published in 1967, Domhoff identified several criteria for membership in an upper class; then he examined the sociological backgrounds of institutional leaders and other key decision makers. He found that members of what he defined as the ruling class—fewer than 1% of the American population—constituted between 25% and 60% of the directors and partners in the largest banks, law firms, and corporations and that, either directly or through those they employed, they dominated the boards of directors of philanthropic foundations, leading universities, major opinion-forming associations, major media, and the executive branch of the federal government.[11] Domhoff has explored and delineated this theme with great care in all the work that has followed—*The Higher Circles* (1970), *The Powers That Be: Processes of Ruling Class Domination in America* (1978), *Political Elites and the State: How Policy Is Made in America* (1990), and others—but *Who Rules America?*, most recently revised in 1998,[12] remains the most concise and comprehensive statement of his methodology and findings, and the most timely.

Perhaps the most succinct statement of Domhoff's perspective comes, however, not in one of his books, but in his response to a critical review of *Who Rules America?* that appeared in 1975 in *The New York Review of Books*.[13]

> Let me make [the case] even more sharply than I have in the past. The owners and managers of large banks and corporations, with a little bit of help from their hired academics, lawyers, and public relations people, dominate everything in this country that is worth dominating—foreign policy through such organizations as the Council on Foreign Relations, Council of the Americas, and Trilateral Commission; economic policy through the likes of the Conference Board, Committee for Economic Development, and Brookings Institution; population policy through such groups as the Population Council, Population Reference Bureau, and Planned Parenthood; environmental policy through Resources for the Future, Conservation Foundation, and American Conservation Association; legal policies through the American Law Institute and committees of the American Bar Association; and educational policy through such entities as the Ford Foundation, three Carnegie foundations, and the Carnegie Council for Policy Studies in Higher Education. Every one of these organizations is financed and directed by the same few thousand men who run the major banks and corporations, and every one of them is pivotal on government policy in its area of specialization.

There is much in this statement that appears as well in the work of the political scientist in question, Thomas R. Dye. But whereas Domhoff believes in the centrality of social class as a determinant of elite status, Dye focuses instead on position itself—on being the one who makes key decisions—as determinative. For Dye, the ruling elite is an organizational phenomenon, not a social one. The difference is suggested, perhaps, in the running main title of the several editions of Dye's book setting out this argument, *Who's Running America?*,[14] as opposed to Domhoff's question of who rules.

Leaving aside the question of class and some differences of method, the structure of Dye's argument is sufficiently similar to Domhoff's, especially as set forth in the most recently quoted passage, that we need not restate it here. But in a key regard, Dye has gone Domhoff one better. . . he has drawn a picture of the mechanism of elite dominance as he sees it. That picture is reproduced in Fig. 1.1.

In Fig. 1.1, which Domhoff has reproduced and evaluated in his own work, Dye delineates the flow of resources and influence—and hence of power— from corporations and the wealthy through a network of intermediary institutions that formulate a limited menu of policy options from which the nation's political leaders are free to select. In brief, Dye believes that corporations and wealthy individuals (whose wealth generally has derived from corporations) support a web of quasi-philanthropic endeavors—family charitable foundations, university research programs, and professorships—as well as policy-generating think tanks, all of which are controlled through selective funding, interlocking directorates, and other inducements and constraints. These institutions work to define, investigate, refine, and instigate public policies that are consistent with the interests of their corporate (and other) sponsors. The resulting university and think tank research and policy proposals are then pumped through the major media—themselves owned and influenced by corporate elites—where their visibility is raised, presumably to the point of inevitability. They then enter the more traditional political process, where they are reviewed, occasionally modified, adopted, implemented, and adjudicated by Congress, the executive branch, and the courts. This political absorption, which receives substantial media coverage in its own right, becomes the focal point for public attention and political involvement. But in Dye's view it comes so late in the process as to be all but meaningless, except as an exercise in generating a sense of political efficacy and governmental responsiveness.

The fundamental dynamic of power in this model is agenda control. Resources are marshaled and channeled to support the development of policy options on a selective basis—with only those deemed acceptable to the funding elites being granted support through research, legitimacy through policy think tanks and councils, visibility through the media, and viability in the halls of government. Dye's is not necessarily a closed system—other ideas and alternative policies can freely percolate—but it is a system of favoritism in which unconventional, or counter-elite, policies are significantly disadvantaged and unlikely to be adopted.

What is missing in both Domhoff's and Dye's views of political power—or more to the point, what is granted only minimal significance, if any—is the

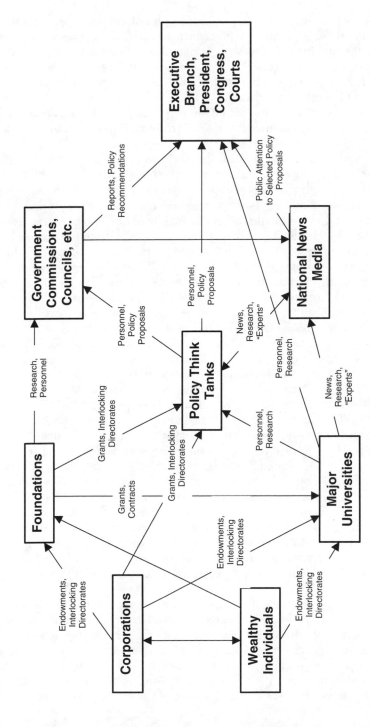

FIG. 1.1. The policy process: the view from the top. *Note.* *Who's Running America 3/E* by Dye, Thomas, ©, Reprinted by permission of Pearson Education Inc., Upper Saddle River, NJ.

very essence of pluralist democracy—the interplay of interest groups, political parties, election cycles, citizen involvement, and government responsiveness and accountability that collectively dominate the myth structure of American politics. Look at Dye's picture of the power structure, and they are nowhere to be found. Saying that another way, what is missing here is democracy, the supposed defining ethos of American politics. Of course, that is the point of the analysis, the critique from the Left, and the thing that has made this line of argument controversial since it was set forth in its initial form by Professor Mills.

Now, it would be a mistake to think that there were no pluralists on the Left, no engaged citizens espousing alternative positions within the democratic institutions that elite theorists portrayed as a mere façade. They had long existed, operating on the Left, but relatively near the center of the dinner plate. Until the 1980s, they were called Liberals, and it was they who were effectively disenfranchised and delegitimized by the Reagan Revolution. It was their loss of face, direction, and influence that created a political vacuum . . . and an opportunity for a new and alternative Left—the Progressive Left—to emerge.

This newest incarnation of the Left traces its origins to two sources. The first are the remnants of what we have termed the Old Left, the left rooted in Marxism–Leninism and in espousing the rising up of the working class to challenge the power of capitalism. For the most part, that Left no longer exists in the United States today, but it does endure in residual and much diluted form through organizations such as the Institute for Policy Studies and the Democratic Socialists of America. The second point of origin for the new progressivism is the New Left—the campus-based movement of the 1960s and 1970s—and it is here that Mills' influence is very strongly felt.

The period from approximately 1957—marked by the emergence of a politically viable and newly radicalized civil rights movement—through 1980—marked by the Iranian hostage crisis—was one of tremendous social and political upheaval in the United States. It was a period of great mass movements and of broad-scale political activism, especially, though by no means exclusively, on the campuses of the nation's colleges and universities. Among these campus activists, the most significant was a group at the University of Michigan who formed a society to debate the nature of, and move to change, a social order they understood to be dominated by elites, and more specifically—per Mills—by major corporations and the privileged and powerful few who controlled them. They called the group Students for a Democratic Society, or SDS.[15]

SDS was not a typical group of tear-down-the-system campus radicals, at least not at the outset. Although the group evolved in that direction, especially during the period of anti-Vietnam War protests, SDS began life as a vibrant intellectual community—a debating society with a radical central tendency, and at the same time a policy-oriented think tank of sorts with an experimental but pragmatic bent and a penchant for activism. SDS was a collection of thinkers who acted and of activists who were at their core philosophic.

In the near term, SDS produced a series of policy and community organizing initiatives, one of which ultimately influenced the development of VISTA, the so-called domestic Peace Corps, now known as AmeriCorps, and one far-reaching document drafted by Tom Hayden and adopted by the group in 1962—*The Port Huron Statement*—that stands today as a clear expression of New Left beliefs *and* as a foundation stone of the contemporary Progressive Left. The document, which in this passage very clearly reflects the worldview of the late Professor Mills, on which subject Hayden had written his master's thesis, opened with a call for student activists to[16]:

> Look beyond the campus, to America itself. . . . The apathy here is, first, subjective— the felt powerlessness of ordinary people, the resignation before the enormity of events. But subjective apathy is encouraged by the *objective* American situation— the actual structural separation of people from power, from relevant knowledge, from the pinnacles of decision-making . . . . The American political system . . . frustrates democracy by confusing the individual citizen, paralyzing policy discussion, and consolidating the irresponsible power of military and business interests.

Then, in a later passage, Hayden's manifesto drives to the core issue, converts Mills philosophical argument into a call for action, and in the process defines an agenda for the New Left that, for reasons explored later, resonates even more strongly today as the central tenet of the emergent Progressive Left. In this critical passage, Hayden argued[17]:

> It is not possible to believe that true democracy can exist where a minority utterly controls enormous wealth and power. . . . We can no longer rely on competition of the many to assure that business enterprise is responsive to social needs. . . . Nor can we trust the corporate bureaucracy to be socially responsible or to develop a "corporate conscience" that is democratic. . . . We must consider changes in the rules of society by challenging the unchallenged politics of American corporations.

This passage represented a subtle, but highly significant, change in thinking on the Left—a redefinition of the problem source, if you will, from people— the capitalist class—who existed for many simply as an abstract concept, to an institution—the corporation—with which most Americans came into daily contact. It was a break with the past, and it ultimately would provide a key bridge to the future of thought and action on the Left. But much had to happen before that could occur.

Some in the SDS—most notably, perhaps, Todd Gitlin and Paul Booth— began to devise direct actions targeted against major corporations. In 1964, Gitlin as president and Booth as vice president of SDS staged a rather business-like demonstration against Chase Manhattan Bank in New York to protest the bank's role in financing the Apartheid regime in South Africa and pressure it, through public embarrassment, to cease this activity. This demonstration served as a prototype for innumerable anti-corporate actions in later years, but it proved to be a one-time event for SDS itself, as the group was soon fully immersed in the anti-war movement, of which it became for a time the leading voice.[18]

Although it was short-lived as a functioning entity, SDS has had a remarkably enduring impact, not only on the Left but on American institutions generally. We have already suggested two examples of this—influencing the creation of VISTA/AmeriCorps and framing effectively for the first time among activists a focus on the corporation as the key anti-social actor. Both of these, and especially the latter, are significant accomplishments. But the greatest impact of SDS is arguably to be found in what, for want of a better term, might be characterized as its alumni association. Many former members—and leaders—of SDS have remained politically active, and they have occupied many positions of influence: Tom Hayden in the California State Senate; Paul Booth, director of organizing, and more recently assistant to the president, of the American Federation of State, County and Municipal Employees, the nation's leading public employees union; Heather Booth, a long-time Democratic Party activist and most recently executive director of USAction, formerly known as Citizen Action, an important progressive advocacy group; Steve Max of the Midwest Academy, a training center for community activists founded by Ms. Booth; Michael Locker, now an influential steel industry analyst; Todd Gitlin and Richard Flacks, who became prominent academics; and others whom we shall encounter as we go along. Due no doubt to its substantial intellectual roots, and to the substantial intellectuals it attracted during their most formative years, the influence of SDS survives to this day through the continuing appeal of some of its ideas and through the continued activism of these alumni, even though the demise of the group itself is decades past.

That longevity owes itself as well to more specific actions that helped to institutionalize the anti-corporate philosophy that was born of C. Wright Mills and nurtured in SDS. Although obscure at the time, one of the most important of these actions was the production in 1970 of a slim volume called the *Research Methodology Guide* by a small New York-based entity, the North American Congress on Latin America (NACLA). The *Research Methodology Guide* was the first how-to manual for researching and attacking corporations to pressure them into changing their policies in ways desired by their critics on the Left. NACLA was a joint venture of sorts created by SDS, the National Council of Churches, and others in 1966 designed to generate information about the ownership and other aspects of specific companies that could be used to advantage in pressure campaigns against them.[19]

Written in part by SDS alumni Michael Locker and Paul Booth, the *Research Methodology Guide* described what it termed "power structure research," the objective of which was[20]:

Identifying the people and institutions which make our lives and the lives of so many others intolerable, . . . locating weak points in the system, . . . suggesting a strategy for resistance, . . . [and] propelling ourselves and others into a higher consciousness of where the nodes of power lie and how they function. Knowledge of such points gives us the leverage to challenge the system effectively with the means at our disposal. Sometimes even an apparently insignificant weakness can be effectively exploited. The public image of a corporation, for instance, can be important to its continued prosperity—investment, government contracts, employee recruiting, etc., can all be affected by a change in this image. (pp. 2–3)

Here, then, is the first clearly delineated strategic doctrine of what I have termed Biz-War—the waging of reputational warfare on the corporation as a means of changing corporate policy company by company and in the process of redirecting public policy through the aggregation of these individual-level changes. This is a critical bookmark in the eventual development of the contemporary Progressive Left, and one to which we shall return later. Before that can be done, however, additional history must be traversed.

THE "VAST RIGHT WING CONSPIRACY," A DEMONSTRATION PROJECT

On January 27, 1998, shortly after allegations had surfaced about her husband's relationship with White House intern Monica Lewinski, Hillary Clinton asked viewers of NBC's "Today Show" to[21]:

Look at the very people who are involved in this. They have popped up in other settings. The great story here for anybody willing to find it, and write about it, and explain it, is this vast right-wing conspiracy that has been conspiring against my husband since the day he announced for President.

The then-First Lady may have been guilty of overstatement—there were, in fact, activists on the Right who saw the undermining of the Clintons as their personal mission, but whether they constituted a conspiracy is at least open to interpretation. At the same time, however, there very clearly was in place by the 1990s at the least a substantial, commonly motivated, well-funded, and more or less integrated network of actors dedicated to pursuing a very conservative agenda. Its roots, however, were considerably deeper than Mrs. Clinton's statement might suggest.

While those on the Left in the 1970s and 1980s were busily looking for ways to undermine the power structure delineated variously by Professors Mills, Domhoff, Dye, and their colleagues, others on the Right were more interested in capturing and controlling it. These individuals were less interested in arguing about the role of social class in molding or programming the power structure than they were in holding sway over the mechanisms of power themselves. If foundations and corporations and media institutions and the like were the key to power, the reasoning went, then might it be possible to establish a network of such actors that were dedicated to the policy goals of social and political conservatives, either as a subset of, or as an alternative to, the Mills–Domhoff–Dye power elite? It was an idea that seemed to some worth a try.

Although there is ample room for argument about the origins of any such movement, let us arbitrarily set the beginning of the systematic conservative backlash against New Deal liberalism in the early years of the administration of President Richard Nixon. Nixon was consumed by a belief that what he viewed as the Eastern liberal-elite news media—by which he meant the major network news organizations, elite newspapers, and newsmagazines—were united in an effort to attack him and his policies and, further, that this "media conspiracy" was out of step with the values of the American people, as was the policy agenda of the Eastern liberal elite more generally, from which, in his view, the media's perspective derived. Nixon, his closest aides, and their supporters were determined to fight back. Part of what they did—for example, constructing a list of political enemies that included journalists like Daniel Schorr and threatening to take away the broadcast licenses of stations owned by the major networks—crossed an important line in political ethics and contributed to Nixon's ultimate downfall. But part of what they did was both legitimate and far-sighted. For during these years there began to rise an infrastructure—from media critics to policy developers—whose function was to advance a more conservative view of government and policy. Some components of this early infrastructure included:

- Pro-conservative advocacy: Accuracy in Media was founded by Reed Irvine in 1969 as an organization dedicated to casting light on the perceived liberal bias of the media. This group continues to the present day and, in 1985 gave rise to a sister organization, Accuracy in Academia, dedicated to revealing liberal bias on university campuses.
- Pro-conservative research: In 1972 the Nixon Administration threw its support behind the then newly established Television News Archive at Vanderbilt University, which maintains recordings of the major network news broadcasts and since has emerged as a significant resource for media scholars. In the words of presidential aide Charles Colson, "This is the first time that TV journalists can be held accountable for what they have said or shown on every newscast. It is . . . not of insignificant interest to those that feel that the news coverage is slanted."[22] There was even consideration given to helping to fund the Archive. Much later, in 1985, a more extensive conservative media analysis operation was established in the form of the Center for Media and Public Affairs, which not only archived network broadcasts (including entertainment) but conducted its own content analysis of them as well.
- Pro-conservative policy development: Easily the most important of the Nixon-era start-ups was the Heritage Foundation, established in 1973 to formulate and advance public policies based on "the principles of free enterprise, limited government, individual freedom, traditional American

values, and a strong national defense,"[23] which is to say, to define the practical alternative to liberalism. It would not be incorrect to suggest that Heritage's job was to define what conservatives were *for* as a complement to what they agreed they were against—liberalism. In the event, the policies developed by Heritage over the decade of the 1970s formed the core of the agenda pushed by the Reagan Administration in the early years of the following decade.

But these and other initiatives of the Nixon years were only the starting point for a much more elaborate construct. From this point forward, a substantial network of conservative organizations was developed very much along the lines of the power structure delineated by Dye in Fig. 1.1.

The key to success for these endeavors was the establishment (or redirection of purpose) of a series of foundations to support conservative causes. This funding network was succinctly described by Sally Covington of the National Committee for Responsive Philanthropy at the 1997 annual meeting of the Council on Foundations. As summarized in the magazine *Philanthropy*, she reported that these foundations saw the establishment of an influential conservative infrastructure and a supportive mass public as an elaborate process of social marketing. To this end, they sought to "invest" in social change by funding scholars, university programs, and think tanks where policy options could be developed, as well as implementation groups to bring these proposals into the political marketplace and eventually to consumers.[24]

> Over the past two decades, Covington contended, conservative foundations have broadly followed such a model, investing hundreds of millions of dollars in a cross-section of institutions dedicated to conservative political and policy change. Her report, accordingly, closely examines the following foundations: the Lynde and Harry Bradley Foundation, the Carthage Foundation, the Earhart Foundation, the Charles G. Koch, David H. Koch and Claude R. Lambe charitable foundations, the Phillip M. McKenna Foundation, the J. M. Foundation, the John M. Olin Foundation, the Henry Salvatori Foundation, the Sarah Scaife Foundation, and the Smith Richardson Foundation. Together, these foundations controlled over $1.1 billion in assets in 1994, awarded $300 million in grants over the 1992-1994 study period, and targeted $210 million to support conservative policy and institutional reform objectives.

> Covington found that, of this $210 million, conservative foundations awarded:

> – $88.9 million to support conservative scholarship and programs, train the next generation of conservative thinkers and activists, and reverse progressive curricula and policy trends on the nation's college and university campuses. Among the top academic sector grantees identified by Covington were the University of Chicago, Harvard, George Mason University and Yale.
> – $79.2 million to build and strengthen a national infrastructure of think tanks and advocacy groups, $64 million of which was directed to institutions with a major focus on domestic policy issues and $15.2 million of which went to institutes focused on American national security interests, foreign policy, and

global affairs. Among the top think tank grantees of conservative foundations
singled out by the report are the Heritage Foundation, AEI [American Enterprise Institute], the Free Congress Foundation, the Cato Institute, Citizens for
a Sound Economy, and the Hudson and Hoover Institutions.
– $16.3 million to finance alternative media outlets, media watchdog groups,
and public television and radio for specific, issue-oriented public affairs or
news reporting. Conservative favorites here are the American Spectator Educational Foundation.... The Public Interest and The National Interest....
Finally, conservative foundations began to support the development of conservative "counter institutions" at a time when the American political system
began to undergo fundamental changes.

This was family money, personal wealth. Bradley, Coors, Koch, Lambe,
McKenna, Olin, Richardson, Salvatori, and Scaife. It derived from corporate money. The Allen-Bradley Company, Coors Brewing, Kennametal Inc.,
Koch Industries, Mellon Bank, Olin Corporation, Vick Chemical, and Western Geophysical. But these were not the Fords and the Rockefellers, the old-
moneyed elite, the "ruling" class. This was new money earned by outsiders
with a point of view. And the infrastructure it supported was not the power
structure that Mills, Domhoff, and Dye envisioned, the system-legitimizing
status-quo-maintaining power structure of the elite establishment, but a rene-
gade alternative meant to achieve specific political objectives in the form
of a more conservative government and policies. The Religious Right of
Pat Robertson and Jerry Falwell, the Right-mouthed talk of Rush Limbaugh
and a countless host of imitators, and even the scandal-mongering attacks
later decried by Mrs. Clinton—these may have been for many the visible
face of the conservative movement of the period, but all were mere window
dressing behind which serious influence-building was under way.

WHAT THE "L"

By the election of 1980, much of this effort had succeeded. For proof, one need
look no further than the election result itself: out with Carter, in with Reagan.
But for those in the center-Left of the political spectrum, there was worse to
come. For at the end of his administration, Ronald Reagan, with assists from
George Bush (the Elder) and political strategist Lee Atwater, among others,
would deprive them of their very essence. With but a little poetic license
we can trace that outcome to the afternoon of August 14, 1988, at 4:15 to
be precise, in Hall C of the New Orleans Convention Center. There, in
what amounted to his farewell address before the delegates of the Republican
National Convention, Reagan declared:

The masquerade is over. It's time to talk issues; *to use the dreaded L-word*; to say
that the policies of our opposition and the Congressional leadership of his party are
liberal, liberal, liberal. [italics added]

"When he recited the L-word himself," observed New York Times reporter E. J. Dionne, Jr., "the President made it sound like an anathema."[25] The headline in the next day's Bergen Record was more succinct: "Reagan Marches In, Gives Democrats L".[26]

This was not the first reference to the so-called "L-word." On the Thursday before Memorial Day in 1988, Republican strategists Lee Atwater, Roger Ailes, Robert Teeter, Craig Fuller, and Nicolas Brady—essentially the GOP brain-trust of the day—brought together two focus groups of prospective voters—15 people in each group, together with a moderator—to "focus" on Democratic presidential candidate Michael Dukakis. Years of careful polling and other research lay behind those two sessions—studies of voting habits, candidate perceptions, media use habits, and the like. But this was the pivotal moment. The themes that would resonate best would be adopted for the campaign. The L-word reference was on the list, and it tested surprisingly well—so well that, over time and with a boost from Reagan, it became the campaign's mantra.[27] So well, in fact, that it wrought the destruction of that it described.

Encouraged by his advisors, Bush began applying the L-word to opponent Dukakis as a label of derision early in the summer, and by July 4 of that year conservative columnist George Will was claiming that Dukakis would, "if necessary, climb a tree to escape from the dreaded 'L' word (L******ism)."[28] The very next day, July 5, Reagan told a White House gathering of conservative leaders[29]:

> The American people understand what liberalism means and don't like it. So our opponents plan to go out to the [voters] incognito. They're putting on political trench coats and sunglasses and will never, even in the lowest whisper, mumble the "L" word again.

Still, it was the convention speech that set the rhetorical direction for the remainder of the Bush campaign and, more to the point, sealed the fate of liberalism itself.

Through a systematic campaign of perception management by Reagan, Bush, and the Republican Right, the "L-Word" became the political equivalent of the Scarlet Letter tattooed on the foreheads of anyone whose politics placed them to the left of the steak, if not of the steak knife. Where it had been a badge of honor among some for two generations or longer to be a Liberal, from the early 1980s on, and especially during and after the 1988 campaign, to be associated with this label was to be a political outcast. By word, gesture, and innuendo, the term was literally forced out of style. It is scarcely uttered by anyone but critics to this day.

In effect, the Republican communication strategy literally deprived the opposition of the right to label itself and in the process seemed to render those previously liberal unable to formulate or characterize with clarity their own views. They lost their collective self-image, their sense of who they were. In a very short time—and indeed, well before their fate was reified in the Reagan–Bush rhetoric of 1988—they became scrambled eggs to the conservative's hard boiled.

As late as 1995 and beyond, this effort at demonizing the Left was still under way. In January of that year, for example, GOPAC, the political action committee established by then-Speaker of the House Newt Gingrich, issued a memorandum, headed "Language: A Key Mechanism of Control," in which the group set forth a lexicon of terms to be applied to its political opponents—terms such as decay, failure, destructive, sick, pathetic, lie, traitors, radical, corrupt, selfish, insensitive, shame, disgrace, and . . . liberal—and others—opportunity, moral, courage, commitment, confident, etc.—to themselves.[30]

By changing the language of American politics in so purposeful, so consistent, and so effective a manner, the Reagan and post-Reagan Republicans changed the character of American politics as well. They moved the center of the debate well to the right. They also left their political opponents in a state of utter disarray—deprived of their legitimacy, of their influence, and even of their name. If not Liberals, who or what were they to be? It was a very confusing and demoralizing time for the American Left—or what was left of it.

SOCIAL SEISMOLOGY

While all this thinking and planning and doing and claiming was going on, the social and economic landscape of the United States itself was shifting. The civil rights movement of the 1950s and 1960s may not have fully addressed the grievances of racial minorities, but it did create new economic opportunities for many, and by the 1980s the racial composition of the workforce and, importantly, the white collar and managerial workforce, had begun to change. Indeed, between immigration and differential birth rates among the races, the United States itself was, by century's end, well on its way to becoming a minority-majority nation with growing African American, Hispanic, and Asian populations claiming a larger share of the political and economic spoils. Similarly, partly as a result of the women's rights movement of the 1970s, but also a result of the economic dislocations of the 1980s, women came to play a far more extensive and influential role in the workplace.

But the workplace, too, was changing. New technologies and new business models were transforming the American economy. Manufacturing and heavy industry were in decline—whether because their products had been displaced by newer ones or their workers had been displaced by cheaper ones. Markets for those products that were still produced domestically were globalized, but so, too, was the manufacturing process itself. Jobs moved offshore, and jobs at Wal-Mart and McDonald's replaced those on the assembly line. Companies downsized to meet the new global competition but also to respond to the new short-term, bottom-line-only perspective that was broadly adopted by the financial markets. Efficiency, cost-cutting, and productivity became the watchwords of the era.

And while all this was happening, the working population of the country was aging, most notably the bubble of so-called baby boomers, born collectively in a fit of mass passion and family-building in the wake of World War II, passing into their peak earning and consuming years in the 1990s, and threatening to overwhelm the government's social safety net of last resort— Social Security and Medicare—beginning just after 2010. To prepare for this foreseeable denouement, but also simply to protect their financial accomplishments, the Boomers (and others) began to invest at a level the United States had never seen. At work, they vested in pension plans and 401(k)s. At home, they bought mutual funds and real estate. The dollar values involved in all this investing are staggering. In 1985, for example, there were 10.3 million participants in 401(k) pension plans, of which there were approximately 30,000 in place. These plans accounted for $144 billion in assets. By 1996, 30.8 million Americans were participants in some 230,000 plans with a total asset value of $1.06 *trillion*. And that does not begin to account for public employees participating in local, state, and federal retirement programs.[31]

But pension funds and other forms of personal investment were only a part of the story. Between 1980 and 2000, the total of what is termed "nonbank" finance—that is the sum of such institutional investments as credit union deposits, life insurance, mutual funds, money markets, and trusts—surged from $2.88 trillion to $26.14 trillion, nearly a ten-fold increase.[32] In a system where money is power—and that is surely the system envisioned by Mills, Domhoff, and Dye—there was suddenly a lot more power out there, or more correctly, a lot more *potential* power. And in a way that had not been true earlier in the nation's history, the resource that lay behind and gave rise to that potential power belonged not to some socially remote elite or ruling class but to the people themselves. They had, however, yet to claim it.

THE LIGHTS GO ON

So there they were, these politicos formerly known as Liberals and their compatriots further to the Left. Split by internal tensions and historical divisions that were as much products of their post-New Deal success as of any failings. Newly sensitized to a clearly delineated view of American democracy as a façade masking an institutionalized elite power structure grounded in prominent, influential, but carefully controlled institutions. Under attack from an increasingly influential New Right modeled after the power elite but bent on an ideological cleansing of the system. Thrown from power by a cowboy politician from the wrong coast. Deprived of their very name by this same ragtag army of what they perceived to be anti-intellectuals and rabble-rousing preachers. Grounded in a bottom-centered political philosophy supporting a working and middle class that was under increasing pressure itself. But one that also had amassed, at least indirectly, unprecedented wealth.

Let's rephrase. A new understanding of how power really worked. A demonstration of how this power structure could be replicated on a smaller scale through strategic wealth management, and yet wield great influence. A similar demonstration of how the construction of an enemy—themselves!—and a concerted attack on that enemy could mobilize support for, and in the process legitimize, an ideological movement that was, at the end of the day, representative of a distinctly minority viewpoint. A prospective and growing base of increasingly disaffected people . . . people who happened to control immense resources.

To rebuild the Left, then, might one not rename the movement in such a way as to abandon the lifeless Liberal label and at the same time broaden its appeal, identify a common and tenable "enemy" against which to organize in counterpoint, build a network of think tanks and advocacy organizations to research and advance a new policy agenda, and fund their activities through private philanthropy but also by gaining functional control over the vast ocean of institutional investments?

Click.

Epiphany.

ENDNOTES

1. Jarol B. Manheim, *Déjà Vu: American Political Problems in Historical Perspective.* New York: St. Martin's Press, 1976, pp. 215–216.
2. These events are described in more detail in ibid., pp. 216–220.
3. Jarol B. Manheim, *The Death of a Thousand Cuts: Corporate Campaigns and the Attack on the Corporation.* Mahwah, NJ: Lawrence Erlbaum Associates, 2001 pp. 2–10.
4. Mark C. Smith, "Mills, Charles Wright," *The Handbook of Texas Online,* found online, December 4, 2002, at www.tsha.utexas.edu/handbook/online/articles/view/MM/fmi37.html.
5. C. Wright Mills, *The New Men of Power,* 50th Anniversary Edition (New York: Oxford University Press, 2002), p. 16.
6. Ibid, p. 17.
7. C. Wright Mills, *White Collar: The American Middle Classes* (New York: Oxford University Press, 1953), p. 328.
8. C. Wright Mills, *The Power Elite,* Second Edition (New York: Oxford University Press, 2000), pp. 3–4.
9. Eugene V. Schneider, "The Sociology of C. Wright Mills," in G. William Domhoff and Hoyt B. Ballard, eds., *C. Wright Mills and* The Power Elite (Boston: Beacon Press, 1968), p. 17.
10. Dwight D. Eisenhower, Farewell Address, *Public Papers of the Presidents, 1960,* pp. 1035–1040.
11. This summary is based on one provided by Domhoff himself in "*The Power Elite* and Its Critics," in Domhoff and Ballard, eds., op. cit., p. 269.
12. G. William Domhoff, *Who Rules America? Power and Politics in the Year 2000* (Mountain View, CA: Mayfield Publishing, 1998).
13. G. William Domhoff, "Is There a Ruling Class?," Letter to *The New York Review of Books,* July 17, 1975, found online at www.nybooks.com/articles/9124, December 4, 2002.

14. Dye's book has been published in seven editions to date, all of which maintain the same main title, but each of which bears a different subtitle to reflect its era. The first edition, published in 1976, was titled *Who's Running America? Institutional Leadership in the United States* (Englewood Cliffs, NJ: Prentice-Hall). The most recent is *Who's Running America? The Bush Restoration*, seventh edition (Englewood Cliffs, NJ: Prentice-Hall, 2001) . Other volumes have focused on the Carter years, the Reagan years, the conservative years and the Clinton years. In each instance, Dye identifies the individuals who occupy the highest positions of influence in the major institutions in each portion of his model, then examines the extent to which their positions interlock, either at a given point in time or over time.

15. For a related discussion of SDS see Manheim, *Death of a Thousand Cuts*, loc. cit. For a far more comprehensive analysis of the group and its influence see James Miller, *Democracy Is in the Streets: From Port Huron to the Siege of Chicago* (New York: Simon & Schuster, 1987), passim.

16. From *The Port Huron Statement* as reproduced by Miller, op. cit., pp. 334–336.

17. Ibid.

18. Miller, op. cit., p. 228, and Todd Gitlin, *The Sixties: Years of Hope, Days of Rage*, revised edition (New York: Bantam, 1993), p. 317.

19. For more details on NACLA, its organization and leadership, and its relationship with SDS see Manheim, op. cit., pp. 6–10.

20. North American Congress on Latin America, *NACLA Research Methodology Guide* (New York: 1970), pp. 2–3.

21. Quote found online at www.cnn.com/ALLPOLITICS/1998/01/27/hillary.today/, December 16, 2002.

22. Memorandum from Charles Colson to Ken Clawson, May 1, 1972. Found in Bruce Oudes, ed., *From The President: Richard Nixon's Secret Files* (New York: Harper & Row, 1989), pp. 436–437.

23. From the foundation's mission statement as found at www.heritage.org/about/, December 17, 2002.

24. "The Plan: Do conservatives have a strategy, or merely a vision?" *Philanthropy* (1:2), Spring 1997, found online at www.philanthropyroundtable.org/magazines/1997/1.2/theplan.html, December 16, 2002. See also "Social Studies: Conservative Crusaders," *National Journal*, April 26, 2003.

25. E. J. Dionne, Jr., "The Republicans in New Orleans: Reagan Promises an All-Out Drive for Bush Victory," *The New York Times*, August 15, 1988, p. A1.

26. *Bergen Record*, August 15, 1988, p. 1.

27. The development of this strategy is described in Jarol B. Manheim, *All of the People All the Time: Strategic Communication and American Politics* (Armonk, NY: M.E. Sharpe, 1991), pp. 49–68.

28. George Will, "Pin the Label on the Donkey," *Newsweek*, August 1, 1988, p. 62.

29. Ronald Reagan, "Remarks at a White House Briefing for Conservative Political Leaders," *Public Papers of the Presidents*, 24 Weekly Comp. Pres. Doc. 897, July 5, 1988.

30. GOPAC, "Language: A Key Mechanism of Control," memorandum, ND, pp. 2–3.

31. *Statistical Abstract of the United States* (Washington: Census Bureau, 2001), Table 535.

32. *Ibid*, Table 1163.

2

Dollar$ to Doughnuts:
Financing Social Change

> 'Twixt the optimist and pessimist
> The difference is droll:
> The optimist sees the doughnut
> But the pessimist sees the hole.
>
> —McLandburgh Wilson, *Optimist and Pessimist*

In 1981, the same year Ronald Reagan ascended to the presidency, a secret meeting was held at a hideaway in the Colorado Rockies. Present were 22 young and wealthy individuals who shared a common concern about the conservative turn the country had taken and a common commitment to try to do something about it. As this somewhat mystical group sat in a circle meditating about how best to engage in effective social action, a doughnut-shaped cloud appeared overhead. Taking this as a sign of sorts, the group dubbed itself "The Doughnuts." The idea they hit upon was to pool their resources and direct them at what they saw as socially and politically desirable programs. Described by one magazine as "a loose-limbed freemasonry of wealthy young idealists trying to heal the wounds of affluenza," the group continued to meet once or twice a year through the 1980s.[1]

In addition to sharing a common concern and commitment, 21 of the 22 Doughnuts had a common friend, Joshua L. Mailman. Mailman had called them together.

THE MAILMAN RINGS THRICE

Born in 1957 and a graduate of Middlebury College, Josh Mailman was 23 years old when he gathered his friends for their mountain retreat. And he was convinced that, by accepting responsibility and marshaling their resources, the emerging generation of philanthropists—his generation—could construct an alternative to the Rightward wave of political reform then sweeping the country.

Joseph L. Mailman, Josh's father, was born in Utica, New York, where he and his brother, Abraham, formed the Utica Knife and Razor Company in 1920. In 1928, they started the Pal Blade Company, an early competitor to Gillette, and in 1934 established the Mailman Corporation, one of the first of a new type of corporation—the conglomerate. In subsequent years, the brothers acquired or gained control of several other companies, among them Air Express International (AEI), the oldest and largest international air freight forwarder in the United States; Gulfstream Land and Development, a Florida real estate development company; and Republic Aviation, a defense contractor best known for its fighter aircraft before it was acquired by Fairchild in 1965.[2]

The elder Mailman was a close friend of cosmetics king Charles Revson and was joined on the board of Gulfstream Land by another prominent industrialist, Canadian liquor mogul Edgar M. Bronfman, chairman and CEO of both Seagram Company, Ltd., and Joseph E. Seagram & Sons, Inc.[3] But the most interesting story of the family business is that of AEI. AEI was the biggest air cargo forwarder at New York's JFK International Airport when, in 1983, the company considered merging with CF Air Freight, a subsidiary of Consolidated Freightways. At the time, freight operations at Kennedy were the objects of attention by organized crime leaders, operating through corrupt Teamsters locals, who offered a trade: labor peace in exchange for a surtax on the fees earned by the air freight companies. It was something of a fee-for-service arrangement. In return for a share of their profits, the companies were offered services such as "recruiting the customers of a competitor, granting immunity from cargo thefts, and providing protection against labor problems." The Mafia even went so far as to establish a telephone hotline for use in case of emergencies such as labor disputes and thefts. The companies were, in fact, paying this "tax," amounting to tens of thousands of dollars annually, which was one factor contributing to a sharp decline in the share of air freight entering the United States through Kennedy (from 41% of all freight in 1977 to 33% 10 years later).

But that was the companies' problem. The proposed merger presented two separate problems for the Mafia leaders. First and most immediately, there was a jurisdictional issue. AEI, with 2,250 workers and annual revenues of $250 million, had contracts with Teamsters Locals 295 and 851, which were controlled by the Lucchese family. But CF Air Freight dealt with two different locals, 707 and 814, which were linked to the Colombo and Bonnano families.

It was thus in the interests of the Lucchese family to prevent the merger. They were aided in this by the fact that they had an inside man at AEI, Vice President John Russo, who was in charge of labor relations at the airport, and by their knowledge that other AEI executives feared Russo because they knew he had Mafia muscle behind him in the person of one Frank Manzo. So it was with some confidence that Manzo instructed Local 295 to strike AEI on the grounds that its contract gave it a veto over any merger that would remove the local as a bargaining agent.

At this point, Russo went to Joseph Mailman, then 82 years old, to tell him that the only way to settle the strike was to pay his "contact"—i.e., Mr. Manzo—$500,000. Mailman agonized over the decision for several days and eventually refused to pay. At this point, the merger collapsed and, on Manzo's instruction, Local 295 demanded that the company hire more union workers. Manzo then stepped in as "peacemaker." He accepted a fee of $50,000, and the union backed away from its demand.

We know this because of the second problem the Mafia leaders and Teamsters officials had at the time—many of their conversations were being recorded through FBI wiretaps. For in 1983 the Federal Organized Crime Strike Force had launched an investigation of racketeering at JFK. In 1986, Russo and other key defendants pleaded guilty; in 1987 Manzo followed suit.[4]

As for the company, after the merger with Consolidated Freightways collapsed, its stock price did the same, dropping by two-thirds, or about $44 million of market capitalization. As owners of about 30% of the stock, Mailman and his family had lost something on the order of $15 million by 1985.[5] Though Mailman remained on the board of directors, he resigned as chairman of the company in 1984.[6]

In addition to their business ventures, the Mailman brothers also developed a tradition of family philanthropy. Joseph, for example, was a benefactor of institutions such as Montefiore Medical Center, Lincoln Center for the Performing Arts, Nova University in Fort Lauderdale, Florida, and the Mailman Center for Child Development in Miami.[7] After his death from lymphoma in 1990 at the age of 88, the family's Mailman Foundation donated $33 million to establish the Joseph L. Mailman School of Public Health at Columbia University.[8] For his part, as he approached his death in 1980, Abraham offered his own daughter, Marilyn Segal, a choice: she could inherit his money herself, or she could use it to establish the A.L. Mailman Family Foundation. She chose the latter.[9]

This was private philanthropy on a moderately large scale—not the Rockefellers and the Fords, perhaps, but serious money nonetheless. Yet at the same time, it was old-style philanthropy, targeted at social, cultural, and educational institutions to help support worthy causes from the arts to basic health care. Josh's vision of the future of private philanthropy was rather different and clearly more political.

It was against this background that he called his friends together in Colorado and against this background that he began to convert his vision into reality. For Joshua Mailman was every bit as entrepreneurial as his father and uncle, but where their innovative thinking went into their businesses, his went elsewhere. Joshua Mailman was—is—a social and political entrepreneur. He told an interviewer in 1989[10]: "People who really wield power use financial resources, the force of their own person and their contacts to achieve substantial social aims.... The heaviest game in town is how people can transform this planet—the environment, the nuclear weapons, the starving people—in the next ten years.... Civilization is in a coma, and I want to awaken it." (p. 36)

CROSSING A THRESHOLD

Mailman was not just a talker. In 1982, shortly after the meeting in the mountains, he established the Threshold Foundation as a focal point for pooling the funds of the Doughnuts. This rather unique arrangement, about which we'll have more to say shortly, provided a mechanism for increasing the leverage of a number of relatively small donors (the minimum amount required of participants annually was set at $500,000). From that point forward, Mailman's life became a literal whirlwind of founding, funding, advising, directing, and supporting an ever-expanding number of business organizations, socially responsible businesses and business ventures, environmental groups, activist foundations, and labor and policy advocates. Table 2.1 provides what is surely but a partial list of these affiliations. Of the many connections and affiliations listed in the table, three are of particular interest, in part because of Mailman's central role in their formation and in part because of their lasting influence in the context of the larger story.

The first of these is, as already noted, the Threshold Foundation, which takes as its purpose the promotion of peace, understanding, and environmental awareness through grant-making and educational activities. The foundation's agenda has three main components. They include support of system-level policy change "where an organization is working to shift the larger, often governmental, structures that create limiting... and unjust frameworks," community-level grassroots initiatives that complement systemic change, and programs that change "underlying cultural and political assumptions" by means that are "radical, sensible and grounded...."[11] More specifically, the foundation has expressed interest in the issues of globalization, campaign finance, corporate accountability, environmental protection, criminal justice and corrections, media independence and diversity, demilitarization, and access to health care.[12]

Unlike the larger, well-established and often better-known family foundations that also fund progressive activism—the Pew Charitable Trusts, for example—Threshold has remained true to its Doughnuts origins, providing a mechanism for pooling the funds of smaller contributors in an effort to maximize their social impact. In the period 1996–2000, the foundation received an average of slightly over $1.6 million in gifts and grants annually. In 2000,

TABLE 2.1

Organizations Associated with Joshua L. Mailman, By Type

Entity	Relationship	Description
Activist foundations		
Joshua Mailman Charitable Trust	Principal	Established in 1998; sometimes referred to as the Joshua Mailman Foundation
Joseph L. Mailman Foundation	Director	This is the family trust established by Mailman's father
Threshold Foundation	Founder	Established 1982 immediately following the formation of The Doughnuts; later merged with the Tides Foundation under a fiscal sponsorship
Ruben & Elisabeth Rausing Trust (UK)	Co-founder, Managing Director	Trust established by Sigrid Rausing
Tides Foundation	Fiscal Sponsorship, Major Donor	Hosts the Threshold Foundation and the Mailman Institute
Activist business organizations		
Social Venture Network	Co-founder, Director Emeritus	Formed in 1987 to encourage pro-social businesses; Mailman also founded SVN's Asian and European counterparts
Business for Social Responsibility	Co-founder, Director	Formed in 1992 as a sort of SVN for major corporations
Network for Social Change	Founder	Self-described as "a British self-help group for rich people who aspire to use their resources to make the world a better place"
Forum Empresa	Co-Founder	A hemispheric alliance of corporate social responsibility-based organizations in the Americas
Social Investment Forum	Donor	Funded report issued in 2000
Environmental advocates and foundations		
International Rivers Network	Director	Activist group that links human rights to environmental issues—eg, through an emphasis on the rights of indigenous peoples; project of the Tides Foundation since 1985
Sierra Madre Alliance	Director	Supports a network of indigenous pueblos and Mexican nongovernmental organizations to resist modernization and preserve the rainforest
Cold Spring Conservancy	Director	Manages a biodiversity reserve

(Continued)

TABLE 2.1

(Continued)

Entity	Relationship	Description
Rainforest Foundation	Director	Supports indigenous and traditional communities in the rainforest
Living Earth Foundation (UK)	Trustee and Patron	Foundation that supports programs emphasizing community empowerment to address environmental issues
Rocky Mountain Institute	Donor	Advocates "natural capitalism," which has to do with efficient and restorative use of environmental resources by corporations and others; founded 1982
Ecological Development Fund	Advisory Board Member	Promotes community-based development and self-determination in tropical ecosystems in Latin America
Green Map Systems	Major Donor	Encourages ecological thinking at the community level by mapping local ecosystems
Other policy and advocacy links		
Human Rights Watch	Director, Donor	Advocacy group that investigates and reports on human rights violations
Corporate Watch	Advisory Board Member, Donor	Anti-corporate webzine and organizing site established by the Transnational Resource and Action Center and the Tides Foundation
Witness.org	Director	Human rights advocacy group that provides cameras, imaging and editing software, satellite phones, e-mail, and training
Press for Change	Donor	Funded 1999 study of Nike labor practices in Indonesia by labor activist and leading Nike critic Jeff Ballinger
Fund for Global Human Rights	Director	Makes grants to activist grassroots human rights nongovernmental organizations
Institute for Multitrack Diplomacy	Donor	Anti-war group that sees diplomacy as having nine components, among which are business, activism, religion, and private philanthropy
Global Partners Working Group	Donor	This was an activity of and sponsored by the Council on Economic Priorities
Reebok Human Rights Awards	Advisory Board Member	Awarded annually to human rights activists selected by the Advisory Board
Americans for Peace Now	Hosted 1991 Program, Presumed Member	APN is the US branch of the Israeli Peace Now movement

(Continued)

TABLE 2.1

(Continued)

Entity	Relationship	Description
Chiapas Media Project	Donor	Provides video gear, computers, and training to indigenous and campesino communities in Chiapas, Mexico, center of the Zapatista movement, to which the group has ties through the Mexico Solidarity Network
Business Leaders for Sensible Priorities	Member	Group opposed to a second U.S. war with Iraq
Internews Network	Funder	International organization to support open media systems, with emphasis on emerging democracies
Mailman Institute	Founder and Major Donor	Conducts strategic planning exercises for activists
Media & Democracy Congress, 1996	Member, Planning and Advisory Committee	First in a series of meetings between journalists and Progressive activists focusing on class-based views of the media, changing roles of journalists, democratization of media, media activism, etc.
Educational activities		
Joseph L. Mailman School of Public Health, Columbia University	Director	School was renamed after major grant from the Joseph L. Mailman Foundation
American Indian Forum	Donor	Funded the 2001 meeting at Cornell University
Alternative Education Resource Organization	Founding Donor	Describes itself as a catalyst for educational change and advocate for "learner-centered" education—e.g., through joint student–teacher decision making
Business ventures and relationships		
Sirius Business Corporation	Founder and Principal	This New York-based venture capital firm is Mailman's primary business enterprise
NextPoint Partners	Investment Advisor	High-tech venture capital firm
Global Telesystems Group	Founding Investor	Pan-European telecommunications network with substantial holdings in Russia
Grameen Telecom	Founding Investor	Operates a cellular network in Bangladesh

(Continued)

TABLE 2.1

(Continued)

Entity	Relationship	Description
Sterling Energy Systems	Founding Investor	Phoenix-based provider of renewable power, including solar dish systems; has partnered with Boeing and US national laboratories on demonstration project
Shaman Pharmaceuticals	Founding Investor	Specializes in developing new therapeutic drugs from the tropical rainforest using indigenous knowledge
Wcities.com	Founding Investor	Provides location-based information services for e-commerce covering 300 cities in 70 countries
Perks4u.com	Founding Investor	No information available
Webmiles.com	Founding Investor	No information available
EHealth Direct	Founding Investor	Provides health care management administrative services; since renamed as DeNovis
Stoneyfield Farms	Founding Shareholder	Producer of yogurt and ice cream using organic products, donates 10% of profits to environmental causes
Earthstone International	Founding Investor	Produces nontoxic cleaning and sanding products
Juniper Partners	Founding Investor	Venture capital firm headed by Lynne Katzman, SVN board member, who chaired the committee that formulated the SVN corporate responsibility standards
Calvert Social Venture Partners	Founding Investor	Investment fund targeting entrepreneurial ventures that find profitable ways of addressing social issues
Utne Reader	Founding Shareholder	Progressive publication
Pepi Co-Generation Company	Owner	No information available; co-generation is a highly efficient process for generating heat and electric power simultaneously from the same source—e.g., biomass
Energía Global	Investor	A renewable energy owner, operator, and developer with assets in Central and Latin America; acquired by Enel Green Power in 2001
Seeds of Change	Investor	Producer of organic seeds, plants, and frozen entrees
World Music Productions	Director	Nonprofit multimedia producer
Afropop Worldwide	First Investor and Director	Nonprofit subsidiary of World Music that focuses on African arts and artists

(Continued)

TABLE 2.1

(Continued)

Entry	Relationship	Description
Sustainable Asset Management	Advisory Board Member	Swiss-based asset management firm that emphasizes investment in sustainability-driven companies; advises banks, insurance companies, pension funds, and private clients
Vegetarian Travel Guide	Supporter	Web site providing information for vegetarians
HP World e-Inclusion	Policy Board Member	A worldwide business development venture of Hewlett-Packard
Goodale Associates	Client	Fund-raising consultancy that also serves the Tides Foundation
Citidel Underground	Advisory Board Member	San Francisco-based publisher of books on subjects such as the drug culture, rock-and-roll music, and Eastern religions

Note: Listed positions are ever-held and not necessarily current or contemporaneous.

for example, the largest donations the foundation received of cash or property ranged in size from $34,000 to $114,000 and totaled slightly over half a million dollars. During the 1996–1999 period, no single donor contributed as much as $250,000.[13] Although these are large numbers in some contexts—wouldn't it be nice to be able to give away $34,000 this year?—in the world of private philanthropy they are minuscule, and, by pooling them, the foundation gives the donors more leverage than they otherwise might possess. The donors— or Doughnuts—in turn rotate into positions on the foundation's board of directors, where tenures tend to be much shorter than is typical of other philanthropic entities. By this device, they share in the prestige and influence of board membership. At least 18 different individuals have served on the Threshold board in recent years.

By 1991, which marked the end of its first decade, Threshold had made a total of $7 million in grants to what were then considered nontraditional causes.[14] By 2000, the foundation was giving away more than $1.3 million per year. The recipients of this largesse included, among many others:

- Alliance for Global Justice—to support the Mobilization for Global Justice, which played a central role in mounting demonstrations in Seattle and Washington against corporate globalization
- The Rainforest Action Network, a leading environmental antagonist of corporations such as Conoco, Freeport-McMoRan, Georgia Pacific, Home Depot, Kimberley Clark, and Mitsubishi
- Friends of the Earth, for its genetically altered foods initiative

- Government Accountability Project, for a program on openness and national security
- United for a Fair Economy, an organization that focuses on the adverse effects of concentrated wealth and power
- Coalition of Immokalee Workers, a group that is campaigning against Taco Bell to gain leverage for Florida tomato workers
- Project Underground, an environmental advocacy group that focuses on the mining and energy industries
- Corporate Watch, a web publication of the Transnational Resource Center
- Essential Information, the core Ralph Nader organization
- The Chiapas Program of the Seva Foundation, which focuses on community organizing and participation
- Institute for Policy Studies, for a program to support grassroots groups in Mexico addressing the globalization issue
- US/GLEP, to support a pressure campaign against Starbucks by coffee workers in Guatemala
- Action Resource Center, to support nonviolent direct action such as blockading timber companies and lumber yards that sell old growth products and hanging banners at oil companies that operate in the rainforest
- Taxpayers for Common Sense, which opposes governmental support of corporations
- International Labor Rights Fund, to advocate for the incorporation of workers' rights into programs of trade expansion
- The Ruckus Society, which conducts training camps where environmental and other activists learn to climb buildings, bridges, and trees to hang campaign banners and engage in other forms of publicity-rich demonstrations.[15]

Many of these organizations have roles to play as our story unfolds.

Whereas some of the foundation's money has supported more traditional educational, artistic, and cultural organizations, recipients like those just listed are clearly different. They are policy advocates and activists in various fields who have in common a commitment to a Progressive-Left political agenda. And that is the real point. What Joshua Mailman and a few others of the same era saw as an opportunity, and what they have accomplished over the past two decades, is nothing less than the redefinition of what it means to be philanthropic. By pooling their funds, not only within foundations, as in the case of Threshold, but across foundations—and there are many such partnerships, some of which are documented later in this volume—they began to create a resource base on which a Progressive-Left counter-revolution could be constructed. Richard Mellon Scaife was not the only one who could play the game.

Although the spirit of the Doughnuts endures—the foundation's web site is found at www.doughnuts.net—and although he continues to contribute significant sums, Mailman himself has not been personally involved in the activities of the Threshold Foundation in recent years. Instead, in addition to continuing as an officer and director of the original family foundation created by his father, in 1998 he established his own Joshua L. Mailman Charitable Trust. And while the family foundation continues to contribute primarily to traditional educational and cultural causes, although in recent years it has made major grants to the Rainforest Action Network and the Tides Foundation,[16] the Joshua Mailman Trust has demonstrated a much more activist bent. It has contributed to groups such as:

- Co-Op America Foundation,
- Project Underground,
- Essential Information,
- Corporate Watch,
- Human Rights Watch,
- Global Exchange,
- Pesticide Action Network,
- Rainforest Action Network,
- Press for Change,
- The Ruckus Society,
- Social Venture Network,
- INFACT, and the
- Tides Foundation.

Threshold, the family foundation and his own trust—a fairly impressive roster of accomplishments for a young philanthropist. But for Mailman there was still more to come. Included among his several Tides Foundation grants, for example—and a great deal more remains to be said about Tides in this narrative—were several that established and funded yet another entity, the Mailman Institute, which conducts retreats for small groups of activist leaders to develop strategic plans to implement their policy goals. Finally, Mailman is the cofounder and managing director of the Ruben and Elisabeth Rausing Trust (UK), an endowed foundation funded by Sigrid Rausing, that makes annual grants totaling approximately $4 million in the areas of human rights, environmental justice and sustainability, and economic justice. Recent grantees include Amnesty International, Human Rights Watch, Oxfam International, and, in the United States, the Center for Public Integrity.[17]

In sum, Mailman has established a career nonpareil as a virtual funding machine for advocates of Progressive-Left causes. Through his philanthropy alone, he has fulfilled the vision that first appeared in that doughnut-shaped cloud. But for Joshua L. Mailman, that was mere prelude.

SOCIAL VENTURE CAPITAL

A second Mailman connection of special interest is the Social Venture Network (SVN), which he co-founded (with Wayne Silby, also co-founder of the Calvert Group and President of the Calvert Social Investment Fund) in 1987. The idea here was at once similar to that of the Threshold Foundation and different. The point of similarity lay in the concept of pooling relatively small collections of resources to achieve a social end. The point of difference lay in the types of resources in question. Where Threshold was a consortium of private philanthropies, SVN was designed to mobilize a network of businesses—mainly small to medium-sized—that were committed to an agenda of social and economic reform. In the words of the organization's membership statement, the goal of SVN "is to create a balanced and stimulating community of entrepreneurs, investors, corporate leaders, public interest innovators, and intellectuals committed to the use of business as a vehicle to create a more just, humane and environmentally sustainable society."[18]

By 2002, membership in the group had grown to approximately 450. Among them (at various times) have been companies such as Afropop Worldwide, Aveda, Ben & Jerry's, Body Shop International, Esprit, Levi Strauss, Next-Point Partners, Reebok International, Shaman Pharmaceuticals, Stonyfield Farms, Tom's of Maine, *Utne Reader* and Verité Inc., and a number of social-responsibility investment fund companies including Calvert Group, Domini Social Investments, Progressive Asset Management, and Working Assets Funding Service. In addition, the membership has included entities such as Citizen Action (renamed US Action after the group was involved in a scandal involving illegal contributions to the reelection campaign of Teamsters president Ron Carey), Co-op America, the Council on Economic Priorities, The Ford Foundation, Friends of the Earth, Human Rights Watch, the MacArthur Foundation, *Mother Jones* magazine, Rainforest Action Network, Responsible Wealth, the Rocky Mountain Institute, Social Investment Forum, the Surdna Foundation, Taxpayers for Common Sense and Witness. Medea Benjamin, founder of Global Exchange, has been a member of SVN, as has Fenton Communications, a Washington-based public relations firm that works on many Progressive advocacy campaigns.

The careful reader will recognize many of these entities as either investment vehicles or philanthropic interests of Mr. Mailman but will have to take it on faith that there are still more examples of both categories. In effect, then, SVN has served in part as a mechanism for integrating Mailman's own interests and, perhaps, for identifying new ones.

SVN was established, and operates, as a project of the Tides Foundation. Among those who have served on its board of directors are Ben Cohen of Ben & Jerry's, Sharon Cohen of Reebok International, Drummond Pike of the Tides Foundation, and, of course, Joshua Mailman. The organization hosts several educational institutes annually where members network and develop their business skills, as well as semi-annual national conferences where members interact with prominent Progressive activists. Other SVN initiatives and activities have included campaigns for organic food and environmental standards, fair trade practices, campaign finance reform, and a living wage, among others. In 1999, SVN published a code of conduct for corporations, a project in which Alice Tepper Marlin of the Council on Economic Priorities (CEP) participated; CEP was at the time engaged in advancing its own, far more elaborate code, known as SA8000. Both Josh Mailman and Drummond Pike took active roles as financial and content contributors to the SVN code, as did many other members.[19]

More interesting in some ways, however, has been SVN's penchant for spinning off related organizations. These include SVN affiliate groups in Europe and Asia; Net Impact, originally known as Students for Social Responsibility, a group of some 5,000 recent MBAs dedicated to new ways of doing business; and the Business Alliance for Local Living Economies, a sort of network of community-based mini-SVNs. Of greatest interest, however, is another SVN spinoff and the third of our key Josh Mailman connections—Business for Social Responsibility (BSR). Where SVN was designed to appeal to and serve primarily small to medium-sized businesses, BSR was designed to draw major corporations into the expanding web of the social responsibility movement. BSR, too, was a brainchild of Joshua Mailman.

HOOKING THE BIG FISH

BSR was founded by Robert Dunn of the Levi Strauss Foundation in 1992 around a core of 50 companies, including some familiar names from SVN— for example, Ben & Jerry's, Body Shop, Calvert Group, Levi Strauss, Working Assets—as well as a number of larger corporations. By 1996, it had grown beyond 800 members, including the likes of AT&T, Federal Express, The Gap, Home Depot, Honeywell, Hasbro, Polaroid, Taco Bell, Target Stores, and Time/Warner.[20] Based in Washington, DC, and San Francisco, the group operated that year on a budget of $2.6 million, about one third from members' dues and two thirds from grants provided by the Ford Foundation, Levi Strauss Foundation, Merck Family Fund, Pew Charitable Trust, Stride Rite Foundation, the US Department of Energy, and the Environmental Protection Agency, among others.[21] Dunn has remained as President and Arnold Hiatt, Chairman of the Stride Rite Foundation, has chaired the BSR board of directors from its inception; Joshua Mailman has served on that board throughout.

Today membership in BSR is something of a must-join for major American corporations, and the membership—now numbering more than 1,400— includes diverse companies such as Chevron Texaco, Chiquita Brands, Citigroup, Coca-Cola, Exxon Mobil, Freeport McMoRan, Gap, Home Depot, International Paper, McDonald's, Nestle, Nike, Phillips Van Heusen, Rio Tinto, Shell Oil, Starbucks, Wal-Mart, and Walt Disney.[22] I have selected these particular companies to make a point. What they have in common is that each has been the target of one or more anti-corporate campaigns—attacks on corporate reputations about which a good deal more is said in chapter 6. This may suggest that at least some companies see membership in BSR as providing a measure of cover, a defense against allegations that they are antisocial actors. For its part, BSR eschews this characterization, preferring instead to emphasize its commitment to working with member companies to promote what it views as more responsible business practices.

In that regard, it is interesting to note that, at least in earlier years (current information is not available), one of BSR's members was Alice Tepper Marlin, a former securities analyst who served as president of CEP, an organization that operated from 1969 through 2001. CEP took a rather more antagonistic approach to companies it regarded as acting irresponsibly. From 1992 through at least 1995, for example, the group launched a "Campaign for Cleaner Corporations," which publicized corporations regarded by the Council as bad actors. One judge of the 1995 "competition," New York University business professor Tom Gladwin, summarized the objectives of the exercise as follows[23]:

> A company's most important asset, that has to be most carefully managed, is its corporate reputation.... And reputation usually counts for about one-third of the company's share price. When that sinks in, listed companies should be at this door kissing our toes. What we have just engaged in today could wipe out a fraction of shareholder wealth. (p. 25)

Participants in the review process that led to these "awards" include some groups whose names have already been encountered in this narrative: Citizen Action, Co-Op America, Friends of the Earth, Government Accountability Project, Pesticide Action Network, Rainforest Action Network, and Working Assets (in this case, Working Assets Long Distance).[24] In other words, CEP established a mechanism by which advocacy groups antagonistic to corporations would judge and score corporate actions in a setting where threats to corporate reputations could be framed and leveraged to adversely affect shareholder value. If that sounds like a blueprint for Biz-War, the similarity is not coincidental.

CEP established processes for monitoring corporate behavior—precursors of the screens used today by social-responsibility fund managers—and in 1996 forged a global network of corporate social responsibility organizations from around the world. Some of the 70-plus people present at the Working Group's organizational meeting included Tim Smith, Executive Director of the Interfaith Center for Corporate Responsibility, one of the earliest players in the war on corporate reputations; Sharon Cohen, public relations vice president for Reebok and a board member of both SVN and BSR; Jon Lickerman of the Calvert Group; and representatives of Friends of the Earth, Progressive Asset Management, Co-Op America, the Ford Foundation and the Investor Responsibility Research Center. Among the sponsors of the session was Joshua Mailman. A principal objective appears to have been developing ways to pressure companies into releasing more information on what was termed their "social performance."[25]

Finally, CEP produced a series of industry- and company-specific reports addressing their respective social performances. Among the companies for which such reports were produced were Chevron and Texaco (since merged),

Citicorp (now Citigroup), Coca-Cola, Exxon and Mobil (since merged), Gap, Home Depot, International Paper, McDonald's, Nike, Shell Oil, Starbucks, Wal-Mart, Walt Disney—13 of the 18 companies listed as BSR members who had been subject to anti-corporate campaigns. More than two dozen other companies tracked by CEP were also subject to such attacks (among a much larger list of tracked companies).[26] Because information on CEP is no longer readily available, and because BSR does not release complete lists of its members or their dates of membership, we cannot know whether these two organizations operated as a collective carrot and stick for corporate social responsibility, an institutional rendition of good cop–bad cop, but the possibility is worth considering as a component of the emerging strategy to redirect corporate policies.

Sometime around 1996, and building on its by then rather elaborate mechanisms for evaluating corporate behaviors, CEP began evolving toward a different sort of organization, one that was less overtly an advocate and more broadly accepted as an arbiter. Later in this volume, I will examine the emergence of what are known as corporate "codes of conduct"—essentially statements of the standards of morality and behavior that various companies adopt as matters of policy. For now let us simply note that CEP staked out a leading role in this emergence through its development of a generic code of conduct known as SA8000 (the SA stood for social accountability). It then established a new entity, the Council on Economic Priorities Accreditation Agency (CEPAA), to evaluate the performance of those companies that signed on to its code. In 2001, CEP itself ceased to exist. CEPAA was succeeded by a nonprofit consultancy known as Social Accountability International (SAI). In this form, it continues to promulgate and accredit signatories to SA8000.[27] SAI has received major financial support from George Soros's Open Society Institute; the Ford, MacArthur, and Rockefeller Foundations; and the US Department of State.[28] Alice Tepper Marlin continues as President of this successor organization.

Although CEP has thus been fairly aggressive in assailing supposed corporate wrong-doers, BSR has restricted itself mainly to a more affirmative approach. The group provides advisory services for member companies such as policy and practice assessments, best-practices benchmarking, staff training, and assistance with reporting on social and environmental practices; conducts annual conferences with programs on topics such as the changing requirements of corporate social responsibility and the associated benefits (what BSR terms ROR or return on responsibility); training workshops on labor practices and corporate social responsibility; issues working groups and various publications.[29] In 1997, the BSR Education Fund and BSR President Robert Dunn, Progressive Asset Management, Joshua Mailman, and others sponsored a conference in Miami that led to the establishment of Forum Empresa to advance the corporate social responsibility agenda in the Western Hemisphere—a sort of BSR for the Americas.[30]

THE ASYNCHRONICITY OF
JOSHUA L. MAILMAN

From just these few of his ventures and involvements, it is clear that Joshua Mailman has played a substantial role in the reemergence of the Progressive Movement over the last twenty years. Figure 2.1 can help understand just how substantial that role has been. The figure illustrates Mailman's connections through his financial largesse to, or personal participation, either direct or at one step removed, in many of the advocacy organizations that carry that movement forward in the policy arena. And even this is an understatement of some magnitude, because many other connections are not included in the figure. (For assistance in interpreting Fig. 2.1, refer to the organizations listed in Table 2.1 and in the lists of foundation grantees that appear earlier in this chapter.)

Add to this web of connections his business investments and activities, which provide examples of the application of the second bottom line of corporate social responsibility, and Joshua Mailman stands as an apt icon of the new economy as imagined by the Progressive Left today—focused on social good as a core business objective—and of the path toward achieving it—by leveraging the assets of the reformers to the maximum extent possible. As Mailman himself put it in a self-revelatory 2002 essay he prepared for a seminar on the future of social change[31]:

> How can private interests be inspired to champion the public good as a key strategy in their global agenda? . . . We should remember that, as social activists interested in the future of social change, it is often necessary to seek the straw that breaks the camel's back, the most effective way to leverage our small resources to make major change. This is what I call asynchronous philanthropy . . . [which] means coming up with ideas that allow relatively small amounts of money to help bring about significant positive change.

Some years earlier, in 1993, he had expressed his views rather more pithily at a meeting of the Social Venture Network. He told his audience at the time that[32]:

> My father always told me that money is like manure. If you pile it up, it stinks. But if you spread it around, it can do a lot of good. If we do not use our wealth and resources to help lessen the gap between rich and poor, when the world looks back on us from the twenty-first century, people with money who didn't do anything will be remembered as the war criminals of the nineties. (p. 153)

Taking him on his own terms, the evidence of Fig. 2.1 suggests that such a charge would not stick to Joshua L. Mailman. Teflon.

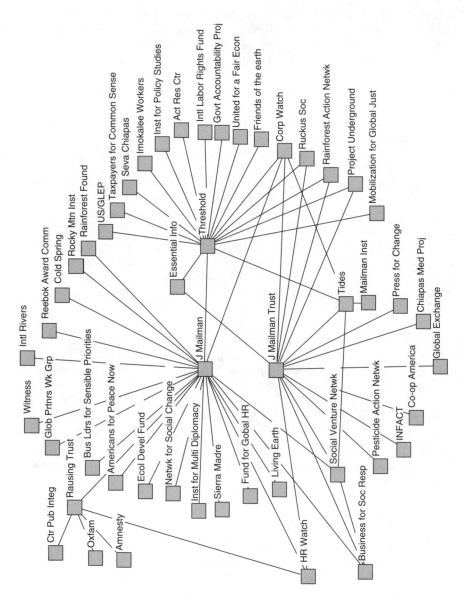

FIG. 2.1. The Joshua Mailman network.

ENDNOTES

1. George Harris and Daniel Yankelovich, "What Good Are the Rich? Charitable Activities of the Affluent," *Psychology Today* (23:4), April 1989, p. 36.
2. "Joseph L. Mailman, 88, Head of Philanthropy," *The New York Times*, July 10, 1990, p. B8.
3. T. J., "A Break in the Clouds?," *Forbes*, August 26, 1985, p. 167, and untitled news release from Gulfstream Land, PR Newswire, September 29, 1980.
4. Roy Rowan, "How the Mafia Loots JFK Airport," *Fortune*, June 22, 1987, p. 54.
5. T. J., op. cit.
6. Untitled news release from Air Express International, PR Newswire, June 21, 1984.
7. Ibid.
8. "Mailman Foundation Commits $33 Million to Columbia University School of Public Health," news release, Columbia University, July 2, 2000.
9. Kathleen Kernicky, "Supernova: Nationally Known Child Development Expert and a Nova Pioneer Steps Down After More than 30 Years of Helping Children," *Fort Lauderdale Sun-Sentinel*, June 5, 1997, p. 1E.
10. Harris and Yankelovich, loc. cit.
11. Threshold Foundation, *Guide for Grantseekers*, 2000.
12. Threshold Foundation, *2002 Committee Guidelines*.
13. Threshold Foundation, IRS Form 990 for 2000.
14. Judith Miller, "Old Money, New Needs," *The New York Times*, November 17, 1991, p. F40.
15. Threshold Foundation, IRS Form 990 for 1997–2000.
16. See, for example, the foundation's IRS Form 990-PF for 2000.
17. Nick Davies, "The Rausing family: what they give to charity," *The Guardian*, April 11, 2002. Retrieved October 4, 2003, from www.guardian.co.uk/uk_news/0,3604,682159,00.html.
18. Found on the SVN website at www.svn.org/memberpolicy.html on May 4, 1997. A later restatement of this objective can be found at www.svn.or/organization.html.
19. Social Venture Network, *Standards of Corporate Social Responsibility*, published in 1999 and found on the web at http://www.svn.org/Initiatives/PDF_standards.pdf, January 22, 2003.
20. This list was found at www.bsr.org/cosizes.html , August 22, 1996.
21. Found at www.bsr.org/bsrfact.html, August 22, 1996.
22. From a partial list of member companies found at www.bsr.org/Meta/MemberList.cfm, January 23, 2003.
23. Quoted in Paul A. Hilton and Alice Tepper Marlin, "1995 Results of the Campaign for Cleaner Corporations," in *Corporate Environmental Strategy* (Vol. 3, No. 3), 1995, p. 25.
24. Listed at www.accesspt.com/cep/research/c3/c3partic.html, April 6, 1997.
25. Information on this meeting was found at www.accesspt.com/cep/news996.htm, April 6, 1997.
26. The complete list as of 1997 appeared at www.accesspt.com/cep/reports.html, April 6, 1997.
27. Found at www.cepaa.org/AboutSAI/AboutSAI.htm, January 23, 2003.
28. Listed at www.cepaa.org/AboutSAI/GovernanceandFinancials.htm, January 23, 2003.
29. Information found at various locations accessible from www.bsr.org, January 23, 2003.
30. Information about Forum Empresa found at www.empresa.org, January 27, 2003.
31. From a seminar on "The Future of Social Change," CLAL Jewish Public Forum, May 20–21, 2002, New York City, as reproduced at www.clal.org/csa64.html, and found on January 22, 2003.
32. Quoted in Kenny Ausubel, *The Bioneers: A Declaration of Interdependence*, second edition (White River Junction, VT: Chelsea Green Publishing, 2001), p. 153.

3

Foundations of
Progressivism

In 1985, the Threshold Foundation switched coasts and affiliated itself with
an innovative and increasingly influential activist enterprise in San Francisco,
the Tides Foundation.

Established in 1976, the Tides Foundation was the brainchild of Drummond
Pike, who at the time was working as executive director of the Shalan Foundation. The concept of the foundation was similar to that which lay behind the Threshold Foundation—pooling the resources of progressive donors
and channeling them toward projects not typically supported by traditional
philanthropy—but his sense of scale was far more grandiose and his vision
more comprehensive. For Pike realized that for the pooling of resources to
work most effectively, someone would need to provide a variety of core
management services, not only for the donors, but for the recipients as
well.

A TAXING MATTER ... OR NOT

The collection of services Pike envisioned had a name—fiscal sponsorship—
and a long history, but at the time, and for the use Pike and other West
Coast activists had in mind, its legitimacy was in question. The idea of fiscal sponsorship is essentially this: A tax exempt charity decides to support
a nonexempt project and in the process extends a sort of umbrella of tax

44

exemption over that project, at least insofar as it retains "complete discretion and control" over the funds and so long as the project itself advances the sponsor's tax-exempt objectives. In this way, activities that do not qualify for tax exemption in their own right can legally benefit from tax-exempt contributions. Put another way, this is a device through which individual or corporate donors can give money to such projects and for which they can receive a tax deduction as if it were a charitable contribution.[1] The sponsoring organization—typically a foundation—might also provide a variety of administrative services to its sponsored projects—things like accounting services, office space, publicity, even fund-raising assistance, all under the umbrella of tax exemption.

It is easy to see why at first glance this might appear to be less than fully legitimate. In the words of one foundation executive[2]:

> Despite its long history, extensive utilization, and potential for efficiency and productivity, a stigma is often attached to the very concept of fiscal sponsorship. Some view it as a tax dodge: a shady sleight-of-hand to slip funds to activities that do not truly qualify as charitable. (p. viii)

But the fact is that such arrangements have long been commonplace, having been used primarily to support the activities of scientists, researchers, writers, artists, and performers. One embodiment of the idea is the university office of sponsored research, which typically helps university faculty to seek support of their research from governments, corporations, and private foundations and then manages the finances and administration of each grant, thereby freeing the researchers to . . . well, research.

By 1993, there was interest, not only in the arts community, which was straining under the financial pressures imposed by Presidents Reagan and Bush as they reduced the role of government in American society, but among the progressive activist community that was positioning itself to stage a counter-revolution, in using fiscal sponsorship to support a broader range of activities. With that and other less politicized objectives in mind, a group of San Francisco-based foundations, several of them already using fiscal sponsorship in some form, convened a meeting to explore the issues associated with such an initiative. Afterward, a local attorney who had not participated in the meeting, Gregory Colvin, was commissioned to write a book outlining several alternative models of fiscal sponsorship and suggesting how they might be put to use within the limits of the tax code. An important part of this undertaking was to find ways of legitimizing fiscal sponsorship as applied to supporting the arts and culture. The result—*Fiscal Sponsorship: 6 Ways to Do It Right*—has become something of a cult classic in the community of philanthropists. As the project developed, Colvin consulted with a small number of interested parties, among them Drummond Pike, who then contributed some comments to the book itself.[3]

To get a sense of just how fiscal sponsorship allows a stretching of the tax exemption boundaries, consider this from the "Fiscal Sponsorship Guidelines" published by the activist Agape Foundation.[4]

> The Foundation acts as a fiscal sponsor for tax deductible contributions to the legal and educational work of grassroots organizations.... Agape employs the pre-approved grant relationship model for fiscal sponsorship. Under this arrangement the individuals and nonexempt organizations do not become a program belonging to Agape. Instead, Agape chooses to further its exempt purposes indirectly, by giving financial support to an organization for a specific project that Agape believes will advance its own charitable goals.
>
> The following are examples of some of the issue areas Agape provides fiscal sponsorship to:

> - Peace—anti-military and anti-nuclear
> - Environmental justice and protection
> - Human rights
> - Economic justice

What sorts of groups fall within this definition? One example is that of Project Underground, which received support in 1998 to conduct campaigns against companies in the mining and petroleum industries.

RISING TIDES

As this more recent example suggests, the initial challenge for Pike and the Tides Foundation arose not from the device of fiscal sponsorship but from the areas of activity to which he sought to apply it. For it was his insight—not unique, but over time uniquely implemented—that this same logic could be used to provide a veneer of tax exemption for contributions to a collectivity of cause-based political activism. Through the Tides Foundation, Drummond Pike and co-founder Jane Begley Lehman[5] set out to gather together under one tax-exempt umbrella a potpourri of progressive projects that were unified and legitimized by their congruence with the stated tax-exempt objectives of the Tides Foundation, to wit[6]:

> Tides actively promotes change toward a healthy society, one which is founded on principles of social justice, broadly shared economic opportunity, a robust democratic process, and sustainable environmental practices.

That statement is unassailable—who in a liberal democracy would be against such things? It is comprehensive, potentially encompassing virtually all aspects of contemporary society. And it is nonpartisan, focusing on social outcomes and not on any specific party or platform. The one thing it is not is apolitical. To the contrary, it is an intensely political mission statement and one that is highly controversial, not at the level of broad and appealing statements of values, but at the level of specific implementation. It is not the words that are prospectively controversial but their interpretation as matters of policy and practice. This was Drummond Pike's key insight . . . and his market niche. The Tides Foundation would become the fiscal sponsor of the Progressive Left.

In 1977, Tides took on its first fiscally sponsored project, a film documentary on women in the military, but it was not until 1980 that Pike began to realize his vision in a more substantial way. In that year, in direct response to the Rightward shift in American politics and specifically to the election of Ronald Reagan as President, Norman Lear and others launched a new Tides project—People for the American Way (PFAW). PFAW began with a campaign of direct mail and public service announcements on the theme of tolerance. PFAW eventually would grow into a highly visible progressive voice in the debate over civil liberties, strong enough to cut its ties with Tides and operate independently. But in this early period, it stood as a marker of the new direction in which Tides would flow. In 1981, the foundation itself became a free-standing operation with a staff of two, and in 1982 it established its first donor-advised fund based on family giving, the 777 Fund, which focused on issues of women's reproductive health (the abortion debate) and the environment.

In 1985, as noted, Tides began providing administrative services as fiscal sponsor of the Threshold Foundation. In that same year, the International Rivers Network—perhaps not coincidentally another interest of Joshua Mailman—organized as a Tides project. Like PFAW, International Rivers became independent in 1992 but continues to receive financial support from the foundation. Then, in 1987, Tides expanded its portfolio still further by managing the operations of philanthropic programs for institutional clients. In 1987, the foundation launched a computer network for activists and non-profit organizations through another of its projects, the Institute for Global Communication (IGC). Through three issue-specific channels—PeaceNet, EcoNet, and ConflictNet—and for a time through a fourth—LaborNet—and by providing access to a long list of organizations, IGC played an essential role in developing the use of the Internet and the Web to mobilize, publicize, and fund progressive activism.

With its package of financial, legal, computer, and general administrative services, the Tides Foundation was positioned by 1990 to fulfill Pike's vision. At that point, Pike was joined by China Brotsky, hired initially as the foundation's Chief Financial Officer but more recently serving as Director of Special Projects, who would come to play a central role not only in the further development of Tides but also in several of its projects. The year before, the foundation had established separate staffs for its fiscal sponsorship projects and its grant-making activities, a distinction that was further institutionalized in 1996 when these components were reorganized into two quasi-independent units—the Tides Foundation, which would focus on grant-making, and the Tides Center, which would focus on fiscal sponsorship. In 1998, Tides launched eGrants.org—now known as Groundspring.org—an Internet-based foundation that functions as an online fund-raising and training center for progressive nonprofits as well as a clearinghouse for issue-based giving opportunities. Also in 1998, Tides established a management strategies and services component to work with family foundations and independent funding institutions. Most recently, in 2001, the Tides Center launched an internal network, TidesNet, to provide real-time financial information for Tides projects—a service closely akin to online banking.[7]

Although this infrastructure development has made Tides unique and highly influential in the Progressive Movement, it is only a part of the real Tides story. For along the way, the Foundation has raised and distributed a great deal of money—more than $225 million in its first quarter century. In 2000 alone, it distributed more than $56 million, *double* the amount awarded in 1999. And in 2000 the Foundation and the Tides Center between them managed 350 projects. Both of these measures have shown nearly uninterrupted growth for 20 years or more.[8]

At the top of the organization chart of the Tides Foundation is the board of directors, among whose members are[9]:

- Drummond Pike, who, as President, retains his active interest in Tides
- Joanie Bronfman (recall Joseph Mailman's friendship with Edgar Bronfman), who previously served on the board of the Threshold Foundation and as founder of Threshold's Social Justice Committee—one of six programmatic foci of the foundation
- Wade Rathke, founder and chief organizer of the activist group ACORN and chief organizer as well of Local 100 (New Orleans) of the Service Employees International Union (SEIU); Rathke is the only board member other than Pike to serve also on the board of the Tides Center
- Joel Solomon, a former president of the Threshold Foundation and a founding member of the Social Venture Network.

The central role of the Doughnuts and the Threshold Foundation in Tides operations is not the only connection between Tides and Joshua Mailman. The Tides Foundation provided a home for another Mailman enterprise, the Social Venture Network, for example, and for its spin-off, Business for Social Responsibility, and the Mailman Institute—Mailman's strategy-development center for activists—is organized as a project of the Tides Center. There is substantial overlap between the groups to which Mailman contributes and those operated or supported by Tides. And, of course, Mailman continues as a significant contributor to Tides.

Table 3.1, which lists a sampling of grants awarded by the Tides Foundation in the period 1998–2000, provides a useful indicator of the breadth and

TABLE 3.1

Selected Grants Awarded by the Tides Foundation, 2000

Recipient	1998 award [1]	1999 award	2000 award	2001 award	1998–2001 total
ACORN	52,121		2,500	140,000	194,621
Adbusters Media Project				28,899	28,899
Alliance for Global Justice			1,000	5,000	6,000
Alliance for Justice	50,000	112,000	325,000	275,000	762,000
Americans for Peace Now				66,050	66,050
Amnesty International USA	102,500	48,172	67,000	57,165	274,837
Applied Research Center	26,000	41,100	172,000	25,000	264,100
Business Leaders for Responsible Priorities		10,000	5,000	300,500	315,500
Business for Social Responsibility (US and Canada)	5,000	20,800		15,632	41,432
Center for Campus Organizing	5,000	12,239	1,000	14,492	32,731
Center for Environmental Citizenship		196,000			196,000
Center for Investigative Reporting	27,300	53,847	3,900	74,000	159,047
Center for Science in the Public Interest				25,000	25,000
Changemakers		6,500	69,500	123,100	199,100
Coalition of Immokalee Workers	5,000	7,600	8,000		20,600
Coalition for Justice in Maquiladoras				55,000	55,000
Co-Op America				10,000	10,000
The Data Center	21,000	10,000	37,500	80,000	148,500
Earth Island Institute	68,999	92,100	188,565	82,637	432,301
Earth Justice Legal Defense Fund	500	41,744	36,500	20,950	99,694
Economic Policy Institute	5,000	5,000	100,000		110,000
Environmental Defense Fund	1,352	4,850	717	129,000	135,919
Environmental Media Services			25,000	80,400	105,400
Environmental Working Group			18,763		18,763
Essential Information	500		8,131	5,000	13,631
Fairness & Accuracy in Reporting	35,629	2,500	32,368	4,220	74,717
Florence Fund				15,000	15,000
Foundation for National Progress				1,000	1,000
Friends of the Earth	141,897		24,500	42,500	208,897
Friends of the Earth Action			43,438		43,438
Fund for Constitutional Government			1,000		1,000
Fund for Investigative Journalism			18,954		18,954

(Continued)

TABLE 3.1

(Continued)

Recipient	1998 award	1999 award	2000 award	2001 award	1998–2001 total
Global Exchange	24,701	8,500	21,910	7,000	62,111
Government Accountability Project	12,500	5,000	7,300		24,800
Greenpeace and Greenpeace Fund	25,000	65,163	5,200	55,772	151,135
Highlander Center	5,000	16,000			21,000
Human Rights Watch	39,756	39,500	42,136	9,500	130,892
Independent Media Institute	1,000	2,500	1,000	25,000	29,500
Independent Press Association		5,000		28,519	33,519
INFACT			13,000		13,000
Institute for Agriculture and Trade Policy	113,320	64,458	41,000	57,400	276,178
Institute for America's Future	20,000	25,000		100,000	145,000
Institute for Media Analysis				51,750	51,750
Institute for Policy Studies		2,500	16,700	15,000	34,200
Institute for Public Affairs	1,000	1,500	1,000	113,500	117,000
Interfaith Center on Corporate Responsibility				14,409	14,409
Inter-hemispheric Resource Center	5,000				5,000
International Media Project	1,000	26,500	16,000	12,000	55,500
International Rivers Network	12,802	2,000	22,450	51,059	88,311
Internews Network	140,000	142,000	140,000	140,000	562,000
Lawyers Committee for Human Rights		2,000	2,000		4,000
League of Conservation Voters & LCV Education Fund	253,000	162,759	140,150	147,734	703,643
Living Earth Foundation		98,400	19,601		118,001
Livingry Fund				8,239,500	8,239,500
Los Angeles Alliance for a New Economy			5,000	95,000	100,000
Mailman Institute		18,725		44,000	62,725
Media Alliance	2,000	7,500	8,000	4,000	21,500
Media Foundation	3,620	68,699	34,565		106,884
Michigan Citizen Action			5,000		5,000
Midwest Academy	1,500	13,790	1,000	2,000	18,290
National Interfaith Committee for Worker Justice				20,000	20,000
National Labor Committee Education Fund in Support of Worker and Human Rights in Central America		13,872	2,000	52,500	68,372
National Lawyers Guild	21,286	2,500		5,000	28,786
National Network of Grantmakers	27,500	34,500			62,000

(Continued)

TABLE 3.1

(Continued)

Recipient	1998 award	1999 award	2000 award	2001 award	1998–2001 total
Natural Resources Defense Council	134,447	30,000	3,000	112,800	280,247
NGO Coalition for Environment			6,000	21,626	27,626
Oxfam America	270,749	82,500	42,057	16,720	412,026
People for the American Way Foundation and Action Fund	4,600	33,694	5,000	20,190	63,484
Pesticide Action Network	61,508	6,900	8,250	17,000	93,658
Political Research Associates	28,000	57,500	46,101	21,500	153,101
Preamble Center & Preamble Collaborative	20,000		13,000	10,000	43,000
Press for Change				1,000	1,000
Progressive America Fund				170,000	170,000
Project Underground		28,551	46,000	15,000	89,551
Public Citizen and Public Citizen Foundation	5,600		74,725		80,325
Public Media Center		1,250	62,000	143,000	206,250
Rainforest Action Network	8,840	17,450	55,778	13,300	95,368
Rainforest Foundation		1,800	2,000		3,800
Rocky Mountain Institute		500		25,000	25,500
Ruckus Society		5,000	18,400	16,000	39,400
Sierra Club and Sierra Club Foundation	495,000	214,500	110,500	29,500	849,500
Sierra Madre Alliance	20,000		19,650	500	40,150
Social Venture Network		3,250	562	500	3,312
Threshold Foundation	306,010	139,775	139,700	125,449	710,934
Transnational Resource and Action Center/CorpWatch		7,000	10,000	25,000	42,000
United for a Fair Economy		63,808	40,500	22,895	127,203
US Public Interest Research Group	250,000	11,000	10,000	15,000	286,00
United States Student Association Foundation			10,000	1,000	11,000
Wilderness Society				51,000	51,000

[1] The data reported here are drawn from IRS Forms 990 filed by the Tides Foundation covering the years 1998–2001. In 1998, the Foundation reported a long list of otherwise unspecified contributions to projects of the Tides Center. These grants ranged in value from $200 to $100,000. In subsequent years, Tides Center grant recipients were identified by name, and several of these appear in the table. Consequently, contributions to these projects in 1998 may be understated. In addition, it should be noted that there is some ambiguity about the flow of funds through the Tides Foundation and other foundations that operate under its umbrella. This has two consequences. First, contributions from Tides to other related foundations—the Threshold Foundation and the Livingry Fund being substantial cases in point—may then be awarded in the form of grants by the second foundation. These awards would not be reflected in this table. Similarly, awards from Tides-related foundations to inside or outside projects are not captured here. Accordingly, both the overall level of support for specific recipients and the list of recipients itself, as reported here, are incomplete.

character of the foundation's philanthropy. Tides has awarded support to a wide range of progressive advocates but has at the same time taken a particular interest in the environmental movement and a recent interest in all manner of projects relating to the media.

A related, but more structural, interest is reflected in the projects of the Tides Center, a few of which are listed and characterized in Table 3.2. While these fiscally sponsored projects share the same progressive political orientation as those supported by grants from the Tides Foundation, they also share a common emphasis on creating a supporting infrastructure for progressive activism—whether in the form of anti-corporate or pro-social responsibility research, message construction, social networking, policy development, strategy formation, or recruitment. Collectively, then, they represent a sort of starter kit for advancing the new-economy notions of the Progressive Left, and the Tides Center serves as an incubator for that activity. Together with the Tides Foundation, it effectively generates new ideas or social change technologies and gives them an opportunity and a nurturing setting in which to prove themselves; then—People for the American Way being but one example—it sends them out into the world. In this, the role of the Tides Foundation is to prospect for, accumulate, and distribute money mainly from relatively small donors such as modest family foundations, which can be leveraged to support project development. At the same time, the foundation supports a large number of independent, but politically like-minded, organizations—sometimes with very large amounts of money.

The nature of this enterprise comes through quite clearly in a retreat that the Tides Foundation has conducted annually beginning in 1999—"Making Money Make Change"—which is billed as "a gathering for progressive people with wealth, ages 15–35." Sponsored by agencies such as Responsible Wealth, the Calvert Foundation, and the Threshold Foundation, in the call for the September 2002 session the Tides Foundation, asked:

- Is this gathering for me?
- Do you have or expect to come into inherited wealth? Do you have earned wealth? Or are you the partner of someone with wealth?
- Do you want to work with others to create a more just and equitable society?
- Would you like to talk with your peers about the opportunities and challenges of having wealth?
- Are you interested in strategic philanthropy, responsible consumption, and/or effective social change activism?
- Do you want to use your resources to transform society and promote innovative social change? [10]

Whereas the Tides Foundation and Center take as a central part of their mission the recruitment of the individually wealthy and the leveraging of their wealth, they are scarcely averse to accepting money from major foundations,

TABLE 3.2

Selected Projects of the Tides Center, 2000[1]

Project	Description
2030 Center	Organizes young leaders to advance a progressive economic agenda and provides services to other like-minded organizations in the form of research, information, and message development
Corporate Sources	Undertakes investigative research on the environmental records of major corporations and publishes company profiles emphasizing lobbying and advertising, environmental records, labor relations, shareholder relations, and compliance with environmental laws
CorpWatch	Previously known as the Transnational Resource and Action Center, publishes the Corporate Watch web site, which campaigns on allegations of environmental and social malfeasance by corporations
eActivist.org	Provides a clearinghouse for electronic actions and tools for electronic activists; objective is to be the focal point of progressive activism on the Web
Economics Working Group	Seeks to create a General Agreement on a New Economy (GANE) based on the principles of environmental sustainability, equity, and full employment; includes focus on the need to curtail corporate power; appears to be modeled after an earlier Tides project, the Environmental Working Group
Institute for Global Communications	Provides computer networking tools for activists organized into four issue-specific networks—PeaceNet, EcoNet, WomensNet, and ConflictNet; for a period included LaborNet; links to an international network of such service providers through the Association for Progressive Communications
Mailman Institute	Conducts small-group discussions among activists to develop strategic plans of action
Net Action	Claims to create coalitions linking online activists with community-based organizations but only activity to date appears to be participation in a campaign coalition with labor and consumer groups and corporate competitors arrayed against Microsoft
New Economy Communications	Packages the agenda of progressive populism in messages that will appeal to the public and policymakers
Pew Center for Civic Journalism	Promotes the notion of civic journalism–i.e., journalism that addresses community concerns and employs community perspectives
Pew Center for People and the Press	Conducts public opinion research on media issues as well as social and political values
Pew Internet and American Life Project	Seeks to be the authoritative source for information on the growth and social impact of the Internet, with an emphasis on issues of education, health care, political participation, and citizenship
Social Venture Network	Promotes progressive business practices; see chapter 2 for details

[1]These profiles are based the listing of Tides Center projects retrieved January 29, 2003, from www.tidescenter.org.

as the inclusion in Table 3.2 of three separate projects supported by the Pew Charitable Trusts might suggest. In fact, Tides has benefited from some rather substantial support from its more traditional and more substantial philanthropic brethren. According to figures provided by one conservative watchdog organization, for example, Tides received:

- $108.8 million from the Pew Charitable Trusts between 1990 and 2002,
- $26.4 million from the Ford Foundation between 1989 and 2002,
- $7.3 million from the Open Society Institute (the philanthropic and social policy arm of the George Soros financial empire) between 1997 and 2002, and
- sizeable contributions from a wide range of other progressive activist foundations, including the John D. & Catherine T. MacArthur Foundation, Florence and John Schumann Foundation, David and Lucille Packard Foundation, William and Flora Hewitt Foundation, Charles Stewart Mott Foundation, Nathan Cummings Foundation, Joyce Foundation, Rockefeller Foundation and the Rockefeller Brothers Fund, Levi Strauss Foundation, Surdna Foundation, Vanguard Public Foundation, Arca Foundation, and Public Welfare Foundation, to name but a few of the roughly 40 foundations that have contributed more than $600,000 to Tides projects.[11]

Indeed, it is fair to say that the accelerating growth evident in Tides grant making is a direct function of this sizeable and increasing flow of "serious" money from more mainstream foundations, which may see Tides as a mechanism for funding activism with which they would prefer to maintain an arms-length relationship.

One analysis—again by a conservative organization critical of Tides—suggests, for example, that one explanation for the substantial flow of Pew money through the Tides Center is the fact that these projects distribute direct grants to for-profit media companies, an activity that is precluded for private foundations (Pew) but not for so-called 501(c)(3) organizations—a designation for nonprofits in the tax code—of which the Tides Center is one. This same critique suggests that another attraction of working through the Tides Center is that, even as each project retains de facto independence, any expenses for lobbying activity in which these projects might engage—and they do lobby to some extent—would be treated for tax exemption purposes not as lobbying by the individual projects but as lobbying by the Tides Center itself. Because the tax code does permit a limited degree of such activity by 501(c)(3) organizations, the multimillion dollar budget of the umbrella organization would ensure that the smaller amounts spent on lobbying by individual projects would not be sufficiently material to be disqualifying.[12] In this view, much of the Tides operation constitutes little more than a scheme to circumvent the tax laws.

The purpose here is not to judge that question one way or the other but rather to understand, from a strategic perspective, the role that Tides, its partners, and its affiliates play in the re-emergence of the Progressive Left. We can safely characterize that role with two words: imaginative and substantial.

FOUNDATION ACTIVISM

That said, as the preceding analysis clearly indicates, there are a lot more players in this game than Tides and many with vastly superior resources to those of Pike and his minions. Although it would be interesting to catalogue the full range of activist foundations, the list is a long one indeed—far too long for this volume. So in its stead, let us focus on just five of the more prominent, more politically engaged, and more interesting participants in this game of funding social change. All except the Schumann Foundation are drawn from the membership of the National Network of Grantmakers, formed by Pike and some colleagues in 1980. Membership in this group can be taken as a primary indicator of a commonality of interest in advancing the progressive social, political, and economic agenda. As we will see, the Schumann Foundation is a member of this group in spirit if not in fact.

The Arca Foundation

Arca, established in 1952, is a primary outlet for the Reynolds family's tobacco fortune. In its early days, the foundation supported projects focusing on population control and human rights, interests of its founder, Nancy Susan Reynolds. More recently, as later generations of the family have joined the foundation's board of directors, the emphasis has shifted toward environmental issues, U.S. foreign policy toward Cuba and Central America, and efforts to curb corporate influence in American politics. In 2001, the foundation had net assets of about $75 million and made more than $3 million worth of grants, enough to make it a meaningful partner, but not enough to make it a dominant force, in progressive philanthropy.[13] In addition to several members of the family, key board members include Margery Tabankin (who also serves as President of the Barbra Streisand Foundation and Executive Director of Stephen Spielberg's Righteous Persons Foundation) and Janet Shenk (Special Assistant to AFL-CIO President John Sweeney and formerly Executive Director of *Mother Jones* magazine, published by the Foundation for National Progress).

The Nathan Cummings Foundation

Nathan Cummings (1896–1985) was the force behind the Sara Lee Corporation, which he built from a small Baltimore purveyor of tea and canned foods into a cake-baking (and much more) powerhouse. He also built a sizeable personal fortune, which is the basis for this foundation dedicated to building "a socially and economically just society that values nature and protects the ecological balance for future generations."[14] The foundation supports projects that contribute toward its goals of fostering concern for the disadvantaged, respect for diversity, cultural understanding, and community empowerment. The board of directors is dominated by members of the family, but headed by President and CEO Lance Lindblom, who joined Cummings from a previous posting as executive vice president of the Open Society Institute. The foundation has assets of approximately $400 million and makes annual awards on the order of $15 million.

Open Society Institute

The Open Society Institute (OSI) is the philanthropic arm of international financier George Soros, who has been described as "the most important philanthropist to come along since Andrew Carnegie"—perhaps because he has pledged to keep giving until his entire fortune, estimated variously at between $3 and $5 billion, is gone.[15] The total amount of grants and fellowships distributed annually by OSI varies widely but is generally on the order of $150 million, placing the foundation far in the forefront of progressive givers. Much of this money is distributed outside the United States, most notably in Eastern Europe and the states of the former Soviet Union, but a sizeable amount—$99 million in 2000 alone—goes to U.S. recipients.[16] In 2002, OSI opened a Washington office with a $2 million annual budget, of which $750,000 was specifically earmarked for lobbying on Capitol Hill.[17]

Public Welfare Foundation

The Public Welfare Foundation was established in 1948 by newspaper publisher Charles Edward Marsh, who endowed it by transferring ownership of three newspapers in Alabama and South Carolina. These were eventually sold to the New York Times Company in 1985. Today the foundation has an endowment of approximately $400 million and in 2001 awarded just under $20 million in grants. The foundation's mission is to help people overcome barriers to full participation in society. Today that is interpreted as comprising three components: service, advocacy, and empowerment.[18]

Florence and John Schumann Foundation/The Florence Fund

Florence Ford was the daughter of a founder of IBM, and John Schumann was a successful businessman who rose to the position of president of General Motors Acceptance Corporation. Their combined fortunes provided the endowment for the Schumann Foundation, which was established in 1961. At the end of 2001, the foundation had assets of approximately $75 million and in that year made grants of approximately $7.5 million. Of particular interest is the president of the foundation, journalist Bill Moyers, who also serves as a director of the Open Society Institute. Moyers has, on occasion, used the pulpit provided by his role as a journalist on PBS to advance anti-corporate Progressive causes, as he did, for example, in a March 2001 program attacking the chemical industry, which was partly based on data gathered by the Environmental Working Group and was followed by a related campaign by Working Assets-affiliated ActForChange.com.[19] The Schumann Foundation is rather less forthcoming about itself than some others but maintains programs focused on effective government, the environment, and the media.[20] In the 1990s, the foundation created the Florence Fund, an independent entity based in Washington and headed by Moyers' son John. The Florence Fund operates a website, Tompaine.com, and also serves as a conduit for funds to a number of progressive advocacy organizations, focusing on those that are judged to have potential for carrying their messages forward through paid media strategies. In 2000, for example, from its total budget of $2.2 million, the fund paid $95,000 to Fenton Communications, a Washington-based communications firm, and $795,000 to the *New York Times*, for what were characterized as advertising expenses. Unlike the other foundations described here, Florence does not have a significant asset base of its own. It ended the year 2000, during which it awarded more than $2 million to projects, with net assets of just $2.8 million. From this it is clear that the Florence Fund is more of a money-transferring vehicle than an independent source of funds in its own right.[21]

A NETWORK OF LIKE MINDS

Recall that four of these five foundations are members of the National Network of Grantmakers (NNG). NNG has a membership of 400 grantmakers who are dedicated to what the organization terms "systemic progressive social change," which it defines as an equitable distribution of wealth and power, and mutual respect for all peoples.[22] Two of the foundations described previously, Arca and Public Welfare, are represented on the board of directors, as is the Tides Foundation in the person of executive director Idelisse Malavé. In a 1998 report, NNG further defined social-change giving, and the common mission of its members, as follows[23]:

> The U.S. now has the widest gap between rich and poor of any industrialized country in the world, and it is increasing every day. However, the vast majority of private charitable giving goes not to help "the needy," but to Ivy League universities, museums, symphonies, think-tanks, private hospitals, prep schools and the like—groups that sustain the status, culture, education and policy positions of the well-to-do. Compared with $13.8 billion in domestic grants distributed in 1997 by the nation's 42,000 private foundations, only $336 million went to progressive philanthropy—just 2.4% of the total. Social change giving is about reaching those that most charitable giving ignores, but who are in greatest need of help. These include: low-income children

and women, the disabled, the elderly, and the poor in general, gay, lesbian, bisexual and transgender communities, and people of color.

It is, of course, one thing to espouse such common cause and quite another to act on the claim. Thus it is not only reasonable, but important, to ask whether this ostensible network of like minds produces a series of shared behaviors. To answer that question, at least in part, let us select the five foundations described previously, plus the Tides Foundation, and examine more closely their grant-giving activity. Specifically, let us identify a market-basket of progressive advocacy or action groups who might be recipients of foundation largesse, and see if their experience evidences common patterns of giving on the part of the foundations in question. This is accomplished in Figure 3.1.

Figure 3.1 is sufficiently complex as to appear all but indecipherable, but that is, in fact, the point. The figure illustrates the connections between the six foundations in question—Arca, Cummings, Open Society Institute, Public

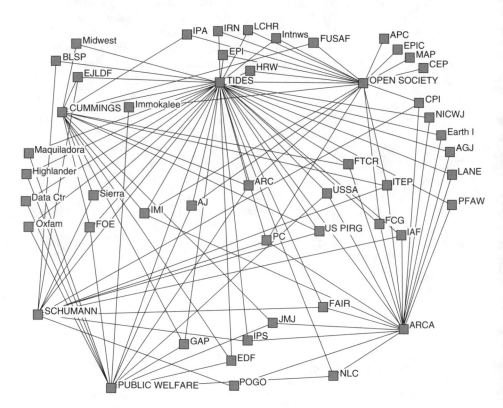

FIG. 3.1.   Selected interlocking program interests among progressive foundations.[24]

Welfare, Schumann (including the affiliated Florence Fund), and Tides, on the one hand, and 44 selected progressive activist organizations, on the other. The foundations are shown at the perimeter of the figure and the recipients of their support in the interior. If there were no overlap in the giving patterns of these foundations, each would be surrounded by a unique cluster of recipients unconnected to the other foundations. What we see instead is a complex web of multisource support.

The recipients shown in Fig. 3.1 have been organized into seven highly subjective and very broadly conceived clusters, including consumer and whistleblower (e.g., US PIRG), Environment (e.g., FOE), progressive infrastructure (e.g., ARC), economics and ideology (e.g., EPI), media and communication (e.g., FAIR), human rights (e.g., HRW), and culture (e.g., Highlander). All but a very few of these groups receive money from at least two of the six foundations, and quite a number are supported by three or more. In addition, note that every one of the other five foundations also contributes money to the Tides Foundation and/or the Tides Center, which may then pass that money through to the same group of recipients—making it appear that the group has broader support than it actually does—or to different recipients—in effect masking the giving pattern of the originating foundation.

THE BOTTOM LINE ON THE BOTTOM LINE

As we come to the end of this stage of our discussion, let us be quite clear. The methodology used here is both subjective and selective. All these foundations—including Tides, Threshold, and the Joshua Mailman Trust—contribute large amounts of money to educational, health-related, cultural, and other traditional causes, none of which is examined here. And all the recipient organizations on which we have focused most recently receive additional significant support from other sources as well. It is not our purpose to argue otherwise. But for all of that, it is also the case that there has evolved over the past two decades a new style of philanthropy, one much more focused on effecting social change through the leveraging of private giving. Recall Joshua Mailman's characterization of asynchronous philanthropy—giving at the edge where the balance might most easily be tipped. That is precisely the exercise in which these and other progressive foundations are engaged, and they are doing it today with several hundred million dollars per year.

Is that enough to achieve their objectives?

At the November 2002 regional meeting in Washington, DC, of NNG, the "trade association" of progressive philanthropists, this question was in the forefront. More specifically, the discussion centered around the following major concerns[25]:

1. The left is underfunded, unprepared, fragmented and not strategic.
2. The left is losing the war of ideology.
3. Progressive funders need to invest more in advocacy and electoral strategies.

Clearly, those whose money is on the line are not satisfied with the results to date, nor are they particularly sanguine about the future. But as we are about to see, theirs is not the only game in town.

ENDNOTES

1. Gregory L. Colvin, *Fiscal Sponsorship: 6 Ways to Do It Right*, second edition (San Francisco: Study Center Press, 2000), pp. 2–3.
2. John Kreidler of the San Francisco Foundation, quoted in Colvin, op. cit., p. viii.
3. Colvin, op. cit., pp. viii, 60.
4. The guidelines were found online at www.agapefn.org/fsguides.html, November 1, 2002.
5. Ms. Lehman was the grand-daughter of R. J. Reynolds, whose tobacco fortune also funds the Arca Foundation and others. She chaired the Tides Foundation until her death in 1988. *Tides: 1976–2001, 25 Years of Working Toward Positive Social Change* (San Francisco: Tides Foundation, 2002), p. 10.
6. From the statement of purpose found at http://www.tides.org/index_tds.cfm, January 27, 2003.
7. This brief history of the Tides Foundation is grounded in the timeline published in *Tides: 1976–2001, 25 Years of Working Toward Positive Social Change* (San Francisco: Tides Foundation, 2002), pp. 8–13.
8. Ibid., p. 5.
9. Annual Report of the Tides Foundation, 2000, p. 36.
10. Information on the meeting was found at www.tidesfoundation.org/mmmc/index.cfm, October 7, 2002.
11. These data were found under the "Tides" file at www.consumerfreedom.com/activistcash/ on January 29, 2003.
12. Patrick Reilly, "The Tides Foundation and Center: Unusual Philanthropies Funnel Money to Activist Groups," *Foundation Watch* (January 1998). *Foundation Watch* is a publication of the Capital Research Center in Washington, DC.
13. Based on the history of the foundation found at http://fdncenter.org/grantmaker/arca/history.html, January 30, 2003.
14. From the foundation's mission statement as found at http://www.ncf.org/aboutncf/mission.html, January 30, 2003.
15. David Callahan,, "George Soros: Open Society Crusader in Retreat?," *Journal: Civnet's Journal for Civil Society* (Vol. 3, No. 2), March-April 1999. Retrieved October 4, 2003, from www.civnet.org/journal/vol3no2/rpgsoros.htm.
16. From IRS Form 990 for 2000.
17. David Bank, "Major Philanthropists Lobby to Promote Their Pet Causes," *Wall Street Journal*, June 19, 2002. p. B1.
18. Information on the foundation was found on its web site at www.publicwelfare.org on January 30, 2003, and in IRS Form 990 for 2001.
19. The program, "Trade Secrets," aired on March 26, 2001, and was supported by an elaborate web site at www.pbs.org/tradesecrets. See the related discussion found online at www.alternet.org/chemicals.html, April 18, 2001.
20. Much of this information derives from the foundation's IRS Form 990 for 2001.
21. From IRS Form 990 for 2000.

22. From the NNG "Vision Statement" and "Mission Statement" found at http://www.nng.org/html/whoweare/mission_table.htm, January 29, 2003.

23. *Social Change Grantmaking in the U.S.: The Mid-1990s*, report prepared by the National Network of Grantmakers, September 1998, and found online at http://www.nng.org/html/ourprograms/research/socchangeppr_table.htm#wscg, January 29, 2003.

24. In an effort to simplify Figure 3.1 to the extent possible, acronyms or short titles have been employed to identify the recipient organizations. They are: AGJ (Alliance for Global Justice), AJ (Alliance for Justice), APC (Association for Progressive Communications), ARC (Applied Research Center), BLSP (Business Leaders for Sensible Priorities), CEP (Council on Economic Priorities), CPI (Center for Public Integrity), Data Ctr (The Data Center), Earth I (Earth Island Institute), EJLDF (Earth Justice Legal Defense Fund), EDF (Environmental Defense Fund), EPI (Economic Policy Institute), EPIC (Electronic Privacy Information Center, a project of FCG), FAIR (Fairness and Accuracy in Media), FCG (Fund for Constitutional Government), FOE (Friends of the Earth), FTCR (Foundation for Taxpayer and Consumer Rights), FUSAF (Families USA Foundation), GAP (Government Accountability Project, a project of FCG), Highlander (Highlander Education and Research Center), HRW (Human Rights Watch), IAF (Institute for Americas Future), IMI (Independent Media Institute), Immokalee (Coalition of Immokalee Workers), Intnews (Internews Network), IPA (Independent Press Association), IPS (Institute for Policy Studies), IRN (International Rivers Network), ITEP (Institute on Taxation and Economic Policy), JWJ (Jobs with Justice), LANE (Los Angeles Alliance for a New Economy), LCHR (Lawyers Committee for Human Rights), MAP (Media Access Project), Maquiladora (Coalition for Justice in Maquiladoras), Midwest (Midwest Academy), NICWJ (National Interfaith Committee for Worker Justice), NLC (National Labor Committee), Oxfam (Oxfam America), PC (Public Citizen), PFAW (People for the American Way), POGO (Project on Government Oversight, a project of FCG), Sierra (Sierra Club), US PIRG (US Public Interest Research Group), and USSA (United States Student Association). Some of these contributions have gone to educational or legal defense funds or to foundations associated with the organization in question. We have already had occasion to mention several of these organizations, and will examine others in more detail as we proceed.

25. Extracted from the summary of the meeting found at www.nng.org/html/conferences/field/nov%2019.htm, January 27, 2003.

4

Archimedes' Lever...and Thor's Hammer

Give me a lever long enough
And a prop strong enough
I can single-handed move the world
— Archimedes

According to the Internal Revenue Service, which collects data on such things, in 1999 the total fair market value of investment assets held by private foundations in the United States was $444 billion; gifts and grants by these foundations totaled $22.8 billion.[1] That includes not only the activities of the progressive activist foundations on the short list in chapter 3 and *all* their like-minded counterparts but the activities of every other private foundation in the country—from the health- and education-centered projects of the Bill and Melinda Gates Foundation (the nation's largest and fastest growing) to those, like the Lynde and Harry Bradley Foundation and the other supporters of conservative causes listed in chapter 1. Indeed, although the Progressive agenda has spread to a great many foundations in recent years, they still account for well less than half of all gift and grant-making activity, which continues to favor traditional charitable causes like the arts, universities, and health care research.

And even with their substantial, growing, and increasingly targeted largesse, these would-be agents of social change are but a drop in the ocean of the American economy. As a point of comparison, consider Citigroup—a financial services company whose components include Citibank, Travelers Insurance, and Salomon Smith Barney, among others—which had total assets as of December 31, 2001, of $1.05 *trillion* and net earnings before taxes for that year of $21.9 billion. Put another way, Citigroup alone, which, by the way, frequently finds itself on the receiving end of pressure from Progressive activists, could, if it so chose, effectively match and better the resources of the entire network of Progressive activist foundations and organizations. And Citigroup is but one of a great many large and highly profitable corporations. That is a core reality of some consequence.

FUTILITY, OR UTILITY?

One of the essential differences between philanthropic wealth and corporate wealth is that the former is largely static, whereas the latter is inherently dynamic. Philanthropic wealth is based on the accreted sum of the assets of philanthropic organizations—the amount of money already residing in foundation hands. It grows over time, but only slowly, through two processes—return on investment and recruitment of new philanthropists. Because foundations are fiduciaries, they are required to invest in relatively conservative vehicles, those that minimize risk to the underlying principal of the funds in trust. With some exceptions—notably the extraordinary growth in value of the stock markets in the 1990s—such investments typically have low rates of return. And while new philanthropists arrive on the scene every year, relatively few—George Soros and Bill Gates being particular exceptions—are wealthy enough to have a significant impact on the aggregated sum of foundation giving.

Corporate wealth, on the other hand, is based on the *flow* of money *through* a company—money that is generated daily through the conduct of the company's business. And where foundations exist to steward their funds, businesses exist to grow theirs—it is their essential raison d'être. To achieve that, corporations are entitled, should they so choose, to assume all manner of risk. They may fail altogether, or they may become Wal-Mart, General Electric, or General Motors. In this game, major corporations are the National Football League, and foundations are high school ball.

Consider: At the end of 2001, the Bill and Melinda Gates Foundation had total net assets of $32 billion and unrestricted net assets (available for programs) of $21.6 billion; during the year the Foundation made grants of more than $1.4 billion. The Foundation had income of $2.2 billion from new contributions and $1.2 billion from investments.[2] The latter amounted to a rate of return on investments of about 5%. In the same year, Microsoft Corporation, the source of the Foundation's wealth, had net *income* before taxes of $11.7 billion (of which $7.7 billion remained after Uncle Sam took his cut) and assets totaling $58 billion. Over the most recent 5 years, the company has *averaged* a rate of return against assets of more than 19%.[3]

If dollars are power—and that is the lesson of Mills and Domhoff and the guiding assumption of the new Progressive Movement—where does more of it reside?

The answer, of course, is obvious to us, and equally obvious to savvy movement builders such as Ben Cohen, Anita Roddick, and Joshua Mailman. Ben Cohen's answer—build a company based on alternative social and economic values, and market it to like-minded consumers. Anita Roddick's answer—donate a share of your company's profits to social causes in which you believe. Josh Mailman's answer—invest in companies that have the potential to grow while serving your social agenda, and invest some of the returns in social-change foundations and organizations. All good ideas, from the perspective of the Progressive Left, but none the "big idea." Yet there were big ideas out there—at least three of them.

The first came from Peter Barnes, Michael Kieschnick, Laura Scher, and Drummond Pike. Why not, they asked in 1983, create a business with substantial cash flow in which a fixed percentage of that flow would be contributed to Progressive causes, with a measure of customer input on their selection? Indeed, why not create a family of such businesses? As they grew over time with the support of millions of customers sympathetic to their mission, they would generate a steady and significant stream of support for Progressive activism. And along the way, they would provide an attractive and straightforward mechanism for recruiting popular support for the movement. Thus was born Working Assets Funding Service (a mutual fund) and its corporate cousins—Working Assets Long Distance, Working Assets Wireless, the Working Assets Visa Card, ShopforChange.com (a sort of Progressive Internet mall), and two related media operations, WorkingforChange.com and RadioforChange. The company has also explored other potential lines of business—local telephone service in the Bay Area,[4] for example, and establishing an electric power-distribution subsidiary (Working Assets Green Power) in Massachusetts and New Hampshire that would emphasize hydro and geothermal generation,[5] but these have since been abandoned. In addition, an online funding venture, GiveforChange, set up as a collaboration between Working Assets and eGrants, a Tides organization later renamed Groundspring.org, for the purpose of facilitating online direct contributions to Progressive causes, folded in 2003.[6]

With the exception of WorkingforChange.com and RadioforChange, which are more focused on broadcasting and distributing Progressive views and perspectives on the Web, each of these enterprises is set up on a revenue-sharing model in which a portion of the money spent by customers is allocated to Progressive causes. For example, 1% of all phone charges paid by long-distance and wireless subscribers are channeled to the company's activism fund. Similarly, 10 cents of every purchase with the Visa Card and between 3% and 5% of every online purchase through ShopforChange.com go to this pool. The shopping options tend to center on smaller retailers but include recognized names such as Amazon.com, Ben & Jerry's, CompUSA, the Container Store, Eddie Bauer, and JC Penney. Public utilities, financial services, and retail—these three sectors have in common one thing: they generate high levels of cash flow.

In the words of co-founder and CEO Laura Scher, "We provide a way for people to become effective activists and philanthropists through their everyday activities, at little or no cost to them." In 1999, the company had half a million customers, more than 100 employees and annual revenues of approximately $140 million.[7] And by the end of 2002, Working Assets had generated $35 million in donations to favored causes.[8]

Working Assets is, like the progressive foundations explored earlier, a member of the National Network of Grantmakers. Not surprisingly, it focuses on areas such as economic and social justice, the environment, civil rights, and peace activism. Among the recipients of its donations have been groups such as ACORN, Adbusters Media Foundation, Amnesty International, Earth Island Institute, Earthjustice, Global Exchange, Greenpeace, Human Rights Watch, Natural Resources Defense Council, Oxfam America, People for the American Way, Rainforest Action Network, and the Sierra Club. If the list sounds familiar, it should.

To select the 50 organizations to which it will contribute each year, Working Assets polls its customers for nominations. Then, as the company explains[9]:

> After an independent foundation evaluates the effectiveness of the hundreds of nominees, Working Assets employees and board of directors select the groups for our annual donations ballot. Customers then vote on how to distribute the donations among the finalists.

The foundation in question is the Tides Foundation,[10] and all the organizations listed previously, as well as a number of others supported by Working Assets, are also the recipients of financial support from Tides.

Working Assets is privately held and reveals little information about itself—including the names of its investors or the directors who select the annual awardees. Among those we can identify as having served as directors sometime during the period 1997–2000 are former Ben & Jerry's CEO Fred Lager; Elizabeth Sawi, an executive vice president at Charles Schwab; Kay Stepp, a former member of the board of the San Francisco Federal Reserve Bank; Sue Swenson, President of Bay Area Cellular One; and co-founders Scher (CEO), Kieschnick (President), and Drummond Pike.[11] Peter Barnes, the other co-founder, and by some accounts the originator of the revenue-sharing model, served for a time as executive vice president of Working Assets Funding Service and as President of Working Assets Long Distance.[12]

In addition to its common founder, Drummond Pike, and its functional connections, Working Assets is closely tied with the Tides Foundation and Center in other ways. Michael Kieschnick served for a time as treasurer of the foundation, and Lawrence Litvak, a member of the Working Assets management team, serves on the board of directors of the Tides Center. Scher,

Pike, and Barnes have all been active in the Social Venture Network, a Tides Center project examined in chapter 2.

In addition to its quasi-philanthropic role, Working Assets plays a more directly political role through efforts to organize the political activity of its subscribers. Among its initiatives over the years have been the following:

- Monthly statements that highlight two political issues and provide customers with the names and telephone numbers of key corporate and political leaders;
- Free speech days—on the first Monday of each month, subscribers could make free telephone calls to political and corporate leaders;
- Letter writing—as a service (for a small fee added to the next bill), sending a "well argued" letter to one of these identified leaders in their name;[13]
- Free phone cards—in 1995, when Republican leader Newt Gingrich and his colleagues reframed the conservative social agenda as a "Contract with America," Working Assets placed a full-page advertisement in the *New York Times* offering a toll-free number—1-800-NIX-NEWT—where callers could obtain a free 10-minute phone card to call Congress and express their opposition;[14]
- Dedicated lines—in a similar 1997 initiative, the company advertised in the *Times* inviting callers to use five dedicated telephone lines to call the Clinton White House and "realign the President" on the issues of tobacco, landmines, global warming, military spending, and a pending Bill on discrimination in employment;[15]
- Flash Activist Network (FAN)—for a small fee, Working Assets will leave subscribers a telephone message advising of pending issues, e.g., in Congress, to which they might wish to respond by contacting officials.[16]

Although the concept that lay behind the establishment of Working Assets, which is to say, the idea of tapping a large, growing, and continuing income stream to support Progressive activism rather than relying solely on the more limited and more static flow of foundation revenue, has shown potential, it has not proven to be the panacea some may have hoped. Working Assets and a small number of other firms with similar intentions remain at the margins of American business and the margins of public awareness.[17] The same cannot be said, however, of another set of commercial ventures based on a somewhat different notion. Collectively, they represent the second big idea of Progressive capitalism, or the so-called "new economy."

BUILDING THE NEW ECONOMY: THE RISE OF SOCIAL-RESPONSIBILITY INVESTING

Suppose you were Ben Cohen of Ben & Jerry's or Anita Roddick of the Body Shop and you wanted to grow your company. What you would need are investors. Some of that need can be filled by venture capitalists—people like

Joshua Mailman—who are willing to invest their own money in socially activist companies. But venture capitalists are, in their way, like private philanthropists—their capabilities are limited by the boundaries of their own resources. There is, of course, a larger capital market, the one in which company shares are publicly traded. But that market historically has tended to be highly skeptical of "do-gooder" companies that are not overtly profit-driven, which is to say, the money tends not to flow in that direction. What are the Bens and Anitas of the world to do? One possibility is to talk with folks like Wayne Silby, Amy Domini, and Bob Monks. We met Wayne in chapter 2 in his role as co-founder with Joshua Mailman of the Social Venture Network. We'll meet Amy and Bob momentarily.

In 1976, Wayne Silby and John Guffey, Jr., founded a new investment management firm, Government Securities Management Company, which began by offering a mutual fund investing in tax-free securities. In 1981, the firm was renamed the Calvert Group after the Washington, DC, street where its offices were located. In 1982, the same year the Threshold Foundation began operating, Calvert created the nation's first social-responsibility investment fund, the Calvert Social Investment Fund (CSIF). The idea was to invest only in companies that met a variety of social and environmental criteria. The original fund since has grown into a family of similar investment vehicles. The company claims a number of social-investing firsts, including:

- In 1982, CSIF was the first mutual fund to take a stand against the practice of apartheid in South Africa. Following Nelson Mandela's call for an end to sanctions, Calvert's CSIF became one of the first mutual funds to invest in a free South Africa in 1994.
- CSIF was the first fund to create a social venture capital program that invests in young, solutions-oriented companies.
- CSIF was the first mutual fund to directly invest a small portion of its assets in communities, providing credit, jobs, and hope for a better quality of life.
- In 1986, CSIF became the first mutual fund to sponsor a shareholder resolution on social issues.
- The CSIF Advisory Council, composed of several internationally known visionaries and activists, provides policy input and regularly assesses the Fund's criteria.[18]

In addition to the customary financial analyses, Calvert screens companies in which it might invest on six areas of social performance—workplace, environment, product safety and impact, international operations and human rights, indigenous peoples' rights, and community relations. In each instance, the firm has extensive criteria. On the environment, for example, the criteria include conducting regular environmental audits of their facilities, reducing or preventing pollution and effective stewardship of natural resources, and having undertaken affirmative environmental actions, among others.[19] On the issue of human rights, the company has even produced its own issue analysis, which sets forth the rationale for its investment decisions.[20] These recommendations are developed by a staff of issue specialists who have come to Calvert from, or participate in, groups such as the Wilderness Society, Food and Allied Service Trades Department of the AFL-CIO, United Food and Commercial Workers Union, World Resources Institute, Human Rights Watch, Greenpeace, and Amnesty International.[21]

By 2003, Calvert, by then a subsidiary of Ameritas Acacia Mutual Holding Company (the parent as well of Acacia Life Insurance), had $8.5 billion under management in one or another of its funds and served 220,000 investors.

In 1995, with support from the Ford, McArthur, and Mott Foundations, CSIF was launched as a separate entity for the purpose of investing in community-level, nonprofit service providers. The Foundation then issued financial notes in its own name as a vehicle for others to invest in these enterprises.[22] More recently, it established the Calvert Giving Fund, a hybrid of sorts in which small investors may establish individual accounts to which they contribute deposits that are invested in the various Calvert social-responsibility mutual funds. Donors are provided access to research on various nonprofit organizations and may then identify those to which they want to make tax-advantaged contributions. The venture is packaged as a sort of low-maintenance de facto family foundation.[23]

Amy Domini came to the game a little later than the folks at Calvert but in a rather more structured way. In 1989, together with partners Peter Kinder and Steve Lydenberg, she developed the Domini 400 Social Index, which tracked the performance of 400 companies selected for their pro-social and pro-environmental policies. The Domini 400 thus was not designed to measure social or environmental performance per se but rather to assess how well socially responsible companies—i.e., those selected for inclusion—were performing financially. The index was launched in 1990, and the following year the group established the Domini Social Equity Fund, which provided a vehicle for investments in a portfolio that tracked the Index. They also launched a new firm—Kinder, Lydenberg, Domini & Co.—to provide social and environmental assessments of publicly traded corporation.[24]

The key players in this firm also have deep roots in the activist community. Amy Domini, for example, has served on the governing board of the Interfaith Center for Corporate Responsibility, which was perhaps the very first organization to promote social-responsibility investing, and has been active in the Social Investment Forum, a project of Co-Op America. Steve Lydenberg is a former Director of Corporate Accountability Research for the Council on Economic Priorities. General Counsel Adam Kanzer has worked with the National Lawyers Guild.[25]

Today Domini operates three funds—focusing on equities, bonds, and money markets respectively—with $1.3 billion of assets under management. Securities are chosen by using similar criteria to those applied by Calvert, although the details vary somewhat. Among other things, Domini funds do not invest in companies that manufacture firearms, tobacco products or alcohol; that operate gambling facilities; that own or operate nuclear power plants; or that are major military contractors.[26]

Between them, then, Calvert and Domini manage approximately $10 billion in investments. They are joined in a growing social responsibility investment community by other firms such as Trillium Asset Management and Progressive Asset Management.

Trillium, originally known as Franklin Research and Investments, was founded in 1982—which, it is increasingly evident, was a watershed year for the Progressive Movement—with much the same mission as those of Calvert and Domini, which this firm characterizes as "financial gain, social equity and ecological sustainability." Trillium's research agenda and screens are perhaps farther reaching than some, including, for example, criteria on animal rights, where the firm has worked cooperatively with People for the Ethical Treatment of Animals (PETA). Trillium is also more likely than other firms to say not only what they are for, but what they are against—companies that engage in or experience "consistent disregard for the environment, evidence of discriminatory practices, anti-union activities, ethics scandals, . . . [and] disregard for human rights." Unlike the other firms we have mentioned, Trillium's services appear to be directed primarily at institutional shareholders—family trusts, foundations, and pension funds—and at "individuals with significant wealth." Joan Bavaria, Trillium's president, was the founding chair of CERES (see chapters 5 and 8) and a director of the Council on Economic Priorities for 12 years; she currently serves on the boards of CERES and the Earth Justice Legal Defense Fund. In 1981 she co-founded the Social Investment Forum, where she served as president for 4 years and as board member for 8. Senior Social Research Analyst Steve Lippman also has movement ties, having come to the firm from Business for Social Responsibility. Amnesty International is a Trillium client. In 1997, Wainwright Bank and Trust of Boston acquired a 30% interest in Trillium.[27]

Progressive Asset Management (PAM) shares with these other firms an emphasis on social responsibility investing, but PAM is not a mutual fund manager like the others. Rather, it is a network of broker/dealers, established in 1987, that provides a variety of social responsibility-related services such as research, screening and advocacy. It also offers pro-social retirement funds.[28] By 1998, PAM was managing an estimated $700 million in assets and serving more than 400 clients.[29] Like the other firms listed here, Progressive is a long-time member of the Social Venture Network.

According to the Social Investment Forum (SIF) and Weisenberger Thomson Financial, a mutual fund tracking firm, at the end of 1998 there were 183 socially screened open-ended mutual funds offered by 40 different companies and covering a wide range of types of investments.[30] According to a later SIF report, by 2001 these funds numbered 230, and collectively had $153 billion under management. More broadly, of a total of $19.9 trillion under professional management in 2001—including those in separate accounts for unions, foundations, religious organizations, and others as well as mutual funds—SIF found that $2.34 trillion, or about 12% of the total, was invested in programs that used at least some degree of social-responsibility screening, up from $40 billion in 1984 when the group first surveyed the industry.[31] Of these funds and accounts, 96% screened out tobacco companies, 86% gambling interests, 83% alcohol manufacturers, and 81% arms producers. Seventy-nine percent screened in some manner for environmental performance, 43% for human rights issues, 38% for labor issues, 23% for abortion or birth control policies, and 15% for animal welfare. Of the investment managers surveyed in 1999, 88% reported using three or more of these screens.[32]

OTHER PEOPLE'S MONEY: ECONOMIC DEMOCRACY AND PROGRESSIVE ACTIVISM

The limiting factor in private philanthropy is that it centers on foundations spending their own money. The great insight of the Working Assets model was that it opened the opportunity to the flow of other people's money, where those other people had a voice, albeit limited and indirect, in how their contributions to the cause were to be allocated. The social investment-oriented mutual funds offer an avenue toward expanding this base, but, in more than 20 years of operation, they have not had much of an impact. For in the context of the American economy, even $153 billion is small potatoes. And even the most inclusive measure offered by SIF—including the separate accounts of institutional investors such as foundations and pension funds—although growing over time, accounted for only one in every eight dollars invested in the U.S. economy.

All these vehicles share one common limitation—they are grounded in the ownership of assets. But what if there were a way to gain effective control over much larger chunks of economic power without having to own the assets that gave rise to them? What if there were a way to turn the private behaviors of not just a few, but many, of the nation's largest publicly held corporations to the service of Progressive social values? Properly wielded, that might be the mechanism of real and fundamental social change. It turns out that there is, in fact, such a mechanism. There really is—at least potentially—a financial equivalent of Archimedes' lever. Its discovery is the third of our big new ideas.

The key insight here was the recognition that shares of stock represent more than simply small pieces of financial interest in a corporation. For publicly held companies, they represent votes.

Under the U.S. system of corporate ownership, each share one owns in a given company that is publicly traded on one of the nation's stock exchanges affords to its owner one vote on matters such as membership on the company's board of directors and the general form of corporate governance and policy. The total number of votes for any particular company is determined by the total number of shares outstanding, which typically is in the tens or hundreds of millions. This amounts to a more or less pure form of economic democracy—one share, one vote—except for two important factors.

First, because they own far more shares than almost any individual investor, institutional shareholders—those are the banks, pension funds, insurance companies, mutual funds, foundations, and the like—tend to have a great many more votes than do individual shareholders. These institutions are generally required to act as fiduciaries, which is to say, they have a legal obligation to invest and to vote their shares so as best to protect the interests of those whose funds they manage—investors, pensioners, etc. Historically, this has been interpreted to mean that these funds must vote their shares with the financial well-being and advancement of each given company foremost in mind. That, in turn, has usually meant that they vote to support positions endorsed by the company's management. Because most companies are majority-owned by institutional investors, this has meant that they have not been subjected to meaningful shareholder pressure to adopt the social agenda pursued by the Progressive activists. On the contrary, they have been pressed to maximize profits irrespective of these considerations. That is not to say that companies have sought purposefully to harm the environment or otherwise chosen to engage in antisocial behaviors but only that they have been structurally bound to place other priorities first.

Second, this economic democracy differs from political democracy in that the voters are allowed to transfer their voting rights to others through what are termed proxies. These are legally binding documents that allow the shares to be voted by one party in the name of another. Typically, most individual investors in a company do not attend the company's annual shareholders meeting, at which time and place the votes are submitted and tallied. To cast their votes, many give their proxies to someone who will be present at the meeting. Most often this is a representative hired by management who agrees to vote as instructed by the shareholder, and most often these votes are cast in favor of board nominees and policies put forward by the officers of the corporation. It is possible to assign proxies to individuals or groups who promise to challenge management positions—to stage what are termed "proxy fights" over matters such as who is elected as a director or how the firm can improve its environmental performance—but, because individual shareholders seldom have anything approaching a majority of votes, these efforts are prone to failure.

In addition to providing financial incentives to progressive companies through their investments, the social-responsibility mutual funds like those discussed earlier have emerged as activist voters in these annual corporate elections and referenda. One of the promises they make to investors, and one of their critical marketing appeals, is that they will use their voting power to advance the Progressive agenda at the companies in which they hold shares. And it is surely the case that $153 billion of assets, although not the loudest voice in the economy, is loud enough to be heard from time to time. Amy Domini of Domini Social Investments has put it this way[33]:

[We] use our shareholders' investments to encourage greater corporate responsibility, both by using social and ethical criteria to select our holdings and by directly engaging corporate management through proxy voting and shareholder dialogues. Since 1994, we have engaged numerous corporations in discussions on a wide range of issues, from sweatshops to the environment. In 1999, we became the first mutual fund manager in the country to publish its proxy votes, so that our investors could hold us accountable for the positions we are taking.

For other institutional investors, however, it is not quite that simple. Recall that such investors have a legal obligation to exercise fiduciary responsibility—to act in the best (usually interpreted as best *financial*) interests of their investors. Because social responsibility criteria generally have not been viewed as meeting that test, these institutions have not only been discouraged from progressive activism (were they so inclined in the first place) but possibly even precluded from it. And that fact presented the Progressive Movement with a conundrum: How to render social responsibility investing and support for the activists' corporate policy agenda sufficiently compatible with the legal requirements of fiduciary responsibility in order to accommodate the needs of institutional investors and to make them more susceptible to influence. In recent years, two answers have emerged.

The first, and most straightforward, was to demonstrate that supporting social responsibility as an investment objective was not inherently irresponsible from a fiduciary standpoint. This would be the case, for example, if the results of pro-social investing could match or nearly match the results of traditional, pro-financial investing. It is this consideration, for example, that gave rise to the series of Social Investment Forum reports on the performance of socially-screened mutual funds and accounts. One such analysis, comparing the performance from May 1990 through May 1999 of two social-responsibility indexes—The Domini Social Index and the Citizen's Index—with a standard measure of performance of the overall stock market, the Standard & Poor's 500 Index, found that the stocks of "socially responsible" companies tracked by the two specialized indexes matched or exceeded the overall performance of the market during these years.[34] If that is true, it undermines the argument that fund managers cannot meet their fiduciary responsibilities by investing in pro-social companies.

The second answer required that the beneficiaries of all this fiduciary responsibility—the people in whose interest the fund managers presumably were acting when they supported traditional markers of corporate success—announce convincingly that they believed their interests to be better served by a new and more socially progressive set of criteria. In effect, they had to tell those charged with stewardship of their money that other things were more important than profits and the growth of capital. In 1998, the AFL-CIO took a giant step in this direction.

The so-called Taft–Hartley pension funds—these are private sector multi-employer funds that manage the pension contributions and benefits of union members—account for a sizeable pool of money. By one estimate in 1997 union pension funds controlled a total of $1.4 *trillion*. Now that is real money—the kind that can get the attention of corporate decision makers. And virtually all the unions with an interest in these funds, accounting for the bulk of the money in question, are members of the AFL-CIO. So when the nation's labor federation speaks on issues related to these pension funds, it speaks with an authoritative voice.

In 1998 the AFL-CIO issued a new set of proxy voting guidelines for the managers of Taft-Hartley funds—in essence, a statement of labor's preferred positions on various issues of corporate structure and corporate social behavior.[35] Some of these include supporting shareholder initiatives that would:

- Ensure that a majority of the board members of a given company are "independent"—a term indicating that their only material connection with the company is their service as a director;
- Make directors personally accountable for meeting their own fiduciary responsibilities to the company (and opposing efforts to limit their personal liability for their actions);
- Eliminate staggered term elections and establish the practice of electing all directors to concurrent terms (thought to make them more responsive to shareholders);
- Establish cumulative voting, a practice that allows shareholders to cast all their votes for a single board member (a mechanism to gain board membership for critics of the company by concentrating the limited voting power of their supporters; i.e., if a company has 15 directors, a shareholder could cast 15 votes for 1 board candidate rather than 1 vote for each of 15);
- Provide for the adoption of principles or codes of conduct relating to matters such as a company's business practices in other countries, to its environmental practices, or to employee health and safety;
- Call for compliance with, and public reporting on, government policies on discrimination and affirmative action, workplace safety and health, the environment, the quality of health care, labor protections, and the like; and
- Call on management to avoid doing business with foreign firms that employ child labor or that fail to meet applicable standards with respect to the wages and working conditions of their employees.

Similarly, the guidelines call on fiduciaries to oppose dual-class voting (in which some shares, such as those owned by members of the family that founded a company, have more votes than others).[36]

These and other positions set forth by the labor federation closely parallel the agenda of pro-social positions advanced by the proponents of social responsibility investing. The correspondence is not coincidental. One purpose of the AFL-CIO guidelines was to lay out in substantial detail its views on this very agenda and to influence the votes of Taft–Hartley and other pension fund managers.

But the larger purpose of the proxy voting guidelines was to provide cover for these fiduciaries when they did, in fact, act in concert with the Progressives. By its very existence, this document legitimizes in some significant measure a claim by any union pension fund manager that he or she was acting in the interests of the fund's beneficiaries when voting in support of change-oriented shareholder resolutions. It provides legal cover against the charge that in so doing, the fund manager acted contrary to his or her fiduciary obligations. In the words of the document itself[37]:

> These guidelines provide standards to help multiemployer pension fund trustees meet their fiduciary obligations when voting their funds' shareholder proxies. . . . By supporting management accountability to shareholders and workers, and encouraging corporate practices that build long-term shareholder value, the guidelines will help provide a secure and decent retirement for all Americans.

John Sweeney, Richard L. Trumka, and Linda Chavez-Thompson (the three top AFL-CIO officers) for the defense. Archimedes' lever seemingly in place. And still the world does not move. Still, corporate management demurs from pursuing the Progressive social agenda. What's a movement to do?

THOR'S HAMMER

Before he was a heavy metal rock legend, Thor was a legendary figure in Norse mythology, the firstborn of Mother Earth. He had three precious possessions— a belt of strength, a pair of iron gloves, and a hammer—of which the latter was most prized. Thor's hammer, known as Mjollnir, represented the focus of Thor's power, the thunderbolt before which nothing could stand. Mjollnir was believed to protect everything the Norse held dear, to defend the world of men and the community from the forces of darkness and chaos, which ever threatened to overwhelm them, and to embody Thor's power to tame the elements.[38] If Archimedes' lever were not enough to change the direction of corporate behavior, might the Progressives find the modern-day equivalent of Thor's hammer? Might they wield a tool before which all of corporate America would tremble?

They may, in fact, have found just such an instrument in the form of a small, obscure, but strategically positioned company known as Institutional Shareholder Services, or ISS.

ISS was established in 1985 by Robert A. G. Monks. Perhaps ironically, in the context of our larger story, Monks had just left the Reagan Administration, where he served in the Department of Labor as Administrator of the Office of Pension and Welfare Benefit Programs, and as one of the founding trustees of the Federal Employees' Retirement System. A graduate of Harvard College, Cambridge University, and Harvard Law School, before his government service Monks' career included a partnership in a Boston law firm, the vice presidency of an investment management firm, the presidency of a family-owned coal and oil company, and service as a director and board chairman of Boston Safe Deposit & Trust Company (later The Boston Company), which he sold to American Express in 1981. Today Monks, in his seventies at this writing, is a prominent author and shareholder activist.[39]

In 1984, while still in the Reagan Labor Department, Monks delivered a speech entitled "The Institutional Investor as a Corporate Citizen" that is widely credited with setting in motion the department's policy of encouraging proxy-voting activism by pension funds.[40] The next year, he founded ISS to advance that activism, challenging management and directors at companies such as Sears Roebuck, Occidental Petroleum, Lockheed, Honeywell, and USX.[41] Monks saw the emerging power of not just pension funds, but institutional shareholders in general, as creating an opportunity for influence. As he told an interviewer in 1988[42]:

> Now that you have a fairly small group of institutions with enormous stock holdings, I think you have the [framework] for something that is a great deal more effective than we have had in the past.

The business of ISS is to provide "independent" advice to the managers of institutionally owned shares on how to vote those shares at corporate shareholders meetings. At first blush, it might not seem that such a service would have any value. Couldn't the fund managers simply decide the issues on a case-by-case basis and vote accordingly? But, in point of fact, institutions typically own shares in hundreds of different companies, and many of these issue their annual proxy statements and hold their annual meetings within a couple of months of one another each spring. When one adds in the increasing number of shareholder resolutions being offered by parties other than management, which vary in number and content from one company to the next, the task takes on a high degree of complexity. To cast each vote in a manner defensible within the limits of fiduciary responsibility requires study and thought—of each ballot question and, in some cases, of each director. That creates a market niche. Enter ISS.

By the spring of 2002, ISS had a full-time staff of 290 employees, supplemented by many additional temporary workers it hired during proxy season. It tracked proxy activity at some 20,000 companies around the world from offices in London, Tokyo, Manila, and Toronto as well as from its home base in Bethesda, Maryland. The company has several divisions, including:

- Proxy Voter Services (PVS). PVS actually started out in 1992 as an independent company. Founded by labor activist Susan Kellock, who had worked with community organizer and anti-corporate activist Saul

Alinsky in Chicago, PVS is in the business of recommending to Taft–Hartley funds how to cast their proxy votes and as acting as their agent to actually cast those votes. Kellock died in 1996, and ISS acquired PVS the following year.

- Social Investment Research Service. This is a social-responsibility portfolio screening service for investment managers that is similar in concept to those described earlier in this chapter. Among other things, it operates a website at www.TrustSimon.com that shows the participation of public companies on social issues.
- Securities Class Action Services. This is another research division, in this instance focusing on companies that are involved in class-action litigation and monitoring the portfolios of client funds with an eye toward filing claims.
- ISS Corporate Programs. This division provides consulting and educational services to corporations to help them anticipate the impact on ISS proxy recommendations to institutional shareholders of various policies or actions they may contemplate or implement. Its IssueCompass service lets clients test their compensation plans against ISS standards, and its IssueBlueprint service helps corporate boards develop governance guidelines.[43]

But we are getting ahead of our story. Back in 1990, just as ISS was gaining substantial influence, Monks came under criticism for what some perceived as a conflict of interests. In addition to the presidency of his own firm, ISS, he served as a director of Lambert Brussels Associates, which held a one third share of the investment firm Drexel Burnham Lambert; on the board of Tyco Corporation; as an advisor to an American subsidiary of Japan's Mitsubishi Corporation; and as a director of Jeffries & Company, a brokerage firm that advised corporate raiders. He resigned from the latter position in that year, although he retained an equity stake in the company. He also served around that time as an unpaid advisor to Dallas investor Harold Simmons in a proxy battle to gain control of Lockheed Corporation and helped another Texas investor, Richard Rainwater, stop two anti-takeover proposals at Honeywell. Critics suggested that such activities were not consistent with his role at ISS. Monks resigned from the ISS presidency, giving way to his frequent collaborator, Nell Minow, who had been serving as general counsel. But he retained for some time yet his ownership of the firm.

In 1991, Monks formed a new firm, Institutional Shareholder Partners, which was based on generating superior results by investing in the shares of underperforming companies with governance shortcomings, pressuring the companies to change their ways, and then profiting from the performance improvements that would result. In 1992, the firm was renamed the LENS Fund. Minow joined Monks at LENS, and Jamie Heard became president of ISS, a post he held until 1996. In the meantime, just to add a new and ultimately significant wrinkle to the tale, a new firm, Proxy Monitor, was established in 1989 to compete with ISS.

By 1994, ISS had added a new line of business—advising corporations on how they might respond to shareholder concerns, such as those raised in their behalf by ISS. This was the origin of the Corporate Programs Division noted previously and was also the focal point of still more concerns about conflicts of interest. In the words of prominent executive compensation consultant Graef Crystal[44]:

> They've got a severe conflict when they work both sides of the street. It's like the Middle Ages when the Pope was selling indulgences. ISS is selling advice to corporations on how to avoid getting on their list of bad companies. There's a veiled sense of intimidation.

ISS, of course, took a different view of the practice, although not always a consistent one. Heard, the ISS president, told the same interviewer[45]:

> If corporations want to come in and understand our policies and the views of institutional investors, we're happy to do that. But if they are looking to get pre-approval for their corporate proxies, they are in the wrong place. We've turned down business that doesn't pass the smell test.

But just a few years later, Patrick McGurn, the firm's vice president and special counsel indicated that ISS acknowledged the problem, but tried to "avoid the conflict by keeping its corporate and institutional staffs and facilities separate."[46]

At this point, our story enters into a series of mergers, acquisitions, and job changes that is reminiscent of the long chain of Biblical begats. Let's take a quick tour in the present tense.

- In 1995, Monks sells ISS to Thomson Financial Services of Canada.
- In 1996, Heard leaves ISS to become CEO of the firm's only competitor, Proxy Monitor.
- In 1997, ISS acquires Proxy Voter Services, the Taft–Hartley advisory service founded by Kellock.
- In March 1998, Monks (via the LENS Fund) enters into a joint venture with Hermes Pensions Management Ltd., to be known as Hermes Lens Asset Management. Time out.

Hermes is about to emerge as an important player in this little drama, so let's take a moment to familiarize ourselves with the company. Hermes is owned by, and serves as investment manager for, the pension funds of British Telecom and the British Post Office. At about that time, Hermes was estimated to have some £40 billion (or $63.5 billion) under management.[47] In the 1990s, under the leadership of its activist CEO, Alistair Ross Goobey, the company was focused on corporate governance reform in very much the same way that Monks was, or perhaps more importantly, in the same way that certain activist pension funds in the United States were. As one British observer summed up the company's credentials, "It has become as inevitably linked to the debate on activism as CalPERS, the Californian pension fund, has in the U.S."[48] Hermes committed to invest $100 million in the new undertaking. And now, back to the begats.

- Speaking of CalPERS, in November 1998 Hermes and CalPERS, a union-controlled pension fund serving public employees in California, announce they will collaborate to push for policy changes at companies in which both hold stock.
- In December 1998, the planned merger of the LENS Fund and Hermes Lens Asset Management is announced. Once implemented, this will have the effect of folding Monks' interests fully into Hermes.
- In March 1999, CalPERS, TIAA-CREF (another activist and highly influential U.S. pension fund), LENS, Hermes, and Pensions Investment Research Consultants (a U.K. proxy voting service) join forces to form the International Institutional Investors Advisory Group, with the stated objective of transforming nation-specific corporate governance guidelines into a set of international standards.[49]
- In 2000, about a year behind schedule, the LENS fund is folded into Hermes. Monks soon becomes deputy chairman of Hermes.
- In July 2001, ISS is acquired by Proxy Monitor, its former (and only) competitor, which is still under the leadership of Heard, its former president. This has the effect of eliminating the possibility that funds might receive differing recommendations from their "independent" proxy advisors. As Marc Schwartz, the founder of Newcastle Partners LP, put it, "It's like going to a doctor and then wanting to get a second opinion, but there is no second opinion. It's a very serious matter."[50]

Now, there was actually a bit more to this deal than met the eye. Proxy Monitor was a closely held firm, and its ownership structure and finances are not readily accessible. What we can infer, however, is that it was not a big enough fish to swallow whole its new acquisition. The deal had to be financed to the tune of $45 million by third parties. And, although not all the details of the financing are public either, we do know that two other companies provided the money to make it work. One was the venture capital firm Warburg Pincus. The other was the British Telecom and Post Office pension fund—Hermes. Following the merger—in which the surviving firm took the ISS name—the company was headed by a board of eight directors, including one from ISS, two from Warburg Pincus, and one from Hermes.[51] The net result, then, was that at the end of all the begetting, Monks found himself second in command in a company that once again had an important voice in his own creation,

ISS. Oh, and did we mention that the new Chairman of ISS is Robert C. S. Monks—aka, Bob junior?

That was surely an ample psychic reward for the firm's founder, whose vision was flowering. But in the grand scheme of things, that outcome is inconsequential. Far more important is this: ISS has now emerged as the only "independent" firm offering proxy voting advice to institutional shareholders in the United States.[52] And ISS is owned and controlled by private interests about whom we know very little except that among them is a British union pension fund with a reputation for progressive shareholder activism. In that light, consider the comments of Richard Trumka, Secretary-Treasurer of the AFL-CIO, when ISS endorsed a workers' rights shareholder resolution at the May 2002 Unocal annual meeting, a resolution sponsored by the AFL-CIO, its British counterpart known as the Trades Union Congress, an international union organization, an American union and a union-owned bank. "We are pleased," said Trumka, "that ISS—*a truly independent expert*—recognizes that Unocal's endorsement of global labor standards would benefit the company and its shareholders."[53]

Mjollnir. Thor's hammer.

ENDNOTES

1. Melissa Ludlum, "Domestic Private Foundations and Charitable Trusts, 1999," *SOI Bulletin*, Internal Revenue Service, Fall 2002, p. 137.
2. *Annual Report* of the Bill and Melinda Gates Foundation, 2001.
3. Data from the online site of the *Wall Street Journal*, found February 3, 2003.
4. Lorna Fernandez, "Working Assets hangs up service: Says PacBell foiled its attempt to break into local market," *San Francisco Business Times*, February 1, 1999.
5. Jim Motavalli, "Power Struggle: Will Utility Deregulation Finally Unplug 'Dirty' Electricity?," *E/The Environmental Magazine*, November–December 1997, found online at www.emagazine. com/1197feat1_sb1.html, December 16, 1997.
6. The concept of this enterprise was described in detail in a news release at the time of its founding, "GiveForChange.com Launches Online Donating to Change the World," October 12, 1999. It's demise was effective January 31, 2003.
7. Marguerite Rigoglioso, "Profile: Sharing the Wealth: Laura Scher of Working Assets," *Harvard Business School Bulletin*, October 2000, found online at http://www.alumni.hbs.edu/ bulletin/2000/october/profile.html, February 3, 2003.
8. Figure provided on the company's web site at www.workingassets.com on January 27, 2003.
9. The description of the procedure was found online at http://www.workingassets.com/recipients. cfm?CFID=4971561&CFTOKEN=36139403, February 3, 2003.
10. "Working Assets donates $1 million to nonprofit groups," Working Assets news release transmitted on Business Wire, April 21, 1994.
11. Some directors in 2000 are listed in Todd Wallack, "Conscience Calls: Working Assets rings up success with charitable giving—critics call it another for-profit phone company," *San Francisco Chronicle*, September 21, 2000. Others were listed on the company's website earlier in its history and were found at www.wald.com/about.html on October 17, 1997.
12. From Peter Barnes' resume as found online at www.skybook.org/author.html, January 21, 2003.

13. Susan E. Kinsman, "Firm puts phone calls, advocacy on same line," *Hartford Courant*, September 27, 1992, p. D1.

14. The advertisement appeared in the *New York Times*, January 19, 1995, p. A17.

15. From a computer notice posted October 24, 1997, on the EcoNet web site operated by the Institute for Global Communications.

16. Described at http://www.workingassets.com/activism/fan/about.cfm?CFID=5012532&CFTOKEN =85460415, February 4, 2003. As of that date, FAN was said to serve 13,000 subscribers.

17. Even psychic Uri Geller—perhaps best remembered for his claim to bend spoons through sheer willpower, has gotten into the act by establishing a dial-up Internet Service Provider (ISP), Peoples Net, that promises to donate 5 percent of the dial-in telephone charges to groups working on issues of health care, human rights, and the environment. The venture even claims an endorsement from Joshua Mailman: "By pledging five per cent of its revenues to voluntary and charitable groups, they are ensuring that the non-profit sector will benefit directly from the growth of the Internet. I'm not aware of any other ISP that has made this commitment." Information found online at http://www.uri-geller.com/imoney.htm, February 4, 2003.

18. This historical profile is based on material posted on the company's web site at http://www. calvert.com/aboutindex_1515.html, and found on February 4, 2003.

19. As described online at http://www.calvert.com/sri_647.html, February 4, 2003.

20. See, for example, the issue brief on human rights found at http://www.calvert.com/621.html, February 4, 2003.

21. The credentials of the staff of analysts were found at http://www.calvert.com/sri_4857.html, February 4, 2003.

22. The history of the foundation was found at http://www.calvertfoundation.org/about/background. html?u=individual;s=aboutus;source=, February 4, 2003.

23. Described at http://www.calvertgiving.org/giving_fund.htm?source=calvert.com, February 4, 2003.

24. From the history found at http://www.domini.com/about-domini/The-Domini-Story/index.htm, February 4, 2003.

25. Biographical information found at http://www.domini.com/about-domini/Management/index. htm, February 4, 2003.

26. Criteria described at http://www.domini.com/Social-Screening/index.htm, February 4, 2003.

27. This summary is based on information found at www.trilliuminvest.com on February 4, 2003.

28. Information on the firm was found at www.progressive-asset.com, February 4, 2003.

29. "Green Company Profiles: Progressive Asset Management," found online at www.lightparty. com/Economic/GreenCompany.html, April 23, 1998.

30. Social Investment Forum, *Screened Mutual Fund Statistics* as of December 31, 1998, found online at www.socialinvest.org/areas/Research/Other/FundStates_12-31-98.htm, February 4, 2003.

31. Social Investment Forum, *2001 Report on Socially Responsible Investing Trends in the United States*, November 4, 1999, found online at http://www.socialinvest.org/Areas/research/trends/2001-Trends.htm, February 4, 2003.

32. Social Investment Forum, *1999 Report on Socially Responsible Investing Trends in the United States*, November 4, 1999, found online at http://www.socialinvest.org/Areas/research/trends/1999-Trends.htm, February 4, 2003.

33. Found at http://www.domini.com/about-domini/The-Domini-Story/index.htm, February 4, 2003.

34. Social Investment Forum, *1999 Report*, op. cit., Figure 6.

35. *Investing in Our Future: AFL-CIO Proxy Voting Guidelines* (Washington, DC: AFL-CIO, 1998).

36. Ibid., pp. 4–12.

37. Ibid., p. i.

38. Dan Bray, "Hammer in the North: Mjollnir in Medieval Scandinavia," found online at www.mackaos.com.au/Articles/Mjol.html, March 13, 2003.

39. Biographical information on Monks was found in many locations, but most succinctly and authoritatively at his personal web site, www.ragm.com, on January 10, 2003.

40. Leslie Wayne, "A Fervent Advocate of the Proxy Battle," *The New York Times*, May 8, 1990, p. D1.

41. Ibid.

42. Quoted in Jube Shriver, Jr., "Called more equitable than fining companies; Plan would punish directors for crime," *Los Angeles Times*, December 6, 1988, p. D8.

43. These services are described more fully on the company's web site, found at www.issproxy.com.

44. Quoted in Wayne Leslie, "Have Shareholder Activists Lost Their Edge?" *The New York Times*, January 30, 1994, p. C7.

45. Ibid.

46. Mary Vanac, "Firm's proxy advice helps big investors decide how to vote," *Cleveland Plain Dealer*, October 3, 2002, p. C4. The quoted material is from the article, but is not a direct quote from Mr. McGurn.

47. Hillary Rosenberg, "An Activist Shareholder Takes on the World," *The New York Times*, March 21, 1999, p. C8.

48. Tony Tassell, "Absence of luxury is a telling story," *Financial Times*, June 17, 2002, p. 22.

49. Richard Donkin, "Powerful support for international guidelines," *Financial Times*, March 19, 1999, p. 4.

50. Quoted in Robin Sidel, "Is Anyone Left to Give Advice After This Deal?" *Wall Street Journal*, July 26, 2001.

51. "At Deadline," *Pensions and Investments*, August 6, 2001, p. 1.

52. In September 2003 the IRRC announced that it was partnering with a proxy research firm, Glass, Lewis & Co., to create a competitor to ISS "free from any conflicts of interest." The viability of this enterprise remained untested at this writing, though the involvement of IRRC would seem to suggest an even more direct grounding in Progressive activism. See "Leading Proxy Advisory Firms Offer new Unbiased Proxy Voting Service," IRRC news release, September 3, 2003.

53. Quoted in "ISS Recommends Unocal Shareholders Vote for Global Labor Standards," news release, International Federation of Chemical, Energy, Mine and General Workers Unions, May 13, 2002. Emphasis added.

5

Them!

*In constructing . . . enemies and the narrative plots that define their place in history, people
are manifestly defining themselves and their place in history as well; the self-definition
lends passion to the whole transaction. . . . To define the people one hurts as evil is to
define oneself as virtuous. The narrative identifies the . . . enemy and victim-savior by
defining the latter as emerging from an innocent past and as destined to help bring about
a brighter future world cleansed of the contamination the enemy embodies.*
—Edelman (1988)[1]

Clever policy-oriented investment strategies and significant influence over
proxy voting may well garner the attention of corporate directors and senior
executives, but they are far too abstract and removed—too bloodless—to
generate much in the way of the popular support that is essential to a resurgent
political movement. For that, one must have an appeal to the heart, or at least
to the gut. Emotion more than intellect powers such movements—emotion
that is generated by what one is for, and whom one is against. The successful
political movement—the movement that is going to displace the established
order and achieve political power—is the movement that stands on the moral
high ground and slays the common enemy.

The Reagan–Bush strategists understood this full well. It was, arguably,
the centerpiece of their attack on liberalism, and the key to its success. By
depriving liberalism of its legitimacy, and then of its name, they redefined the
moral high ground in American politics, and they claimed it.

A ROSE BY ANY OTHER NAME WOULD STILL HAVE THORNS

There were two obvious elements to this linguistic initiative, and both were essentially definitional. Who are we? Who are they? From the answers would flow the framework of understanding for the Reagan–Bush era, the enduring conflict of us versus them.

In reverse engineering the Reagan revolution, then, it would naturally fall to the defeated forces of the political Left to reinvent themselves and their movement under a new label and to select for that purpose a label that would at once provide historical and connotative legitimacy for their own movement and clarify for all observers the forces they opposed and the fundamental evil those forces represented. Light. Darkness. Hope. Despair. Generosity. Greed. Self-Enobling. Self-Aggrandizing. Caring. Callousness. Humane. Impersonal. Pro-social. Anti-social. Benevolent. Malevolent. Angels. Demons. Us. Them!

The label they chose accomplished all of this and more, for not only did it define the forces of good and evil in the abstract, but, by virtue of its unique positioning in American history, it also defined and positioned a natural enemy that perfectly suited the needs of the new activists. The label they selected was "Progressive," or, less commonly, "Progressive Populist."

A hundred years before, an earlier generation of social critics and reformers had begun to coalesce around an agenda that ranged from improving the condition of labor to protecting consumers and the environment. The times were different, but the problem confronting the activists of that era was the same—how to generate sufficient popular support for their cause(s) that the momentum of an entire society might be redirected. They, too, needed a name. And they found it largely by accident in the writing of Ray Stannard Baker. Baker, a well-known journalist, was himself a reformer. In the first of a series of articles on the rail monopoly that appeared in *McClure's* in November 1905 he wrote[2]:

> We are at this moment facing a new conflict in this country, the importance of which we are only just beginning to perceive. It lies between two great parties, one a progressive party seeking to give the government more power in business affairs, the other a conservative party striving to retain all the power possible in private hands. One looks toward socialism, the other obstinately defends individualism. It is industrialism forcing itself into politics.

This, according to historian Edmund Morris, marked the first time that "progressive" came to be applied as a political label, rather than merely an adjective.[3]

As a statement of affirmation in a more contemporary setting, the beauty of the Progressive label is multifaceted: It is inherently high minded and forward looking. It captures more than adequately the substantive thrust of the activists' agenda and provides them with a claim to deep historical roots.

It resonates with the public and is sufficiently ambiguous that a great diversity of issues and positions can reside in its shade. It conveys a philosophy without itself being philosophical. It masks ideology, a quality little valued in American politics, as pragmatism and problem solving, which are greatly valued. It aligns the interests of the activists with the interests of the people. And best of all, in the same process and by virtue of the same historical associations, it defines the enemy and deprives it of all trust, confidence, good will, and legitimacy. We have seen the enemy—for lo these hundred years—and it is the corporation. Not only is the corporation a natural enemy for the Progressive Left, but it is the perfect foil for its agenda.

Corporations depend on at least two types of resources to prosper. The first, as we have seen at some length now, is money in the form of investments, profits, cash flow, and the like. The second is popular acquiescence. In contemporary American society, corporations have been afforded a privileged status. Corporations provide jobs, produce the overwhelming majority of goods and services, and provide a substantial portion of the tax revenues that sustain popular government. They also exercise a considerable degree of political influence, much of which is directed at maximizing their own freedom to make decisions based on their economic self-interest. In the United States, in particular, corporations make campaign contributions through their political action committees, they lobby Congress and the state legislatures, they litigate, they propagandize, and they generally do whatever is legitimately within their power to secure their position in the social order. They are legally protected through de facto citizenship, protective regulation, and commercial speech. They are powerful. They are ubiquitous.

Such actions inevitably have consequences for individuals living within a given society. In effect, corporations determine the scale, nature, and quality of employment; the types of goods and services that are produced and (through their advertising) the demand for them; the form and extent of the exploitation of natural resources and the balance between economic production and environmental quality; and other similarly significant outcomes. So when viewed from the perspective of the individual citizen, corporations are powerful actors whose interests may or may not correspond with their own and whose policies and actions are highly consequential. And, precisely because they are the repository of so much economic, political, and social authority, they are widely distrusted, disliked, and in some quarters even reviled.

Progressive is the perfect label. Corporations are the perfect enemy.

As noted, this is not a new idea. In fact, it was the very idea around which the original Progressive Movement in the United States was organized—which is, of course, the point. The Progressive Era of the early 1900s established a popular expectation that trusts would be busted and corporate scoundrels hounded from their lairs, that consumers would be protected and the environment preserved, all in the name of protecting the public interest from the avarice and corruption of the wealthy and powerful. Much of the regulatory structure that is government today—and that which the Reagan and Bush administrations partially dismantled—was set in place precisely to institution-alize these protections. That, at least, was the popular rationale for the growth of big government, and it contained more than a small element of truth.

Over the years, of course, corporations learned to live quite comfortably with the agencies that had been established to keep them on the straight and narrow. And over time, a balance of sorts was struck between the public's need for protection and the companies' need for relative independence of action. It was that balance that was disturbed by the Reagan administration's assault on the Liberal Left, and the resulting disequilibrium that powers the attack on the collective corporate reputation today. This is a different kind of proxy war from those we have examined earlier in this volume, one in which corporations are proxy targets of convenience, stand-ins for the conservative policies (and for some, the capitalist ideology) against which the Progressive Left now rebels. And truth be told, corporate America has made itself more vulnerable to attack than it might have been.

Most Americans have never held major corporations in particularly high regard. Over the period 1973–2002, for example, when asked by the Gallup Organization how much confidence they had in big business (among other institutions), the proportion of respondents indicating they had "a great deal" or "a lot" of confidence has never exceeded one in three. In June 2002 it stood at 20%, as compared with 32% who said they had very little or no confidence.[4] Similarly, a July 2002 Gallup Poll found that only 23% of respondents believed that most CEOs of large corporations could be trusted.[5] Finally, Gallup reported in November 2002 that only 17% of respondents in a national survey judged the ethical standards of business leaders as high or very high. In fact, over the two decades between 1983 and 2002, there was only 1 year when as many as a quarter of survey respondents held such a favorable view.[6]

But added to this generally low regard has been a series of corporate scandals and misadventures of which Enron, with its massively fraudulent practices and falsified records, is but the most prominent. On issues from accounting im-proprieties to auditing oversights to energy market manipulation to excessive compensation of top executives, corporations have laid themselves open to attack. They might as well have painted bulls' eyes on their chests and issued weapons. It does not matter in the public mind that most companies may not engage in such practices. That subtlety of distinction is lost in the noise. What matters is that the media are filled with stories of those that do.

SOME NOT-SO-ANCIENT HISTORY

For Gordon Gecko, the avaricious corporate raider in the movie *Wall Street*, the mantra might be "greed is good." For the American corporation in the opening years of the twenty-first century, greed—even the perception of greed—is vulnerability. That is the case not only because the public is ready to believe the

worst about corporations, but because the sentiment and the events coincide
in time with the emergence of a movement that is at once conditioned and
positioned to exploit them to the fullest. Advocates of the new progressivism
have, in fact, been at it for quite some time—since long before they became
"Progressives."

Even before the Reagan administration launched its attack on labor, Liberals, and the Left, innovative thinkers on the other side had begun to target
corporations as prospective agents of social change. Examples included the
civil rights sit-ins at Woolworth lunch counters in the southern states to force
integration in the 1950s;[7] the attack on Eastman Kodak led by community organizer Saul Alinsky in Rochester, New York, to force the company to expand
its minority hiring through local community organizations in the 1960s;[8] and
the church-led movement for reform driven by private interests, and eventually for divestment, in South Africa to force an end to the Apartheid regime
there in the 1970s and 1980s.[9] The idea in each instance was that, if they
lacked the resources to force governments to change *public* policy directly,
the advocates of these causes nevertheless could achieve their objectives by
motivating private institutions to change their *private* policies and behaviors
on such a large scale as to constitute a de facto change in public policy. The
target of choice: corporations.

As noted in chapter 1, in 1966 the National Council of Churches (NCC)
joined with the Students for a Democratic Society and others to form the
North American Congress on Latin America, or NACLA. Housed in NCC
headquarters in New York City, NACLA served as a think tank of sorts for
anti-corporate activism. At about the same time, NCC created and spun off
the Interfaith Center for Corporate Responsibility (ICCR), whose function
was to carry the fight for morally responsible corporate behavior to individual
companies through proxy solicitations and other shareholder-directed actions.
Yet another spin-off—this one from NACLA—the Corporate Data Exchange
(CDE)—was created to conduct extensive research on corporate ownership
and provide the data on which future pressure campaigns would be based.

Two other consequential developments paralleled this activity. In late 1969,
a Boston-area synagogue asked financial analyst Alice Tepper Marlin to create a list of companies that were not producing materials being used in the
Vietnam War. The synagogue then advertised the resulting "peace portfolio" in *The New York Times*, which generated inquiries from more than 600
individuals and organizations. News organizations began reporting the portfolio story, and interest snowballed. Marlin obtained a small grant and formed
the Council on Economic Priorities (CEP) to serve as a clearinghouse for economic research on what came to be known as "socially responsible" investment
opportunities.[10]

Finally, in 1970 the Project for Corporate Responsibility announced that its
members, a group of young lawyers who collectively owned 12 shares of stock
in General Motors, were submitting nine corporate-reform resolutions to be
voted on by the company's shareholders. Their initiative came to be known

as Campaign GM and marked a watershed in the use of shareholder resolutions and proxies in attempting to alter corporate behaviors.[11] In concert
with the NCC, NACLA, ICCR, CDE, CEP, and other like-minded advocates, the Project for Corporate Responsibility set the course for pressuring
corporate management through sophisticated and carefully targeted attacks
on key stakeholder relationships. In each instance, the economic pressure
brought on corporations through their investors, their customers, and others
was augmented by a moral argument for social change. Mammon and largesse.
Self-interest and altruism. Misanthropy and philanthropy joined forever like
the circling partners in a binary star. It was a pattern destined for repetition
but that had yet to be wrapped in a package of progressivism.

It is not the argument here that some revisionist Left-braintrust gathered
around a giant conference table and, over bowls of Ben & Jerry's Cherries Gar-
cia, viewed the results of focus groups, tested alternative message points, and
arrived at a collective judgment that "progressive" was the label of the future.
That image is not only contrapuntal but is most probably wrong. Or at least
if it happened, I have not heard about it. But there are some very gifted and
sophisticated communicators in what is now the Progressive Movement, and
even if this imaginary scene did not take place, the degree of careful observation and thought that it suggests no doubt did take place, albeit incrementally.
And from this has emerged something of a consensus.

Interestingly enough, one of the earliest adopters of the new nomenclature was a company—one of the new-age, high-tech startups called Progressive Networks. Founded in February 1994 by Yale and Microsoft alumnus
Rob Glaser and Washington politico (Naderite and fellow Yale grad) David
Halperin, Progressive Networks set out to bring audio and video to the then-
nascent Internet. The company—you know it today as Real Networks—was
funded at the outset by private individuals, principal among them Mitchell
Kapor, founder of Lotus Development Corporation and the Electronic Frontier Foundation, and received second-round external financing of $5.7 million
from Accel Partners, a venture capital firm, in October 1995.[12] But this was
not your typical Silicon Valley company and not merely because it was based
in Seattle. Nor was Glaser your typical CEO. A former "leafleteer" for the
United Farm Workers union (with which he once considered taking a job
as an organizer), protest organizer, and long-time member of the board of
the Foundation for National Progress—publisher of the left-leaning magazine
Mother Jones—Glaser was an early convert to the Ben & Jerry's school of corporate management, which is to say, to using the structure and cash flow of
his company to advance a social agenda. In Halperin's words, "It's fair to say
that our original objective was social revolution."[13]

In that light, the name of the company—Progressive Networks—was something of a play on words. For even as he pushed the envelope of Internet software technology, Glaser (Halperin abandoned the revolution and returned to
Washington in 1995) also set out to create one of the earliest social networks
of Progressive-Left activists. It took the form of web hosting for innovative

activist groups like the Council on Economic Priorities that were pioneers in establishing a presence on the World Wide Web, and a weekly interactive web publication, Web Active, that was designed to connect Progressive activist groups with other like-minded individuals and organizations. In the words of a 1998 Web Active promotion[14]:

> In addition to its work on cutting-edge multimedia technologies, Real Networks aims to bring the networking power of the World Wide Web and the Internet to bear on social and political issues.

Although it is by no means the most visible or influential network of Progressive groups today, Web Active is still available on the web, where its links to activist organizations and publications now number more than 2,100. But its pioneering role as an agent of social networking on the Left and as a purveyor of web-based services has attracted considerable competition. Today the most influential of these is probably the Association for Progressive Communications (APC). APC was formed in 1990 to coordinate activist computer networks in the United States, England, Sweden, Canada, Brazil, Nicaragua, and Australia. By 1997 it comprised 25 member networks in 133 countries, providing e-mail, web hosting, conferencing, news and other services for activists, nongovernmental organizations, and others. In many ways, APC was modeled on IGC—the Institute for Global Communications—a project of the Tides Foundation that was established in 1987, which is the affiliated network in the United States.

Once the core thematic of the Progressive Left was established in the mind of the activist community, the challenge shifted to one of implementation—of finding ways to exploit the new packaging and, in the process, to regain hegemony in the political system. The best way to do that, clearly, was to identify mechanisms that underscored and made self-evident the moral differentiation between the new forces of light and the established forces of darkness. Two such mechanisms—the corporate code of conduct and the anti-corporate campaign (and, in particular, its central theme structure)—are worth a close look, in part because both have roots in the history of the Left itself, in part because they provide a direct connection between the packaging of progressivism and the kind of investor activism we have detailed in earlier chapters, and in part simply because they have become ubiquitous in the public sphere. In the balance of this chapter, we look at the first of these mechanisms, the code of conduct, and at an extended example of its use. In the next chapter, we turn our attention to anti-corporate campaigns.

CORPORATE CONDUCT UNBECOMING[15]

At least since the days of the Ten Commandments and the Code of Hammurabi, civil society has depended on codes of conduct—on rules that set forth the proper roles of the individuals and institutions within that society and that define the limits of acceptable thought and action. Whether in the form of oracular revelation, fundamental law such as a constitution, more transitory legislative and regulatory guidelines, or less formally defined social mores, these rules of social propriety set the boundaries of social, political, and economic life and give sanction to a more or less broad array of activities within each sphere. Indeed, societies are literally defined by the scope and nature of their respective codes and by whether these codes are voluntarily accepted by the people and institutions they govern or, in the alternative, must be imposed by real or implied force of arms.

A *corporate* code of conduct is a statement of the standards of behavior to which a given company or industry aspires. It is a document that codifies the ethical or moral code by which business will be conducted. Thus, it is similar in purpose or effect to a broader societal code. But it is different in the sense that, where a societal code prescribes behavior for an entire population from the top down, a corporate code prescribes behavior for a single actor from the bottom up. The former is a public and collective accord, the latter a private and singular pledge.

The potential value of such codes to the companies that adopt them is suggested by a recent survey that showed that of all the factors most influencing public perceptions of individual companies, the most important is the company's apparent social responsibility on issues such as labor practices, business ethics, and environmental impacts, factors cited by 56% of all respondents.[16] Set against this is the potential danger of adoption, which arises from the fact that in the real world, no company of any scale can reasonably hope to fully and invariably conform to its own code, even where it tries assiduously to do so. Thus, for businesses that adopt such codes—and many do—they represent, in effect, the corporate version of the moral high ground but also an unattainable ideal that, when not achieved, becomes the basis for attacks on their reputations. This is a dilemma not easily resolved and helps explain why, even as some companies and industries have adopted codes of conduct voluntarily and on their own initiative, others have adopted codes only under some degree of duress from third parties—typically unions, churches, environmentalists, human rights advocates, and other activists—aka, the Progressive Left, and still others have resisted altogether.

The first multinational corporation to adopt a code of conduct was Levi Strauss & Company, which committed itself to a set of "Global Sourcing & Operating Guidelines" in 1991. These guidelines addressed general issues such as ethical standards, compliance with legal requirements, environmental responsibility, community involvement, and employment standards and were applied as a matter of company policy to "every contractor who manufactures or finishes products" for Levi Strauss.[17] In the years since, many other companies have followed Levi's lead.

As exercises in corporate ethics and good business practices, the adoption of such codes is unassailable, and the codes themselves are ready symbols of corporate rectitude. But, for companies that find themselves in confrontations with unions or other Progressive-Left advocates, these codes can also create a focal point of corporate vulnerability. As Saul Alinsky put it in one of his "rules for radicals"[18]:

> Make the enemy live up to their own book of rules. *You can kill them with this, for they can no more obey their own rules than the Christian Church can live up to Christianity.* (p. 128)

Alinsky's point was purely strategic: The values that corporations espouse through a code of conduct are impregnable, but precisely because they are so lofty, their institutional agent—the corporation, and the enemy—is inevitably going to fall short of achieving them. The result will be a vulnerability worthy of exploitation.

That is the key to understanding the strategic significance of such codes. The code of conduct defines the moral high ground of business practices— whether pertaining to labor and the workplace, the environment, political action, or any other cluster of issues—*and* provides the basis for attacking the company that adopts it. The code defines for each company the nature of what might be termed "conduct unbecoming" a socially responsible business, symbolizes the company's acceptance of that standard, and virtually ensures that any antagonist will be able to identify irresponsible corporate actions.

SWEATSHOP DAYS AND PHILIP KNIGHT[19]

One of the best illustrations of the strategic use of codes of conduct is found in the apparel industry, where organized labor has teamed with a cluster of human rights and other nongovernmental organizations to bring pressure primarily against companies that market goods in the United States but manufacture them through contractors in developing countries where labor costs and conditions are generally below those in the United States. The principal mechanism of pressure here has been the newly reinvigorated anti-sweatshop movement, and the principal objective has been to drive companies to adopt progressively more restrictive codes of conduct that make offshore manufacturing less attractive as they improve wages and working conditions abroad. It is a perfect case of a high-ground thematic serving both an altruistic objective and a vested economic interest. The poster child of this movement, and an excellent exemplar of its dynamic, is Nike.

The Nike story begins for our purposes in the mid-1980s, when that company joined the surge of American corporations investing in the Asian countries of the Pacific Rim. For many, this was a defensive move intended to counter Japanese firms' investment in the region and offset the worsening balance of trade with countries such as South Korea and Indonesia. As many companies saw it, the choice was between displacing their own American workers by shifting production offshore or having those workers displaced by competitive forces that harmed the companies as well. The typical response was to act to retain market share by exporting production. Between 1980 and 1982, for example, American companies invested $4.8 billion in the region, increasing their holdings by 71%. But still they were losing share to Japanese competitors. So, with the encouragement of the Reagan administration, they stepped up their rate of investment—and of job displacement—even further. Among the companies riding this wave were shoe manufacturers Adidas, Reebok, and Nike.[20]

Economic activity within East Asia had its own dynamic during these years, driven in part by a wage differential across countries—in 1990, for example, there was a 93% disparity between the minimum wage in Taiwan ($600 per month) and that in Indonesia ($42 per month)—and in part by the growing aggressiveness of unions in some countries, most notably South Korea. As a result, production facilities—many of them Korean owned—moved from one country to another in pursuit of the lowest labor costs. It was at about this point in time—the late 1980s—that the Indonesian government launched an initiative to attract new factories with a series of development-friendly policies. That initiative landed, among other U.S. companies, Adidas, Reebok, and Nike. By spring 1990 both Reebok and Nike were ordering 400,000 pairs of shoes a month from contractors in Indonesia.[21]

For Nike, the shift to Indonesian production helped spur a surge in profitability. After weak performances through the mid-1980s, the company's profits rose sharply in 1989.[22] Through the 1990s, Nike came to dominate the market for athletic shoes and diversified its product line. This attracted the interest of Wall Street, where Nike stock emerged as a favorite. It also attracted the interest of organized labor.

In 1989 the AFL-CIO dispatched to Indonesia a young and aggressive labor-lawyer-slash-organizer named Jeff Ballinger. Over a 4-year period, Ballinger worked through indigenous social and religious groups to meet secretly with many Indonesian workers—mostly young women—collecting anecdotes about working conditions and abusive employers. He produced a series of reports focusing in particular on conditions in the factories of Nike contractors that he distributed to the media, to Nike management, and to many of the athletes who endorsed Nike products.[23] These reports, in effect, served to develop the core messages of the subsequent campaign against Nike, the anti-sweatshop movement of the late 1990s, and the contents of the codes of conduct that would later be pressed on the apparel industry generally.

Ballinger's mission was but one part of a much larger labor initiative aimed at reducing outsourcing in the apparel industry. In 1989, for example, the Made in the USA Foundation (MUSA) was established. This organization, with close ties to UNITE—the clothing and textile workers' union—soon launched its own campaign against Nike with a $1 million advertising campaign urging consumers to send their smelly old shoes to Nike CEO Phil Knight accompanied by notes asking him to shift production back to the

United States.[24] And at the urging of the International Labor Rights and Education Research Fund and the human rights group Asia Watch, the Office of the U.S. Trade Representative held hearings in September 1992 that focused further critical attention on Nike.[25] But it was Ballinger who scored the major hit of the campaign when, in 1993, he was invited to accompany a crew from the CBS television program *Street Stories* to Indonesia, where they interviewed a number of Nike contract workers and produced a highly critical report that generated a drumbeat of media pressure.[26]

More recently, much of the campaign against Nike has been coordinated by the Campaign for Labor Rights (CLR), a coalition that includes UNITE, other union and labor organizations, and ideological groups such as CISPES (the Committee in Solidarity with the People of El Salvador, a remnant of the anti-Reagan Left of the 1980s). It has included sponsorship of U.S. tours by Nike contract workers, various media events such as picketing at Nike stores and other retailers, and even personal attacks on the Nike CEO. CLR, in turn, is part of a broader coalition, the so-called "Working Group on Nike," which also includes, among others, the Coalition of Labor Union Women, Amnesty International/USA, Global Exchange, the Interfaith Center for Corporate Responsibility (ICCR), the National Organization for Women, and the pension board of the United Methodist Church.[27] Through this period, Nike became a primary icon of a broader movement linking outsourced production with sweatshops.

In August 1996 President Clinton invited apparel industry executives and labor leaders to the White House to discuss ways to eliminate sweatshop conditions in the garment industry. The President called on those assembled to report back to him in 6 months with a plan to accomplish this purpose. This initiative came to be known as the Apparel Industry Partnership (AIP). In April 1997 the group returned with a series of recommendations, among them a draft "Workplace Code of Conduct" to which the participating companies— including Nike—pledged to subscribe through a new organization, the Fair Labor Association (FLA). In return, their goods would carry a "No Sweat" label assuring consumers that they were not produced by sweatshop labor.[28]

Among the practices proscribed by the AIP code were the following:

- Forced labor, including prison labor;
- Employment of workers under the age of 15;
- Sexual, physical, or verbal harassment or abuse;
- Discrimination on the basis of gender, race, religion, age, disability, sexual orientation, nationality, political opinion, or social or ethnic origin;
- Unsafe or unhealthy working environment; and
- Mandatory work hours or overtime beyond stated limits.

More affirmatively, the code required employers to recognize workers' right to organize and bargain collectively, to pay at least the minimum wage in every country, and to compensate workers at a premium rate for overtime work. Employees were also guaranteed the right to report noncompliance.[29]

As the parties returned to the bargaining table to produce a final document, two components of this agreement led to immediate controversy. The first was a dispute over requiring payment of a "living wage" rather than the minimum wage, an outgrowth of an AFL-CIO initiative to raise the wage base in the United States by establishing not a minimum wage, but, in effect, a minimum standard of living. The second was a dispute over monitoring— over who was to assure compliance with the code and by what process. In the latter regard, the draft code placed substantial emphasis on internal monitoring in consultation with local human rights, labor, and religious groups, as opposed to independent monitoring by such third parties, and provided for the results of any monitoring to be held in confidence rather than made public.[30]

Medea Benjamin, director of Global Exchange, condemned the draft code as "a lousy agreement" that "gives the impression to consumers that things are going to be better when things are going to be exactly the same."[31] But UNITE President Jay Mazur initially described the agreement as "historic."[32] Final negotiations, expected to take 6 months, dragged on for a year and a half until, in November 1998, a subset of the original AIP membership produced a final draft of its code that did not commit to a living wage and fell short of labor's demands about monitoring. Mazur, AFL-CIO President John Sweeney and other labor participants declined to support this draft, and the unions launched a counterattack.

The counterattack centered primarily on the nation's university campuses, where much of the anti-sweatshop movement was by then based and where some administrators had already yielded to student pressure to require vendors of their logo goods to subscribe to the FLA code. The first shot was fired at Duke University, where the AIP guidelines were superceded by those of the Collegiate Licensing Corporation Sweatshop Task Force, which was viewed as more labor-friendly.[33] Then, United Students Against Sweatshops (USAS), a student group established and supported by organized labor, issued its own statement of principles, based on a draft by Global Exchange and Sweatshop Watch, which began by stating that "[t]he Duke Code is a Floor for continuing work on Codes of Conduct" that must be improved by providing for a living wage, full public disclosure of factory locations and monitoring reports, independent external monitoring, and, significantly, formation of an organization independent of the manufacturers and marketing companies with the responsibility to interpret the code and to coordinate monitoring and enforcement.[34]

Such a group—the Workers' Rights Consortium (WRC)—was later formed and has become the rallying point for subsequent campus-based activism in which universities are pressured to subscribe to the WRC and its labor-friendly code rather than the FLA and its industry-friendly code. In the last few years, this has become a widespread and coordinated movement on university campuses that has generated a great deal of news, most of it carried primarily in student newspapers. In a 2-week span in March 2000, for example, pro-WRC student actions occurred at Middlebury College, Temple University, Western Michigan University, Boston University, the University of Colorado, Michigan State University, UCLA, Penn State, the University of Kentucky, Syracuse University, the University of Iowa, Miami University, Purdue University, the University of Wisconsin, and the University of Massachusetts. At Kentucky, students stripped to boxer shorts and bikinis to make their point, while at Syracuse a group of clearly more avant-garde protestors staged a naked bicycle ride through the university quad.[35] Protestors at Wisconsin occupied a campus building for 4 days, while Purdue students staged a pro-WRC hunger strike.[36]

As a primary marketer of university logo goods, including team uniforms, Nike has remained a prime target of these demonstrations. In April 2000, a coalition comprising UNITE, Global Exchange, USAS, and others issued a report alleging that Nike routinely violated even its own code of conduct and staged a demonstration outside the Niketown store in midtown Manhattan.[37] As more universities added their voices to the pro-WRC drive, Nike responded—by canceling a promised $30 million gift to the University of Oregon, canceling a licensing agreement with the University of Michigan, and canceling a contract to provide equipment for the Brown University hockey team—all within a 3-week period in April 2000.[38]

The Nike case illustrates several of our arguments about the strategic use of codes of conduct. First, both the AIP/FLA code *and* the USAS/WRC code represent statements of the moral high ground on the issue of sweatshop labor. But they represent *alternative* statements of morality, one of which is more advantageous to one set of interests, and the other to another. This suggests that the definition of the high ground in such situations is, at least potentially, a competitive undertaking.

Second, the moral high ground draws the eye from less attractive territories occupied by those who would define it. In this case, whatever the level of genuine industry commitment to workplace reform in developing countries, the AIP/FLA code provides symbolic cover for any inevitable failures in achieving a code-defined perfect world. But at the same time, whatever the level of genuine activist commitment to workplace reform in developing countries, the USAS/WRC code provides symbolic cover for opposition to the forces of globalization that constitute a serious threat to the position and influence of organized labor in the United States.

Third, whatever the merits or shortcomings of a given code, those propounding it must build supportive coalitions of highly regarded allies whose participation in the establishment and enforcement of the code lend a luster of legitimacy to the exercise. For the industry in this instance, at least initially, that role was played by UNITE, other labor groups and the Interfaith Center for Corporate Responsibility, all of whom endorsed the early AIP efforts. It was their collective withdrawal of support later that opened the nascent partnership to the continuing subsequent string of attacks on its credibility. For labor, the same role has been played by ICCR, USAS, and several human rights groups whose presence in the pro-WRC coalition has helped to mask labor's more clearly vested interest in this alternative code.

Finally, in the escalation of demands once the industry had agreed to some terms in the AIP/FLA code, we see the strategic risks and opportunities—depending on one's perspective—that are associated with codes of conduct. It was not until the industry leaders had subscribed to one code that they apparently determined to be reasonable that they were confronted with another far less to their liking. Whether purposeful or not, this was accomplished through the expedient of dividing the legitimizing coalition of labor and other activist groups and playing out a game of good cop (UNITE)–bad cop (Global Exchange) to increase the pressure. In the end, the coalition re-formed around the more stringent—and to the industry, the less acceptable—alternative and continued pressing for further advantage. This dynamic is captured quite explicitly in the USAS statement of principles, which, recall, called for treating the Duke University code, already advanced beyond that of the FLA, as a "floor."

USING THE POWER OF LANGUAGE

In the new world of Progressive, anti-corporate activism, as in the world of politics generally, the control of ambiguity is the key to achieving power. Think of a spectrum of language that varies in its degree of ambiguity. At one end of the spectrum are general statements of value and purpose—acting ethically, serving the interests of society, fulfilling a company's obligations to its customers and communities, and so forth. Commitments like these are not only easy for a company to accept, but they are *expected* of a company by virtually all its stakeholders. What company, after all, would announce that its mission is to exploit its employees, rape the environment, cheat its customers, and profiteer at the expense of the national interest? A company like that would find itself on the outside looking in, scrambling for workers and customers, trying to stay one step ahead of the regulators and the courts, and facing a barrage of public outcry. It is easy, after all, for literally everyone to agree on the undesirability of these behaviors, and it is easy to mobilize those who believe a company is engaging in them.

That, of course, is precisely the point. Because the language of commitment at this level is so ambiguous, everyone can "understand" it and come together in a community of purpose based on that shared understanding of what values the company stands for and whether they are, in some fundamental way, good or bad. The problem is that the language on which there is so much agreement remains ambiguous. The agreement may rest on a quicksand of what are in reality *different* understandings of the *meaning* of the language. Is a community's interest best served, for example, by employing many people at the minimum wage, or fewer people at a so-called "living" wage that is substantially higher? Is the national interest best served by employing an admittedly "dirty" technology that damages the environment of a very small geographic area to extract a mineral that is vital to the national defense if that is the only technology that is economically viable, or perhaps the only one that is available? Is a company acting responsibly when it tries to recover its research and development costs by charging a price for its products—say pharmaceuticals—that is higher than the actual cost of production plus a normal profit?

Reasonable people will disagree on the answers to each of those questions and thousands like them. But the same people will agree that each of the companies in question should act responsibly. As we move along the spectrum away from the abstract principles on which there is broad agreement toward ever more precise specifications of how those principles will be incorporated in everyday decision making by a given company, we move toward areas of greater and greater potential disagreement. It is at this low-ambiguity end of the spectrum that outcomes are actually determined. It is here where the winners and losers are found. If a company adopts a living wage policy, some workers will earn more money, and some will be unemployed. If a company chooses to extract a mineral but damage the local environment, the nation will be militarily stronger, but some of its citizens may contract diseases or suffer a lower quality of life as a result. If a company does not recover its R&D costs, it may reduce its research effort, and opportunities to aid sufferers of certain diseases may be forgone.

These are real and important things, but they are, at the same time, potentially divisive. At the abstract level of social-value pronouncements, everyone has a common purpose and everyone wins. But at the concrete level of policy formulation, purposes diverge and some gain advantage over others. It is at this second level that the true results of a code of conduct are determined and at this second level that the interests of those pressing companies to adopt such codes are defined. It follows that it is to the advantage of corporate antagonists to argue their case to the public at the abstract level, using the broad support for pro-social values—justice, fairness, dignity, responsibility—as leverage, while it is to their advantage to negotiate with the company at the specific level where the real benefits reside. And that is precisely what they do.

THE PROPONENTS

Although many activist organizations have become involved in efforts to advance or impose corporate codes of conduct, a small number of such groups are regular participants in these efforts and play significant and rather specialized roles. What follows are brief sketches of a few of the more important of these groups. As we consider them, the linkage between codes of conduct and the types of pro-social investment and proxy efforts we examined earlier will become clear.

Coalition for Environmentally Responsible Economies (CERES)

CERES is a coalition formed in 1989 that brought together 15 major U.S. environmental groups with organized labor, activist public pension funds, social-responsibility investors, and more than 200 Protestant denominations and Catholic orders. The coalition's objective is to supplement governmental efforts at environmental protection by changing private corporate policies and behaviors. The means to this end has been through shareholder resolutions intended to impose on corporate management compliance with a code of environmental conduct known as the "CERES Principles."[39] This is precisely the kind of two-fisted approach—proxy votes to advance codes of conduct and policy changes—we have been suggesting.

In general terms, these principles commit a company to reduce environmentally damaging discharges, conserve nonrenewable resources and emphasize the use of renewable ones, recycle and reduce the waste it generates, conserve energy, use safe and environmentally sound technologies and processes, consult with their communities and inform the public of environmental problems associated with their operations, take no actions against their employees who become environmental whistleblowers, and conduct annual self-audits of their compliance.[40] In the years since the CERES Principles were set forth, they have become something of a gold standard for corporate environmental responsibility and are often now incorporated into other codes of conduct simply by reference.

On the one hand, these principles cut a broad swath through the environmental practices of any company that accedes to them. On the other hand, their emphasis on internal auditing makes them relatively less challenging for a company than other codes that may be propounded. Initially, the CERES Principles were adopted only by companies such as Ben & Jerry's and the Body Shop, which have themselves played active roles in promulgating codes of conduct and related forms of activism. In 1993, Sunoco became the first *Fortune* 500 company to adopt this code. At this writing there are more than 70 signatories, including American Airlines, Bethlehem Steel, Ford and General Motors, Polaroid, and Sunoco.[41]

Social Accountability International (SAI)

This is the recently renamed successor to the Council on Economic Priorities (CEP). As noted earlier CEP was founded by Alice Tepper Marlin in 1969 for the purpose of identifying investment opportunities untainted by connections to the Vietnam War. In later years, it evolved into a visible and influential purveyor of ratings and evaluations of corporate performance on a variety of issues including environmental policies and practices, treatment and compensation of women and minorities, philanthropic activity, helping employees to balance the demands of work and family, general working conditions, and public disclosure.[42] CEP produced a series of technical research reports as well as occasional books, the latter beginning with a 1986 volume rating hundreds of products and companies on a variety of social responsibility behaviors that evolved into a series titled *Shopping for a Better World*.[43] The essence of these volumes was nicely captured in the promotional materials for the 2000 edition[44]:

> Companies will receive letter grades (A's, B's, C's, etc.) for each issue area, based on a quantitative rating system developed by the Council on Economic Priorities.... [The book] will also include alerts about companies that test their products on animals, have significant military contracts, or irresponsibly source their labor overseas.

Around the time those words were being written, CEP was working on the "next big thing" in codes of conduct—a common, globally applicable standard that incorporated all issues from the workplace to the environment and beyond. Known as SA8000, this global code was positioned as a core statement of internationally recognized fundamental rights and corporate obligations. It was grounded in positions that have been adopted over the years by the International Labor Organization, in the *Universal Declaration of Human Rights*, and in the United Nations *Convention on the Rights of the Child*—all of which add weight, legitimacy, and universality to its appeal.

SA8000 derives its power from the elegance and simplicity of its presentation and from the evident reasonableness of its requirements. But as is the case with the narrower codes we have considered, the packaging masks some highly controversial content. Indeed, this international meta-code adds an entirely new dimension of complexity and potential leverage, for it raises at least implicitly the question of how broadly or narrowly markets are defined, whether national or international standards are most applicable, and if national standards are to prevail, which nation's standards they are to be.

Even as it raises these issues, however, SA8000 provides for their resolution. To receive a certificate of compliance with the provisions of the code, companies must submit to an external audit of their practices and, once they have been certified, must submit to follow-up audits each year. And who is authorized to conduct these audits? SA8000 specified as its "accreditation agency" the Council on Economic Priorities, or as it is now known, Social Accountability International.

Interfaith Center for Corporate Responsibility (ICCR)

As noted above, ICCR was one of the earliest players in this particular game. Consistent with its origins in the National Council of Churches, ICCR is a coalition of 275 Protestant, Catholic, and Jewish denominations, religious communities, agencies, pension funds, health care systems, and dioceses—allied with several union pension funds; CalPERS and other public pension funds; a number of social responsibility investment firms and funds (including the now-familiar Calvert, Domini, Progressive Asset Management and Trillium); and other like-minded foundations and organizations (Tides Foundation, Working Assets, Proxy Monitor/Institutional Shareholder Services)—who seek, through the organization, to add the weight of their moral authority to efforts at corporate reform.[45] This is accomplished through the ownership of stock—by the members, but not by ICCR itself—and the introduction and promotion of shareholder resolutions. In 2003, for example, ICCR and its members sponsored 240 such resolutions at 157 companies. The subjects of these resolutions were wide ranging. Topic areas included, among others[46]:

- Corporate governance and executive compensation,
- Environmental practices, including adoption of the CERES Principles,
- Diversity and equal employment opportunity,
- Supplier standards (i.e., codes of conduct for contractors), and
- Implementation of global human rights standards.

In 1995, ICCR joined with two other faith-based organizations—the Ecumenical Committee for Corporate Responsibility of the United Kingdom and the Taskforce on Churches and Corporate Responsibility of Canada—to produce its own code of conduct, *Principles for Global Corporate Responsibility: Bench Marks for Measuring Business Performance*. This 80-page code, which covered the full range of civil, political, social, and economic rights and responsibilities, was intended more as an external yardstick for evaluating corporate behaviors than as a document to which companies would be expected to subscribe.[47]

Global Exchange (GX)

Founded in 1988, GX differs from the other groups described here in that its appeal is not to shareholders, institutional investors, or corporate officers and board members but to street-level activists. The group's agenda incorporates positions on human rights, labor rights, environmentalism, and corporate responsibility, especially as these issues take on a North–South dimension in the international system. As reported previously, GX has played a central role in the anti-Nike campaign and in the anti-sweatshop movement more generally. It was also a central participant in the anti-WTO demonstrations in Seattle in December 1999 and the anti-IMF and World Bank demonstrations in Washington, DC, the following spring. Issues relating to international trade and global outsourcing are particular focal points of GX concern and actions. We will have more to say about this organization in chapter 8. In the present context, GX is most noteworthy for its role, together with the labor-based Sweatshop Watch, in drafting and promulgating the model code of conduct for universities that has been adopted by United Students Against Sweatshops.

Verité

The organizations listed to this point have in common their interest in establishing codes of conduct and increasing the number of companies that adopt them. Once such codes are in place, however, a separate issue arises— verification, or what is generally termed, compliance monitoring. As noted earlier, this is a significant issue in which signatory companies must find a comfort zone somewhere on a continuum from total internal control with limited credibility to total external control with substantial credibility. From a purely strategic perspective, the selection carries considerable risk because codes of conduct often are adopted only under pressure from the company's antagonists and because placing control over compliance in the hands of such antagonists leaves the company open to continued attack, this time legitimized by the very code it has adopted. Verité represents an effort to address that issue.

Verité was established in 1995 for the express purpose of monitoring compliance with codes of conduct. Although established and operated as a non-profit organization, it has, in effect, positioned itself as a consulting company that provides monitoring services to other companies and to client nongovernmental organizations. Verité's market niche is captured in the following passage from its promotional materials[48]:

> No company wants to be known for sweatshop or child labor abuses, yet few have the capacity to monitor every one of their subcontractors worldwide. Verité can work with your in-house staff and suppliers to ensure that goods sold under your trademark meet international human rights standards in production. . . . Verité's programs are customized to the needs, expectations and values of each client. We offer an integrated, comprehensive set of services to manufacturers and retailers engaged in global outsourcing.

Verité maintains a network of ties to other code-active organizations, including SAI and GX, as well as to organized labor.

PROGRESS IS OUR MOST IMPORTANT PRODUCT

In truth, the struggle between the activists of the Left and their corporate opposites is inherently ideological. Some on the Left are genuinely anti-capitalist and are offended by the very existence of the corporation as a form of economic organization. Most are merely pro-social and offended by what they perceive to be the anti-social actions taken by corporations in the name of economic self-interest. But both are motivated in some measure by the same affirmative vision—of a political system in which corporations, to the extent they are tolerated, do the bidding of the people acting as and through communities. Those on the Right—which in the eyes of the Left includes corporations themselves—are more generous in the grant of rights they would make to companies and have a more individual-centered vision of the polity.

Most Americans, however, are not advocates of either view and generally do not tend to think in these terms at all. They are much more concerned with solving everyday problems than with big philosophical ideas. Yet these "undecideds" constitute the majority of voters, the majority of investors, and the majority of consumers. It is for their hearts and minds that the struggle between Left and Right is waged, and it must be waged on terms that will appeal to them. That is the reason the Left has felt obligated to recast itself as a new "Progressive" movement, and it is the reason corporations are so much concerned with image and reputation. Through the promulgation and adoption of codes of conduct, both sides are able to achieve at least some of their objectives. But as we see in the next chapter, there is another mechanism in play in this struggle—the anti-corporate campaign—that is very much more a zero-sum game.

ENDNOTES

1. Murray Edelman, *Constructing the Political Spectacle* (Chicago: University of Chicago Press, 1988), p. 76.
2. Quoted in Edmund Morris, *Theodore Rex* (New York: Modern Library, 2001), p. 426.
3. Ibid.
4. Reported in a Gallup Poll conducted June 21–23, 2002.
5. "Americans Express Little Trust in CEOs of Large Corporations or Stockbrokers," Gallup News Service, July 17, 2002.
6. "Effects of Year's Scandals Evident in Honesty and Ethics Ratings," Gallup News Service, December 4, 2002.
7. David Vogel, *Lobbying the Corporation: Citizen Challenges to Business Authority* (New York: Basic Books, 1978), p. 24.
8. Saul D. Alinsky, *Rules for Radicals: A Pragmatic Primer for Realistic Radicals* (New York: Vintage, 1971), pp. 172–178.
9. Vogel, op. cit., pp. 150–151, 164.
10. Vogel, op. cit., pp. 130–131.
11. Vogel, pp. 71–75.
12. Information found online at www1.real.com/corporate/pressroom/pr/finance.html on September 23, 1998.
13. Robert H. Reid, "Real Revolution," *Wired*, Issue 5.10 (October 1997).
14. "About Web Active," found at www.webactive.com/webactive/about-wnia.html, September 24, 1998.
15. Much of the balance of this chapter is based on and drawn from Jarol B. Manheim, *Corporate Conduct Unbecoming: Codes of Conduct and Anti-Corporate Strategy* (St. Michael's, MD: Tred Avon Institute Press, 2000).

16. Environics International, *The Millenial Poll*, May 1999.

17. "Global Sourcing & Operating Guidelines," Levi Strauss & Company, found on the company's web site at www.levistrauss.com/about/code.html, June 26, 2000.

18. Alinsky, op. cit., p. 128.

19. This section is drawn from Manheim, *Corporate Conduct Unbecoming*, pp. 39–46, and parallels and extends the Nike story as recounted in Manheim, *The Death of a Thousand Cuts*, pp. 71–74.

20. Bruce Stokes, "U.S. Lags Behind Japan in Competition over Investing in East Asia Production," *National Journal*, Vol. 16, No. 7 (July 7, 1984), p. 1300.

21. Paul Charles Ehrlich, "Indonesia seeks investors for footwear field," *Footwear News*, August 7, 1989, p. 98; Paul Charles Ehrlich, "Korea may act on shoemakers' exodus; footwear outsourcing shifting to Southeast Asia," *Footwear News*, August 24, 1989, p. 26; and Paul Charles Ehrlich, "Indonesia is moving up in export lineup; athletic shoe industry," *Footwear News*, April 23, 1990, p. 23.

22. "Shoemaker gets kick from fitness," *Journal of Commerce*, July 18, 1989, p. 4A.

23. Caroline Brewer, "From One Voice to a Roar for the Workers," *Bergen Record*, May 31, 1998, p. L1.

24. Jamie Beckett, "Dunk Nike is Theme of New Ad Campaign," *San Francisco Chronicle*, November 2, 1992, p. C3; and Christy Fisher, "Made in USA Tells Nike: Come Home," *Advertising Age*, October 26, 1992, p. 3.

25. Charles P. wallace, "Doing Business: New Shots Fired in Indonesia Wage War," *Los Angeles Times*, September 22, 1992, p. 2.

26. Brewer, op. cit. See also "Just Do It: Nike Cheap Labor Factories in Indonesia," CBS News Transcripts, July 2, 1993.

27. The complete membership of this coalition was listed online at home.inreach.com/mochi/nike/napp5.html.

28. "White House Fact Sheet on Apparel Code of Conduct," April 14, 1997.

29. *Preliminary Agreement Charter Document, Fair Labor Association*, Apparel Industry Partnership, April 14, 1997, pp. 19–20. Found at www.lchr.org/sweatshop/aipfull.htm on July 30, 1999.

30. Ibid., pp. 20–23.

31. "No Sweat," *The NewsHour with Jim Lehrer*, PBS, April 14, 1997.

32. Ibid.

33. Maureen Milligan, "College consortium nears final sweatshop code," *The Chronicle* (Duke University), November 11, 1998.

34. "Provisional Statement of Principles," United Students Against Sweatshops, found at home.sprintmail.com/~jeffnkari/USAS/principles.html, August 2, 1999.

35. Tracy Kershaw, "U. Kentucky students strip for sweatshop cause," *Kentucky Kernel, March 24, 2000*; and Nicholas Steffens, "Naked bike riders protest sweatshops at Syracuse U.," *Daily Orange*, March 27, 2000.

36. Alicia Hammond, "Protesters stage hunger strike at Purdue," *Badger Herald* (University of Wisconsin), March 29, 2000.

37. "New Report Document's Nike's Continued Use of Sweatshop Labor Practices in Asia," news release from UNITE, April 25, 2000; and "Growing Economic Justice Coalition to Bring Last Week's Washington Protests to New York's Niketown on Tuesday," news release from UNITE, April 25, 2000.

38. Steven Greenhouse, "Nike's Chief Cancels Gift to University Over Monitors," *The New York Times*, April 25, 2000; and Mark Asher and Josh Barr, "Nike Cuts Off Funds for Three Universities," *Washington Post*, May 4, 2000, p. A1.

39. Drawn from information found at www.ceres.org/about/index.html on June 14, 2000.

40. The CERES Principles are listed at www.ceres.org/about/principles.html, as found on June 14, 2000.

41. Drawn from information found at http://www.ceres.org/about/endorsing_companies.htm on March 17, 2003.

42. These evaluative dimensions are detailed, along with current rankings of various companies on each, at www.cepnyc.org/criteria.htm.

43. Steven D. Lydenburg, Alice Tepper Marlin and Sean O'Brien Strub, *Rating America's Corporate Conscience: A Provocative Guide to the Companies Behind the Products You Buy Every Day* (Reading, MA: Addision-Wesley, 1986).

44. This description was found at www.cepnyc.org/sbw.htm, June 14, 2000.

45. Members, sponsors, affiliates and donors are listed in the ICCR's 2001–2002 *Annual Report*, which appeared as Volume 30, Numbers 8–9 of the organization's publication, *The Corporate Examiner*.

46. Found online at http://www.iccr.org/products/proxy_book03/03statuschart.htm, April 2, 2003.

47. "Religious Groups Propose *Principles for Global Corporate Responsibility*, ICCR news release, September 19, 1995.

48. "Purpose and Programs," found on the Verité web site at www.verite.org on June 14, 2000.

6

Capital Punishment

As we saw in the previous chapter, codes of conduct are icons, and can become battlegrounds over control, of the moral high ground in a dispute between a corporation and its critics or antagonists. But whichever role they play, there is at least some agreement on both sides that most or all of the broad values that tend to be expressed in such codes are commonly held by both sides and by the public as well. The same cannot be said of a second mechanism by which Progressive activists attempt to pressure corporations to adopt their preferred policies and practices, the anti-corporate campaign. Here the strategy of attack is more likely to be of the take-no-prisoners variety, and although such campaigns tend to be waged within a frame of pro-social themes, the emphasis is much less on moving toward common values than on exposing and redressing supposed corporate evil-doing. Indeed, where such campaigns are being waged, a debate over a code of conduct, and for that matter the use of financial and proxy-voting pressures by socially motivated funds and organizations, may be but one or two theaters of war in a far broader conflict.

PUNISHING CAPITAL: CORPORATE AND ANTI-CORPORATE CAMPAIGNS

The phenomenon known as the corporate campaign was developed primarily within the labor movement beginning in the mid-1970s. The central idea was that, by identifying and undermining a target company's most critical stake-holder relationships—with its customers, suppliers, bankers, and the like—and by effectively waging war on its reputation, a union could bring a great deal of pressure on management that might, in turn, result in a better contract than otherwise might have been possible or, for nonunion companies, convince the company to facilitate unionization of its workers. To this end, the union, often working with allies and surrogates, would bring lawsuits or other actions against the company, boycott its products, attack its credibility on Wall Street, or engage in any number of other actions that had at their core an effort to embarrass those who did business of any sort with the target company, turn-ing each of these stakeholders into pressure points against management. In theory, and often in practice, as the pressure built to an intolerable level, the company would yield.

In the course of conducting what is by now well over 200 such campaigns, labor recruited to its support a large number of environmental, human rights, consumer rights, and other Progressive activist groups, some of which began to learn the techniques used in such campaigns and to appreciate the potential they had to influence corporate decision makers. Over the last few years, these groups have begun conducting increasing numbers of their own campaigns, sometimes, but not always, with the participation or support of organized labor.

But for all their similarities, there is a difference between these two sets of campaigns that suggests the value of applying different labels to them. Although there are notable exceptions, in most of the campaigns conducted by organized labor, the objective is typically economic—jobs, compensation, work rules, union membership, etc. For this reason, at the end of the day there exists some measure of common interest between the target company and the campaigning union, at least to the point that both have an interest in preserving the viability of the company. This tends to place some limits on what the union is prepared to do in its attacks on the company.

The same cannot be said of campaigns waged against corporations by Pro-gressive activists. As noted earlier, some of these groups would view destruction of the corporation as a social institution as beneficial to society. Others—the clear majority—take a narrower but nonetheless antagonistic view, seeing spe-cific corporations or industries such as mining or petroleum as net evil-doers whose elimination, or at least whose reduced success, would benefit society. These ideological and programmatic activists have no inherent stake in the viability of their targets and, as a result, are less constrained in their selection of tactics. Even though they may resemble in many ways their labor-initiated cousins, because of this alternative set of motives and objectives, we can think of the campaigns waged by these nonlabor activists as *anti*-corporate campaigns.

Historically—and the history here is one of perhaps three decades—corporate campaigns by organized labor have been relatively well-funded undertakings compared with anti-corporate campaigns. Indeed, some union campaigns have been well funded by any standard, as the labor movement has developed mechanisms to channel literally millions of dollars into some of these efforts. Environmental, human rights, and other activists' campaigns have been less well-funded and typically substantially so. As a result, though their objectives and tactics may be more extreme, and are surely more political, their impact on corporate behavior has been comparatively small.

But that may be changing. For one way to look at the expanding system of fund raising and expenditure described in the early chapters of this book—at the activities of organizations like the Tides Foundation and Working Assets, at interpretations of fiscal sponsorship, and at the many other extant and emergent agencies of activist finance—is to view them as institutionalized mechanisms to generate ever larger and more predictable pools of funding in support of anti-corporate activism. This, too, follows a path first hewn by organized labor, but it may, in the end, lead in a very different direction.

DIMENSIONS OF THE ANTI-CORPORATE CAMPAIGN

In an earlier volume,[1] I described at length the strategies and tactics of the corporate campaign, mainly as practiced by organized labor. I do not propose to replicate that analysis in full here. However, to assist in developing the argument of the current volume, there is some benefit to providing a brief and selective summary of that analysis as it applies in the context of the anti-corporate campaign. As we do that, it is worth recalling that, even though its techniques were perfected by organized labor, the anti-corporate campaign was first conceived by the forerunners of today's Progressive Left—the anti-war, anti-apartheid, and other activists who drafted that first how-to manual for attacking corporations, the NACLA *Research Methodology Guide*, and its roots reach deep within what is now known as the Progressive Movement.

The starting point and strategic key to the anti-corporate campaign is what its practitioners refer to as "power structure analysis." In conducting a power structure analysis, one identifies all the stakeholder relationships on which a targeted company depends in the conduct of its daily business; studies each relationship with an eye toward identifying its strengths and weaknesses and its centrality to corporate well-being; matches these observations up with the needs and capabilities of the antagonist itself, with its resources and with any special events or opportunities that may be available to use in support of the campaign; and arrives at a prioritized list of action items that will constitute the campaign plan. The next step is to begin implementing the plan.

This initial stage of the campaign is illustrated in Figure 6.1. The company is shown as a junction point at which intersect the interests, needs, and supports of a large number of other actors—workers, consumers, investors, vendors, regulators, community leaders, and so forth. If one thinks of a corporation as a social institution whose function is to produce goods and services that recognize and respond to the interplay of these forces, then the essence

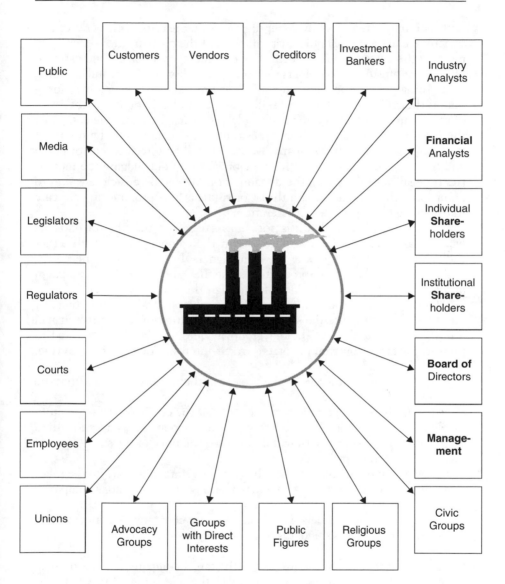

FIG. 6.1.   Power structure analysis. *Note*. From *The death of a thousand cuts* (p. 196) by J. B. Manheim, 2001, Mahwah, NJ: Lawrence Erlbaum Associates. Copyright 2001 by Jarol B. Manheim. Reprinted with permission.

of the strategy is revealed: By disrupting one or more critical elements of this structural equation, the antagonist can prevent the company from effectively meeting the expectations or needs of one or more stakeholders and can mobilize those affected stakeholders to express their dissatisfaction and, in doing so, to bring pressure on the company. That pressure can take many forms— taking their business elsewhere, selling shares and driving down the price of the company's stock, tightening regulatory oversight, suing the company; the list is nearly endless. As these pressure points accumulate, the theory of the campaign holds, the company eventually will be forced to sue for peace and to accept the demands of its antagonists. Without judging the moralities or legalities in any way, the dynamic of influence here is closely akin to extortion—the generation of a threat or risk that one promises to eradicate in exchange for a specified consideration.

A key insight here is that it is not—*not* —necessary that the stakeholders who are assigned this intermediate role in the campaign agree with either the tactics or the objectives of the campaigners. Indeed, it is not necessary, and it may even be counterproductive, that they are aware of the campaign at all. Rather, the idea is to identify through the initial assessment of each relationship the interests that drive the stakeholder to deal with the company and then to so structure the situation that those interests are at risk. It will follow, then, that the stakeholder group in question will be motivated to pressure the target company out of its own self-interest. Consider the following:

- The environmental regulator who sees in the media allegations that the company is a polluter,
- The individual shareholder who hears that the company is having problems and sells the shares of its stock in her portfolio, an action that, repeated by many others, will drive down the price of the stock in a sort of self-fulfilling prophecy,
- The consumer who hears that the company's products may not be safe,
- The retailer whose stores are picketed because it sells the target company's products, or
- The community leaders who hear that the company does not comply with human rights standards in its dealings in foreign countries.

Each of these actors has an interest in the target company, and few of them have any way to test or otherwise evaluate the allegations. But what they have in common is a desire to minimize their own risk or embarrassment. In each instance, then, to the extent the allegations are widely disseminated and become part of the business environment in which the company must operate, these attacks have the potential to weaken one or more stakeholder relationships or perhaps sever them altogether. The chances that this will occur are enhanced if the allegations against the company are in some measure credible, and most such attacks are grounded in some level of truth or evidence, but the simple fact is that the mere presence of the allegation in the public discourse may be sufficient to damage a corporation's reputation or relationships regardless of its validity. The launching of multiple allegations, then, is an essential element of campaign strategy.

Sometimes the credibility of attacks on the target company is established not by the facts or the evidence but by the source of the allegation. In corporate campaigns undertaken by labor unions, this is often a special problem because the unions themselves are not held in especially high regard. They solved the problem by releasing information through allies or surrogates, which, if you will recall, is how many of the Progressive activists got into the campaign business in the first place. For many of the non-labor activists, this is not a problem, or, if it was, it has been solved by the very device of choosing to label themselves as Progressives—as opposed, for example, to radicals, the New Left, or revolutionaries, each of which labels has been used by similar groups in years past. But quite aside from that, many of these groups have their own high-sounding names and high levels of public regard, and they do not need to operate through surrogates: Friends of the Earth, the Sierra Club, Human Rights Watch, Consumers Federation of America. What's to be against? In still other instances, groups that carry some political or historical baggage, small groups that want to leverage their participation, or groups that share common or overlapping agendas will follow the lead of organized labor and work through coalitions. These, in turn, invariably have socially appealing names:

- Campaign for America's Future
- Global Survival Network
- Media and Democracy Congress
- National Religious Partnership for the Environment.

The campaigns themselves contain many tactical elements, some of which we have already suggested. In general, these fall into seven broad categories: legal, regulatory, legislative, political, financial, commercial, and public relations.

Legal Tactics

One of the tools commonly used in anti-corporate campaigns is the lawsuit. In union campaigns, the issues that give rise to such litigation typically are related to workplace conditions or wage-and-hour-type issues, most of which tend to be of only limited interest to the broader community. But Progressive activists have a far wider range of issues available on which to seek redress through the courts, and most of these have, if not always a far larger appeal, at the very least a wider ranging potential impact. Lawsuits over the extent and impact of pollution in a community, the effects of smoking tobacco, and victimization by a faulty or dangerous product are but three of the possibilities, and these alone should be sufficient to suggest the breadth of the effects such actions might have on the company named as a defendant. These effects are only enhanced when the lawsuit in question is certified as a class action or when the plaintiffs include groups that have a special resonance with the public. In its campaign during the late 1990s against BP Amoco's plan for offshore development of Alaska's North Slope oil resources, for example, Greenpeace joined with indigenous Alaskan communities in a lawsuit to stop the project. Greenpeace also joined with a group of farmers in 1999 in filing suit against Monsanto as part of a worldwide campaign to force the company to halt its program of genetic engineering of plants. The following week the company agreed to a merger with a pharmaceutical firm and spun off its agricultural components. And as part of a campaign by the International Rivers Network and others pressuring Texaco to cease its operations in Myanmar (Burma), a group of indigenous Ecuadorian tribes brought suit in the U.S. courts under an eighteenth century law, the Alien Tort Claims Act (ATCA), alleging that Texaco was a major polluter in Ecuador.

ATCA, by the way, is a rather unique statute. Written in 1789, it was one of the very first laws passed in the United States. The statute comprises a single sentence:

> The district courts shall have original jurisdiction of any civil action by an alien [a non-citizen of the U.S.] for a tort [a personal injury] only, committed in violation of the law of nations [international law] or a treaty of the United States.

Translating from legalese, this means that, under ATCA, U.S. courts have jurisdiction to hear disputes involving violations of international law and can award compensation. The defendant in an action must be physically in the United States when the legal papers are served, but otherwise neither the complainant nor the accused need be a U.S. citizen, or even a resident. It is, to be sure, a rather extraordinary law, extending a claim of U.S. jurisdiction around the world, but historically has been little used. In recent years, however, ATCA has been at the center of several human rights claims targeting corporations with U.S. operations (Shell and Unocal, for example, in addition to Texaco).[2]

A number of activist organizations are either set up as de facto law firms themselves, set up as so-called legal-defense funds through which tax exempt funds can be raised and channeled to legal initiatives, or have such entities as affiliates or subsidiaries. For example:

- The Media Access Project (MAP), formed in the mid-1970s by some alumni of Ralph Nader's consumer activism movement, describes itself as a "non-profit tax exempt public interest telecommunications law firm which promotes the public's First Amendment right to hear and be heard on the electronic media of today and tomorrow." As one might expect of such an entity, MAP works in the courts and the Federal Communications Commission to influence public policy on broadcasting and cable issues, the Internet, and new technologies. But it also plays an active role as organizer or member of a number of activist coalitions that engage in outreach, lobbying, and educational initiatives far beyond any courtroom.[3]

- EarthJustice, a similar public interest law firm, began life in 1971 as the Sierra Club Legal Defense Fund, an arms length affiliate of the Sierra Club with a separate board of directors and budget, and was renamed in 1997. Its slogan: "Because the Earth needs a good lawyer." Over the years it has challenged companies such as Disney and Unocal, and has pressured the Environmental Protection Agency and other government agencies to impose stronger limits on the development of lands and resources.[4] Listed among clients of EarthJustice in its 2002 *Annual Report* were well-known groups such as Environmental Defense, Friends of the Earth, Greenpeace, National Trust for Historic Preservation, National Wildlife Federation, Natural Resources Defense Council, Public Citizen, and, not surprisingly, the Sierra Club, and also dozens of lesser-known and mostly local environmental activist groups. Nor is the practice of public interest law necessarily a small-scale enterprise. In 2002, for example, EarthJustice had a total operating budget of approximately $24 million, of which just over $17 million was spent on programs. Of the latter, $11 million was spent on litigation, $300,000 on lobbying, and $5.8 million on public information—a good indicator of the range and priority of these diverse activities.[5]

- The National Lawyers Guild (NLG), although it still falls within this general category of activism, is a somewhat different enterprise in that it is primarily ideological in character rather than programmatic or policy driven. (Critics on the Right refer to the Guild as a communist front or, in one instance, as "the chief legal bulwark of the Communist Party."[6]) An indication of the group's ideological focus is provided by the Guild's Committee on Corporations, the Constitution & Human Rights, whose mission statement proclaims[7]:

> In a democratic society, living human beings are sovereign and are the basis of all government authority. The fundamental premise of a democracy is that political power resides and must remain in the hands of the people. Artificial entities such as corporations, which were created for functional purposes—for example, to produce and provide economic goods—are vital for any modern society. However, unlike human beings, they are neither intrinsically valuable nor do they have any legitimate claim to share in or be able to avoid democratic sovereignty.
>
> Corporations have in recent decades acquired increasing economic and political power such that they have begun to usurp the powers of government and undermine the principle of democratic sovereignty. The Committee's mission is to work toward restoring sovereignty in the hands of the people, to put human beings back in charge as they should be in a democratic polity.

Among the specific objectives of the committee are eliminating the legal fiction that corporations are persons, outlawing the use of corporate funds to influence the political process, and opposing treaties that would substitute international law for local regulation of corporations.[8]

One of the most interesting and potentially most significant uses of the courts by activists, in recent years was a case involving Nike and arising from the issues summarized in the previous chapter. In April 1998 a California activist, Marc Kasky, filed a lawsuit in state court under California's unfair trade practice and false advertising statutes alleging that Nike made false and misleading statements in describing the working conditions in the overseas factories where its shoes are manufactured. Kasky asked that the company be forced to disgorge the profits it made in the state as a result of these claims. Because the statements in question amounted, in essence, to the company's public relations effort to defend itself against the campaign being waged against it by labor and other activists, and because such statements routinely have been treated by the courts as a form of protected speech, the lawsuit represented a systemic challenge to the speech rights of corporations generally. Although perhaps not intended as such, this is an example of precisely the sort of issue being raised more generally by the NLG, for it is a question of the extent to which corporations have the same right to free speech as humans.

The trial court held that Nike's speech was, in fact, protected under the First Amendment and threw the case out. This decision was upheld at the appellate level. In May 2002, however, by a vote of 4 to 3, the California Supreme Court reinstated the case, saying that Nike's public relations fell under the lesser protected category of "commercial speech," which could therefore potentially be found to constitute false advertising under the law, and ordered that the case go to trial. Nike appealed to the U. S. Supreme Court and found quick and widespread support in the form of supporting legal briefs from such diverse interests as the Chamber of Commerce of the United States and the American Civil Liberties Union. It is almost unheard of for the U.S. Supreme Court to accept on appeal a case that has yet to be tried in the lowest court, but in this case the Justices did precisely that in January 2003.[9] A few months later, however, the Justices stepped back, returning the case to California for trial.[10] Shortly afterward, Nike and Kasky settled, with the company agreeing to contribute $1.5 million to support the work of the Fair Labor Association in exchange for withdrawal of the litigation. Yet because the settlement left the California Supreme Court's ruling untested and the underlying law in place, it was sure to have a chilling effect on corporate communications in the state.[11]

In Nike's case, for example, the company withheld release of its 2002 social audit of its contractors—the latest in the very series of reports it was pressured by the activists to produce as part of its acceptance of a code of conduct—because it feared release of the document might be determined by the courts to constitute an actionable statement.[12] Yet if that form of speech is chilled by the outcome, the activists may find themselves with something of a Pyrrhic victory. That, however, appears to be a risk at least some are prepared to run. In the words of California anti-globalization activist Jeff Milchen, "Corporations have a legitimate role to play in society by doing business. But they do not have a legitimate role in influencing public policy. Corporations do not have any claim to the protection of our Bill or Rights."[13]

Regulatory Tactics

The regulatory agencies and departments of government, at both the state and federal level and internationally, provide another, somewhat similar set of venues in which activists can challenge corporations. Perhaps the most interesting example of state-level action was the petition filed with the Attorney General of California in 1998 by the NLG and others asking that the state revoke the corporate charter of Unocal because of the company's operations in Myanmar. Among those elements of the government that come into play with some regularity at the federal level are the Environmental Protection Agency (EPA), the Department of Justice (DOJ), the Securities and Exchange Commission (SEC), and the Federal Trade Commission (FTC). The DOJ and FTC, for example, have been drawn into attacks on corporate mergers or business practices when activists claim the outcome would constitute a monopoly. Consumer activists, advocates of so-called "free software" and others, for instance, helped to draw the DOJ into bringing suit to force Microsoft Corporation to open its software code to competitors and make other changes in its policies, while Greenpeace pressed the FTC to oppose a merger of BP Amoco with ARCO. Similarly, the EPA is alternately pressured or recruited to investigate and criticize chemical, petroleum, and other types of companies targeted by the activists. And as we will see momentarily, the SEC is brought into play as a mechanism for opening corporate proxy statements to shareholder proposals on both governance and policy—the sorts of initiatives described in chapter 4. At the international level, in its campaign against Monsanto, Greenpeace lobbied the European Union regulatory authorities to ban genetically modified food products. In each instance, the idea is to gain leverage in the campaign by mobilizing the forces of government—far more powerful than the activists themselves—as allies in the effort to pressure the target company.

Legislative Tactics

In this arena, unlike some others, Progressive activists are at a disadvantage relative to their labor counterparts, largely because labor is much more effectively organized to influence the electoral process. Nevertheless, the issues of interest to the activists do have some appeal, especially to Democratic legislators, and from time to time they are able to stimulate a Congressional hearing, a letter of inquiry to a regulatory agency, a "Dear Colleagues" letter on Capitol Hill, the introduction of legislation, or some other such action. In 1999, for example, Human Rights Watch worked to get a House subcommittee to hold hearings on Chevron's operations in Nigeria, which the group was pressing the company to terminate. But perhaps the best example of legislative activity in the present context was the introduction in the House of Representatives in June 2000 of the Corporate Code of Conduct Act. That legislation, had it passed, would have required that all "nationals of the United States that employ more than 20 persons in a foreign country" must implement a corporate code of conduct including the following elements:

1. Provide a safe and healthy workplace.
2. Ensure fair employment, including prohibiting the use of child and forced labor; prohibiting discrimination based on race, gender, national origin, or religious beliefs; respecting freedom of association and the right to organize independently and bargain collectively; and paying a living wage to all workers.
3. Promote good governance and good business practices, including prohibiting illicit payments, ensuring fair competition, and revoking corporate charters when corporations fail to serve the public good and general welfare.
4. Comply with all internationally recognized worker rights and core labor standards.
5. Uphold responsible environmental protection and environmental practices, including compliance with internationally recognized environmental standards and with all Federal environmental laws for similar operations that would be applicable if the operations were located in the United States.
6. Comply with minimum international human rights standards.
7. Require, under terms of contract, partners, suppliers, and subcontractors of the national of the United States (including any security forces of the national) to adopt and adhere to the principles described in paragraphs 1–6. In addition, require full public disclosure of information relating to location and address, corporate name, applicable financial arrangements, worker rights practices and labor standards, working conditions, environmental performance, and applicable investments of partners, suppliers, subsidiaries, contractors, and subcontractors of the national.
8. Implement and monitor compliance with the principles described in paragraphs 1–7 through a self-financing program internal to the business.[14]

The bill goes on to provide that "any person may at any time file a petition with the appropriate Federal official" alleging a failure to comply, at which point an investigation *must* be undertaken unless the official in question finds the petition to be frivolous under a specific definition included in the bill. Appropriate officials as defined in the bill included the Secretaries of Commerce, Labor, and State, and the Administrator of the Environmental Protection Agency.[15]

In effect, then, this proposed legislation went even SA8000, which we examined in the preceding chapter, one better. For, although it included all the essential provisions of that and other less global code initiatives, the bill invited allegations of noncompliance, virtually required that every such allegation lead to an investigation, and, most important, would have added the full legal weight and power of the U.S. government, rather than simply the moral weight of a cluster of nongovernmental organizations, as a mechanism of enforcement. In that it is a stellar exemplar of the reason why activists sometimes pursue legislative initiatives and of the potential stakes that are present when they do.

Political Tactics

If by political one means electoral campaigns, then politics is not—or at least not yet—a realm in which Progressives are especially active or influential. Of course, electoral politics was the preferred field of action for Liberals, and electoral politics was the field of action from which they were driven mercilessly by the Reagan revolutionaries. But in truth, politics is a much larger game than mere elections, and there many are other interesting ways in which to play. The Progressive activists are only beginning to explore some of these, although not all among them acknowledge the value of doing so. The Rainforest Action Network, for example, in its ongoing campaign to force Occidental Petroleum to end its operations in the Andes Mountains, accused the company of supporting paramilitary death squads who killed American activists in Colombia, and later staged a sit-in that shut down the Gore for President headquarters in New Hampshire during primary week in 2000. In that same 1999–2000 time period, the Natural Resources Defense Council conducted a letter-writing campaign addressed to the government of Mexico as part of an effort, eventually successful, to force Mitsubishi Corporation to close a salt extraction facility in Baja California because of its effects on sea life.

Financial Tactics

We have already had quite a bit to say about the use of financial pressure by activists to force changes in corporate policies. But at this point it might be useful to take a brief look at the change in a Securities and Exchange Commission (SEC) regulation that greatly expanded the potential use of these tactics, especially with respect to the use of shareholder resolutions to influence public policy. The regulation in question is known as Rule 14a-8, which allows shareholders who meet certain floor criteria to submit and have included in a company's proxy materials a proposal they would like to have adopted and a 500-word supporting statement. Before 1998, the SEC routinely held that companies could exclude from their proxy statements any such proposals that dealt with workplace-related social issues—things like the environment or protection of human rights. But in May 1998, the Commission changed the rule to permit some of these social-policy resolutions to go before shareholders, even over management objections. One of the drivers of the change: 2,000 letters to the SEC from activists.[16] The rule change was followed by a period of confusion and conflict between companies and activists over the precise meaning of the new language, specifically over which types of resolutions companies could continue to exclude. So in July 2001 the SEC issued a document explaining for the benefit of companies and shareholder activists alike how the Commission would interpret the rule going forward.[17]

An expected outcome of the rule change was that both the number and proportion of social policy shareholder resolutions would increase, and that is precisely what has come to pass. In 1997, the year before the revision of Rule 14a-8, a total of 869 shareholder resolutions were submitted to companies, of which 582 related to issues of corporate governance and 287 to issues of social policy. Of the 869 resolutions, 376—including 49% of the governance resolutions and 31% of those pertaining to social policy—were actually put to a vote.[18] In comparison, in 2002, the first proxy season following the SEC's clarification bulletin, a total of 712 resolutions were filed, including 428 on governance issues and 261 on social policy (plus a few hybrids). Of these, 548 were submitted to shareholders for a vote, including 84% of the governance resolutions and 66% of the social policy proposals.[19] Thus, whereas the overall number of resolutions submitted appears to have declined, a much larger percentage of those in both categories is reaching shareholders for a vote. It is still the case, however, that very few of these resolutions, which generally are opposed by management, are actually adopted.

Commercial Tactics

Falling into this category are attacks against the target company's day-to-day business operations—its dealings with customers, suppliers, and others, and, especially in the case of consumer products companies, its products and brands. These marketplace-based tactics can take a variety of forms, of which the most common is the consumer boycott. The tactic was first developed (in its contemporary form) in the civil rights movement and was applied by an early anti-corporate activist group, INFACT, to Nestle in the 1970s and 1980s to force changes in its infant formula advertising, and to General Electric in the 1980s and 1990s in an effort to curb its production of nuclear weapons. In 1996, Friends of the Earth and other environmentalists called for a boycott during the Christmas season of consumer products manufactured by Siemens, which was, at the time, upgrading nuclear power facilities in Russia and Eastern Europe, a line of business to which the activists objected. The timing was designed to leverage whatever limited and short-term impact such a boycott might have—and these things are seldom massively effective—by focusing on the very brief but most profitable period for the sales of such goods. At this writing, according to one advocacy group that tracks such things, there are active boycotts against companies such as

- The GAP—This company is being boycotted by San Francisco-based Save the Redwoods, which objects to the clear-cutting of redwood forests by Donald and Doris Fisher, who founded the company.
- Altria—Never heard of it? This is the new name of the company formerly known as Philip Morris, which has long been the target of boycotts and other actions by INFACT. The boycott extends to the entire family of brands owned by the company, among them Kraft, Nabisco, Maxwell House, Jell-O, Miller Beer, Oscar Mayer, Post Cereals, and even Kool-Aid.
- Neiman Marcus—The company's sale of furs is being targeted by a group called Compassion Over Killing, which has posted stickers on stop signs and elsewhere in the vicinity of the company's stores and also maintains a web site at www.neimancarcass.com.
- *Vogue Magazine*—PETA (People for the Ethical Treatment of Animals) has targeted *Vogue* because the magazine "accepts the use of fur as fashion," has published pro-fur editorials, and has refused to accept advertising from animal rights advocates.[20]

Public Relations Tactics

In some ways, every campaign tactic listed to this point can be seen as having more or less direct public relations value. But in addition, Progressive activists are highly skilled at generating public attention more directly through media and other publicity efforts. One such tactic used with some regularity is exploiting the value of celebrity. When the Natural Resources Defense Council sought in 1999–2000 to stop Mitsubishi's salt extraction operations in Baja California, for example, its efforts were endorsed by Glenn Close, Pierce Brosnan and, in this instance perhaps most telling of all, famed oceanographer Jacques Cousteau. Other tactics have included staging demonstrations at the stores of target companies, as the Rainforest Action Network did when it was pressuring Home Depot to stop selling lumber from old-growth forests; issuing "white paper" reports like the one issued by INFACT summarizing the lobbying and public relations efforts of what was then Philip Morris; naming target companies as "Merchants of Shame," as the National Organization for Women did in its campaign against Smith Barney, the brokerage firm; or advertising in *The New York Times* and other major media, as the International Rivers Network and the Committee for the Defense of the Amazon did when they were pressuring Texaco. In addition, many activist groups engage in puppetry and street theater, as they have done in demonstrations against the International Monetary Fund, the World Bank, and the World Trade Organization.

From time to time, certain groups, most notably drawn from the environmental movement, engage in what might best be termed daredevil publicity stunts—things like hanging banners—and themselves by ropes—from trees, bridges, and tall buildings. There is, in fact, a group known as the Ruckus Society whose principal function is to provide training to those who would engage in such acts. Founded in 1995 by two long-time environmental activists, this organization conducts training camps where activists learn climbing and other physical skills, as well as ways to use them in building organizations and attracting media attention.[21] The Ruckus Society, you may recall, receives support from both the Threshold and the Tides Foundations, as well as from the clothing maker Patagonia, which offers its employees civil disobedience training provided by the group.[22]

TRUTH, JUSTICE, AND THE AMERICAN WAY

Overlaying all these tactics, and drawing not only individual anti-corporate campaigns but their collective character and presence into a more or less unified whole, is a fairly concise and frequently repeated thematic structure centering on the establishment of justice, the protection of rights, the expression of community values, and the advancing of socially responsible behavior—none of which the targeted companies are credited with undertaking on their own initiative. Rather, these corporate pariahs, these outlaw institutions, are portrayed as acting pro-socially only under duress. This is, of course, yet another expression of the enemy construction discussed earlier and a direct link to the high ground staked out through codes of conduct and similar mechanisms. But it also provides the essential patina of morality that is necessary to legitimize the Progressives' highly negative anti-corporate campaigns.

Of these themes, the most important are clearly appeals to justice and rights. To take just one very crude indicator, if we examine the names of the recipients of grants from the Tides Foundation in the year 2000, we find 21 separate groups with the word "justice" in their names. Among them:

- Alliance for Global Justice
- Alliance for Justice
- Center for Health, Environment and Justice
- Center for Law and Justice
- Citizens for Consumer Justice
- Citizens for Tax Justice
- Earth Justice Legal Defense Fund
- Equal Justice America
- Justice Resource Institute
- National Conference for Community and Justice
- Redwood Justice Fund
- Social Justice Center, and
- Environmental and Economic Justice Project

Similarly, as many as 36 of the beneficiaries of Tides largesse in 2000 were organizations with the word "rights" in their names, typically, but not exclusively, a reference to some aspect of human rights. Eight grantees had the word "community" in their names, but a far greater number were actually community-based organizations in California and elsewhere, and others were based in ethnic or indigenous communities. Five recipients had references to "responsibility" or "accountability" in their names.

These counts are based only on specific words in the names of grantees of one Progressive activist foundation in one year, and it is clear that this informal methodology greatly understates the use of such labeling. But we should not understate its significance. For it was this capacity for high-sounding labels that attracted the activists to the overarching rubric of progressivism in the first place, and that also contributed to the renewal of the historic relationship between labor and the political Left, which occurred through, and at the same time facilitated, the transfer of anti-corporate campaign techniques from the unions that most fully developed them to the activist groups that are now using them with increasing frequency. Indeed, the two best examples of groups labeled with a justice reference are two that played pivotal roles in the transfer of that social technology—Jobs with Justice and the National Interfaith Committee for Worker Justice.

Jobs with Justice was established by a union, the Communications Workers of America (CWA), in 1987 as a significant effort at reaching out to local religious, civic, educational, cultural, and political leaders in communities where the union had an interest. These local notables were recruited to speak and act in support of the union and, importantly, to serve as surrogates for the CWA in situations in which the union itself lacked either credibility or clout. In the years since its formation, the organization has come to serve the needs of a number of other unions, but in each instance the same dynamic has been used. The National Interfaith Committee was established in cooperation with the leadership of the AFL-CIO just months after the election of John Sweeney as president. Sweeney's election marked a new commitment among federation unions to organizing through an increased reliance on corporate campaign-type attacks, and, like Jobs with Justice, this organization was established as a loose confederation of local leaders, primarily clergy in this instance, who would, by the very act of engagement, add a moral dimension to the positions taken by organized labor in any given dispute. Over time, both groups have recruited many local activist influentials to the cause of organized labor. And in the process, both have also educated these local advocates in the techniques of pursuing not just labor-related agendas but other issues such as the environment and human rights. And because so many of these advocates have been ministers, priests, women religious, rabbis, and other religious leaders, it is they who have done much to develop the power of the social justice thematic and related appeals.

Yet, as noted earlier, there is an important difference between these and other Progressive activists, on the one hand, and labor activists on the other. It has to do with legitimacy and credibility, both of which arise from differing public perceptions—of unions and labor leaders as inherently self-interested, and of clergy and environmentalists (and others) as inherently public regarding. This means the non-labor Progressive activists have a strategic advantage over their counterparts in the labor movement, one that their selection of campaign themes and frames does much to exploit. More than that, their apparent ability to wage war against corporations without their own reputations and images being dragged down owes a great deal to the assumptions about their motives that the public makes, and seldom questions.

ENDNOTES

1. Jarol B. Manheim, *The Death of a Thousand Cuts: Corporate Campaigns and the Attack on the Corporation* (Mahwah, NJ: Lawrence Erlbaum Associates, 2001). .
2. For a more complete characterization of the activists' perspective on ATCA, see the discussion at www.hrw.org/campaigns/atca/, found online July 29, 2003. The courts, however, have begun narrowing the scope of the law. See Mark Hamblett, "2nd Circuit Clarifies Boundaries of Alien Tort Claims Act," *New York Law Journal*, September 9, 2003, retrieved September 8, 2003, from www.low.com. September 8, 2003.
3. Information found at http://www.mediaaccess.org/about/, April 8, 2003.
4. Information found on the organizations web site at www.earthjustice.org, April 8, 2003.
5. From the 2002 annual report, found online at http://www.earthjustice.org/about/2003_AR.pdf, April 8, 2003.
6. S. Steven Powell, *Covert Cadre: Inside the Institute for Policy Studies* (Ottawa, IL: Green Hill Publishers, 1987), p. 17.
7. From the mission statement found at http://www.nlg.org/programs/corporations.htm, April 8, 2003.
8. Ibid.
9. Maureen Tkacik, "High Court May Hear Nike Case on Protection of PR Statements," *The Wall Street Journal*, January 10, 2003; and Linda Greenhouse, "Supreme Court to Review Nike Case," *The New York Times*, January 10, 2003.
10. Linda Greenhouse, "Nike Free Speech Case is Unexpectedly Returned to California," *The New York Times*, June 27, 2003.
11. Adam Liptak, "Nike Move Ends Case Over Firms' Free Speech," *The New York Times*, retrieved September 13, 2003, from www.nytimes.com/2003/09/13/national/13NIKE.html.
12. Gary Young, "'Nike' Ruling: Just How Chilling Is It?," *The National Law Journal*, January 24, 2003.
13. Liptak, op. cit.
14. "Section 3. Responsible Business Practices of United States Nationals in Foreign Countries," H.R. 4596, 106th Congress, Second Session.
15. "Section 5. Investigations of Compliance with Corporate Code of Conduct," H.R. 4596, 106th Congress, Second Session.
16. Cynthia J. Campbell, Stuart L. Gillan and Cathy M. Niden, "Current perspectives on shareholder proposals: lessons from the 1997 proxy season," *Financial Management*, Vol. 28, No. 1 (March 22, 1999), pp. 89ff.
17. *Staff Legal Bulletin* 14, issued by the SEC's Division of Corporate Finance on July 26, 2001, as referenced in "Shareholder Proposals in Proxy Statements," a client memorandum issued by Fried, Frank, Harris, Shriver & Jacobson, November 30, 2001; found online at http://www.ffhsj.com/cmemos/113001_proxy.htm, April 9, 2003.
18. Ibid.

19. *Towards a Shared Agenda: Emerging Corporate Governance and Social Issue Trends for the 2002 Proxy Season*, report of the Investor Responsibility Research Center and Shareholder Action Network of the Social Investment Forum Foundation, March 2002, p. 5.

20. These and other boycotts were found in an online listing at http://www.boycotts.org/grid.htm, April 9, 2003.

21. Information about the Ruckus Society was found at www.ruckus.org, April 9, 2003.

22. Philip Bourjaily, "Patagonia: Green Business Practices," Environmental News Network, November 30, 1999.

7

Left, With the Right's Stuff

In the opening chapter of this book we suggested that, beginning in the early 1980s, in response to the defeat of liberalism by the Reagan Right, and after groping for a model of reconstruction, the Left reconstituted itself as a latter-day version of progressivism. This was not the result of a single decision by some maximum leader or leadership cabal, nor does it appear to have been the result of a purposeful debate in some wider circle that resolved itself in a consensus on nomenclature. Rather, it was a bit of a messy process—at least in the sense that key individuals and groups on the Left struggled for a time to overcome their shock at what had befallen them, then staggered forward, gradually regaining their rhetorical footing. Coming from a variety of directions and with varying pace, the policy activists, the ideologues, the social philanthropists, and the altruists who compose what we now think of as the Progressive Left slowly converged on their new language and on the strategy it opened up for rebuilding their movement.

But to say there was no grand scheme, no overarching plan, guiding these developments is not to say that they were random. Indeed, they were not. For despite the divergent paths that led so many thinkers and doers to the same place, they shared a more or less common point of origin—the Reagan–Bush attack on the Left—a common historical moment, a common setting, and a common model of action. The origin and moment were important in the short term. They lit the fuse. But it was the setting and the model of action that defined (and saved) the movement.

The setting in which this transition occurred was partly institutional and partly intellectual and most especially composed of the interplay between the two. In particular, we have argued, it took the form of a recognition—at a practical level by some and a conceptual level by others—that the power structure in the United States is best characterized not in terms of the electoral system and other visible political attributes, but rather in terms of the financial system and its influence on political decision making through a variety of intervening institutions. Recall that, in the years leading up to the early 1980s, this was a subject of some considerable interest, as well as some considerable debate, among social scientists, most notably C. Wright Mills, G. William Domhoff, and Thomas Dye arguing the elitist view in various formulations, with Robert Dahl and other pluralist thinkers taking the opposing view.

For the present purposes, we need not resolve, nor even take a position on, this so-called elitist-pluralist debate. We need note only that it was the elitist theory that those on the Left adopted as closest to their view of how the world really works. Best evidence? Professor Domhoff was among the 100+ founders of one notable hub of Progressive networking, the Campaign for America's Future (CAF). He was recruited to CAF by former SDSer Richard Flacks, whom he met while visiting at the University of California at Santa Barbara. As a co-founder of CAF he joined Todd Gitlin, then on the faculty of New York University (one of the pioneers of anti-corporate activism during his SDS days); leaders of organizations such as the Institute for Policy Studies, the Environmental Working Group, the Midwest Academy, and the Institute for Agriculture and Trade Policy; and a large number of intellectuals, union leaders, and other activists. So not only was his work widely reviewed in publications read by the intellectual Left (as we saw earlier), but it was familiar as well to the activist Left.

And just what did this elitist theory hold? In general, it suggested that institutions and actors such as political parties, the mass media, traditional interest groups, and public opinion were important only at the margins of the political system. Rather—and let's take Dye's characterization here because we presented it in some detail earlier—the political system is powered by large volumes of money expended by corporations and wealthy individuals, which they channel through a collaborative network of private foundations, universities, and policy-development think tanks to generate a menu of policy options that are subsequently addressed by policy makers on Capitol Hill, in the executive branch, and even in the courts. Control over the flow of money is exercised directly—by deciding which institutions do or do not receive it— but also and importantly indirectly, through interlocks among the directors of the various companies, foundations, and other institutions. The exercise of power in this world view is subtle and seldom transparent. By selecting the issues that move through the system and by shaping the ways they are studied and framed, the rich (and therefore powerful) are able to place boundaries on the range of policy choices available to those who operate the expressly political components of the system.

The appeal of such a model of politics to individuals who are predisposed to distrust corporate power in any event should be apparent. But the big step as far as movement building was concerned was not acceptance of this perspective per se, but what amounted to its reverse engineering. *If money could be used to such effect to advance the interests of the Right as seen by the Left, why could a parallel system not be created to advance the interests of the Left itself?*

It was with this question—argument really—that we began the present exercise. Now, as we near the end, it is fair to ask whether we have made the case. To do that, let's take a look at each of the critical components of the Dye model as set forth in Chapter 1—the purposeful application of private wealth, the role of foundations as combiners and distributors of that wealth, the formulation of a policy agenda by think tanks and other agencies, interlocking among the leaders of key institutions, the marginalization of pluralist institutions, and the making of policy decisions aligned with the objectives of the wealthy interests at the head end of the process. But this time we will apply the model not to the establishment power structure but to the institutions of progressivism that we examined in earlier chapters. What we find is a system of influence that is still in a relatively early stage of development but that shows clear signs of creating precisely the sort of parallel universe envisioned by the Progressives, even as its proponents use that same knowledge to guide their attacks on the foundations that underlie the extant power structure.

LAYING THE FOUNDATIONS: THE PEW CHARITABLE TRUSTS

From the outset, Progressives understood that their greatest disadvantage was money—the other side had a great deal more of it. More than that, the Right had an ideology that assigned social value to monetary wealth, while the Left had an ideology that disparaged it. So the first challenge was clear—to obtain, or at the very least gain control over, large sums of money in ways that harmonized with a critical view of capitalism.

This is where the Joshua Mailmans of the world came in. Mailman was raised with wealth derived from family businesses that were not in themselves progressive. But he was also raised within a family tradition of philanthropy. His key insights were two: that philanthropy could be defined more broadly to address issues of social policy as well as social need and that others of his generation might be brought to the same conclusion. It was these twin insights that led to the gathering of the Doughnuts, the formation of the Threshold Foundation, and in some measure the full development of the Tides Foundation.

Mailman was what students of the diffusion of innovation refer to as an early adopter, but he was not alone. Drummond Pike of the Tides Foundation, for one, with whom Mailman eventually collaborated, was developing similar ideas on the opposite coast, and there were other small-scale philanthropists beginning to think along similar lines. At the same time, less innovative but far more powerful philanthropic forces were gathering on nearby ground. Some of the nation's largest foundations—the Pew Charitable Trusts, the Ford Foundation, some of the Rockefeller charities, and others—were coming under new leadership that began moving their giving in new directions. Pew, in fact, eventually formed a partnership with Tides to support environmental and other activist programs.

What is interesting about the latter group of social philanthropists is that they found ways to redirect giant pools of old money into causes that would have been anathema to the exceptionally conservative industrialists from whose fortunes they derived. Consider the example of the Pew Charitable Trusts.[1] Measured by the amounts of money it distributes, Pew is the nation's second-largest charitable foundation. The Pew family, for whom the collective trusts are named, and more specifically Joseph N. Pew, Sr., started the Sun Oil Company (Sunoco) in the Pennsylvania oil fields in the 1880s. From early days, Sun Oil and its affiliated companies have explored and developed oil and gas wells, operated pipelines and refineries, developed the first petroleum-based asphalt for paving, built oil tankers, and operated a deep-water Gulf Coast shipping facility as well as all the other functions associated with a vertically integrated petroleum company. When the elder Pew died in 1912, the company remained under family control and continued to grow. The Pew Memorial Foundation, predecessor to the current series of interrelated trusts, was established in 1948 by the four children of Joseph N. Pew, Sr., in memory of their parents, and they funded it with 880,000 shares of Sunoco stock.

The Pew Memorial Foundation was typical of many such institutions, devoted to charitable causes such as building hospitals and endowing universities. The founding donors had interests in four general areas: science, charity, religion, and education, and until their generation passed from the scene, all grants reflected this traditional philanthropic agenda. In addition, the family, which had managed to remain independent of the Standard Oil Trust that dominated the petroleum industry in the early years, was devoted to the notion of free trade and free competition. Joseph N. Pew, Jr., in particular, became a major opponent of President Franklin D. Roosevelt and a bulwark of conservative politics in the Republican Party. Reflecting this perspective, the foundation was an important source of support for conservative policy think tanks such as the Hoover Institution, the American Enterprise Institute, and the Center for Strategic and International Studies. In other words, Pew was one of the very foundations that Dye and others identified as facilitating rule by the power elite of the era.[2]

In 1979, after the death of the last of the founding generation of Pews, the foundation's governing Committee on Grants held a special meeting to set the direction for the future. Much of what was decided then and subsequently pertained to management of the foundation and especially to a commitment to enhanced professionalism in all operations. But over time, there came as well a rather fundamental redefinition of the Pew mission. This redefinition has been cast in what best can be described as obfuscatory language and accompanied by efforts at rationalization. But the bottom line is that a foundation that was established by prominent advocates of free trade and limited government is now a leading funder of policy initiatives that generally are opposed by advocates of those same positions today. In the words of one Pew document[3]:

> As the trusts entered the last decade of the twentieth century, the principles and determination that guided the founding Pews and their grantmaking continued. They sought to promote the benefits of a free market system and encourage its adoption throughout the world. They sought to spread religious faith where it appeared lost, and charity where despair ruled. They sought to improve institutions of higher education in order to assure the intelligent democracy that Thomas Jefferson postulated, and to build institutions of medical research and service to heal and succor. *They demonstrated their will to change society by means of the grants they bestowed.*
>
> The new era posed different problems and different challenges from those that confronted the founders. The 1980s brought changes for which no one was prepared. . . . *[H]istory tells us that the founders sought to improve the world they lived in. The stewards of their philanthropy carry on in that tradition.* [emphasis added] (p. 35)

Rough translation: It is not the defined objectives of the founders we need to follow but the fact that they wanted to change the world. So it is okay to use their legacy to support or encourage change, even if what is being changed is the very world—i.e., the Reagan–Bush world of free trade and limited government—the founders sought to create.

In 2001, for example, one of the seven Pew Trusts, the Joseph N. Pew, Jr., Charitable Trust, made the following grants (among others):

- Earthjustice Legal Defense Fund, $571,000
- Environmental Defense Fund, $1.07 million
- Friends of the Earth, $300,000
- National Religious Partnership for the Environment, $320,000
- Sierra Club Foundation, $280,000
- US Public Interest Research Group Education Fund, $3.475 million

Recall that it was the namesake of this fund who became a focal point of opposition to Franklin Roosevelt, and (to quote the foundation's own characterization) whose "participation in the affairs of the Republican party placed him at the center of American political life for nearly three decades."[4] It is a strong rationale indeed that reconciles these grants with the intent of the original donor. And just to be sure the message gets through, the official history of the Pew Charitable Trusts, a 44-page opus, makes no fewer than 27 direct assertions of the fact that the current trustees are acting in a manner consistent with the intent of the founding donors.[5]

In the 1990s, Pew backed up its new-directions rationale with a new, dual approach to programming, one that was much more aligned with the Progressive activism then emerging with the Trusts' support. Quoting from the same document[6]:

> The board [of directors] . . . wanted to focus efforts on a few key issues of importance to the American people and use the panoply of resources at their disposal—talent, intellect, dollars—to tackle those issues. On some issues, the Trusts would serve, through their grantees, as an advocate. On other issues, their investments would support work of a neutral expert or honest broker, disseminating nonpartisan, fact-based, scrupulously unbiased information on major public and social policy concerns. (p. 36)

Let's think about that one for a moment. For starters, the foundation is acknowledging that it is adopting an activist stance and using its grantees as surrogate spokespersons for its social agenda (a characterization that goes beyond the quoted material but is supported by the document from which it is drawn). But at the same time, the contrasting words here give at least the appearance that this advocacy may not be fact-based and reliable. How is one to know which role the Trusts are playing in any given instance? Or more to the point, how many people will recognize that the honest-broker function, to the extent it is used, serves to legitimize and mask the purpose of the advocacy function when that is in play?

This positioning resolves, for the Pew Charitable Trusts, a set of issues that confront many foundations today and does so with a rationale that clearly serves the new philanthropy on which the Progressive resurgence so depends. The debate itself was clearly articulated by Rebecca W. Rimel, President of the Pew Trusts, in a speech she delivered to the American Philosophical Society in Philadelphia in April 2001. In Rimel's words[7]:

> The most recurring controversy concerns donor intent. The terms of any foundation are set by its indentures. And donor intent should be honored, as a matter of law and of good stewardship.
>
> But . . . . [t]he law recognizes that circumstances change over time. It gives what lawyers call "an affirmative duty" to find a way to continue to honor donor intent, and it assumes that honoring donor intent is a dynamic process. The Pew Trusts believe in our stewardship of our donors' intent. It is through our current work that we honor that intent. . . .
>
> A . . . growing area of debate is the role of foundations in advancing or informing public policy. Foundations may lessen the burden on government as a supporter of social services. But should they be able to use their resources to try and educate and inform and affect policy outcomes?
>
> One side of this debate argues that foundations give voice to many and often opposing points of view and that they serve the causes of pluralism in our democracy. The other side points out that foundation officers and boards are not elected and that foundation money is not subject to taxes. Therefore, they are not "neutral" from a policy perspective and should not enjoy an important and potentially pivotal

position in shaping public policy. The outcomes of these debates will determine much of the future of American philanthropy.

More than resolving this debate with respect to its own purposes, Pew has become fully engaged in the Progressive Movement and has programmed into its activities an expectation that grantees (and the Trusts themselves) will engage in effective networking and outreach. Pew prides itself on what it terms "results-oriented philanthropy," by which it means that projects will be supported only if they lead to some measurable and desirable outcome. The foundation offers six criteria by which grant opportunities will be evaluated, including what it terms "leverage." This criterion means that the effectiveness of each project should be enhanced "through increased interest from the public, the media and policymakers, as well as support from additional organizations, including other philanthropies and individuals."[8]

The Pew Charitable Trusts now make approximately a quarter of a *billion* dollars of grants annually. In 2001 alone, Pew made more than $30 million in grants through its Public Policy program as well as tens of millions of dollars in other grants with clear policy-related objectives on the environment, science and technology policy, and other issues. And Pew is but one example of the phenomenon of redefining—or, viewed from another perspective, interpreting in a contemporary context—the founders' original intent. In these cases, then, not only are the new Progressives building an alternative financial structure with which to take on the Right, but they are doing it with resources that were once controlled by the Right itself. Not only a plus for the Progressive Movement, but an actual takeaway from the other side.

THE EVOLUTION OF LEFT-BRAIN THINK TANKS: INSTITUTE FOR POLICY STUDIES AND COMPANY

If the Left was, as we have argued, in the business of emulating the power elite model in a parallel universe, in addition to building financial supports it would need to construct an activist-intellectual infrastructure of ideas and policies designed to advance its agenda. It would need a set of Progressive-Left think tanks where policy research and development could occur and where Progressive thinkers could find succor. And there is, in fact, such an infrastructure, although parts of it were in place long before the central events of our narrative transpired. In one study sponsored by the New World Foundation, for example, researchers delineated what they termed "an impressive infrastructure" providing research and policy analysis in support of the Progressive Movement. They listed literally dozens of national and regional organizations that were engaged in this activity, including many advocacy groups that also performed research, but also a number of organizations that would clearly qualify under our notion of think tanks. Paralleling the role of universities in the Power Elite model, their report also identified approximately 50 university research centers and scholars engaged in this work.[9]

The earliest and best example of this sort of institution is the Institute for Policy Studies (IPS). Founded in 1963 by Richard J. Barnet and Marcus G. Raskin, IPS substantially predates both the Reagan Revolution and the Progressive resurgence, not to mention the emergence of the so-called New Left in the late 1960s. So it is fair to consider IPS as an institution of the Old Left, the class-based, labor-oriented American Left of the post-World War I era. And for all of its four-plus decades of existence, IPS has been viewed by the Right as an important center, perhaps even the epicenter, of Left-think in the United States. Characterized in 1971 in the annual report of the House Committee on Internal Security as "the far-left radical 'think tank' in Washington, DC," IPS has been singled out for criticism by numerous conservative analysts, not least the Heritage Foundation, framer of the Reagan agenda, which issued a series of extensive reports on IPS beginning as early as 1977.[10] These were followed in 1983 by an examination, in the conservative journal *Human Events*, of IPS's links to the media, which ranged from op ed campaigns and training sessions for mainstream journalists to direct support of *In These Times*, which described itself in that era as an "independent socialist newspaper."[11] And in 1987, IPS was the subject of a scathing, book-length attack by S. Steven Powell in his *Covert Cadre: Inside the Institute for Policy Studies*.[12] Set against this tide of criticism, IPS has had as well a corps of defenders and supporters, who have viewed the Institute in far more salutary terms. This support is perhaps best captured in the words of the late I. F. Stone, who dubbed IPS "an Institute for the rest of us."

For our purposes, it does not matter which view one takes. Rather, what is of interest is the common ground on which stand critics and defenders alike—an agreement that IPS has been an influential center of thought, planning, and policy development on the ideological left. It is the premier example on that end of the spectrum of precisely the sort of organization Dye and others saw as playing an essential role in the elitist model of politics—the yang to the Heritage Foundation–CATO Institute–American Enterprise Institute–Brookings Institution (etc.) yin of the political establishment. To say that IPS is the equivalent of such institutions, of course, is not the same as saying that it is their equal, especially in the area of budgets. In 2001, for example, IPS had income of approximately $2.8 million and expenditures of $2.2 million. In comparison, Brookings alone had revenues of some $35 million and spent $30 million, and the Heritage Foundation's endowment of $104 million was about 100 times that of IPS.[13] But functionally IPS very closely resembles its better-healed counterparts to the right. And it does have some deep pockets on which to draw. The Institute has received substantial support over the years from Samuel Rubin, founder of Faberge Perfumes (and after his death, from the Samuel Rubin Foundation and from his daughter, Cora Weiss), and Sears heir Philip Stern (and later the Stern Family Fund), both of which fund many of today's Progressive activist organizations. Indeed, IPS was more than a cause funded by Rubin and his daughter—it was an organization to which they devoted much time and energy as well.

There is no question that IPS has solidly (Old) Left credentials. It rose to prominence when it was targeted for special attention by the Nixon Administration, which is to say, it received similar treatment to that afforded others of Nixon's perceived political enemies. In 1974, IPS actually sued several administration officials in federal court—among them Attorney General John Mitchell, presidential advisor John Ehrlichman, and FBI Director William Webster. The settlement that ended the case five years later is instructive, if only as a reminder of the tenor of the times in which today's ideological struggles were forged. Among other things, the agreement provided that:

1. [The] Director of the Federal Bureau of Investigation, his successors in office, and his agents and employees agree that they will undertake no investigation of [IPS] unless in accordance with statute, executive order, or other lawful authority.
2. The process of investigation . . . includes, but is not necessarily limited to, any or all of the following investigatory techniques:
   a. Electronic surveillance;
   b. Physical surveillance, including photographic surveillance;
   c. Recruitment or placement of informants;
   d. Search or seizure of plaintiffs' real or personal property;
   e. Mail covers as well as other techniques involving searching and examining mail;
   f. Interviews of persons having, or thought to have, knowledge of a subject's activities and associations;
   g. Trash covers.
3. The Federal Bureau of Investigation shall not collect, gather, index, file, maintain, store or disseminate any information regarding the plaintiffs, their associations, speech or activities except in accordance with federal statute, executive order or regulation in connection with the authorized investigative or administrative functions of the Federal Bureau of Investigation.[14]

Holding office at the very height of the Cold War, the heavily ideological Nixon administration saw IPS as a bastion of socialist (at the time not distinguished from Communist) thinking. And, in fact, the expression of socialist and other leftist views were the Institute's very raison d'être. So it came as no surprise in 1975 when IPS recruited as a Fellow Orlando Letelier, who had served as Defense Minister and Ambassador to the United States in the socialist Chilean government of Salvador Allende. Allende had been killed two years earlier in a bloody coup by the forces of General Augusto Pinochet, who was widely believed to have had the support of the CIA. In March 1976, Letelier was named as director of the Transnational Institute, an IPS affiliate organization. In September, he and IPS staffer Ronni Moffitt were assassinated by a car bomb in Sheridan Circle in Washington, DC. The blast was blamed on the Chilean secret police. This event, too, contributed to IPS's cachet on the Left. By the mid-1980s, it's position was well established. In the words of then *Washington Post* journalist Sidney Blumenthal, "The Institute for Policy Studies is the Pluto of think tanks, the one farthest from the Reagan sun."[15]

But it is the Institute's own institution building that has cast its prominence in cement and enabled it to remain influential even as the political landscape underwent a sea change. For IPS is something of a mother ship for left-leaning organizations, many of them active in the attack on the corporation. Examples:

- Foundation for National Progress—This organization is the publisher of the Progressive magazine *Mother Jones*. It began life as the West Coast affiliate of IPS, although it is now independent.[16] (It is perhaps worth noting parenthetically that the law firm in which Greg Colvin, author of the monograph on fiscal sponsorship, is a partner is the legal counsel for this organization.)
- Government Accountability Project—Initially established in the 1970s as an IPS project to aid government whistleblowers, this organization has since come under the umbrella of the Fund for Constitutional Government, an activist support system funded in large measure by Stewart R. Mott.[17] GAP has since expanded its activities to include supporting some corporate whistleblowers. Although independent of IPS, it is worth noting that, as recently as 2000, Mott and other members of the FCG board of directors were joined on that body by IPS Executive Director John Cavanagh.[18]
- *In These Times*—Started in 1977 as an "avowedly socialist weekly newspaper," this publication was taken over by IPS in 1978.[19] Like other entities listed here, it has since become independent of IPS, operating today through the Chicago-based Institute for Public Affairs.
- Transnational Institute (TNI)—TNI is the international arm of IPS, and, unlike the other affiliates listed here, maintains close ties to the Institute in Washington. Formed in 1973, TNI is based in Amsterdam, and provides a forum paralleling that of IPS for research, discussion, publication and policy formulation, and for ties to activists on a variety of issues.

These and other IPS projects are designed to interact with one another in a more or less seamless web, the outlines of which are not necessarily transparent. For example, as long ago as 1980, *Forbes* columnist John Train offered the following account.

Recently in a bookstore in London I encountered a lot of reports put out by Counter Information Services, a British organization specializing in anticorporate propaganda. One of the most elaborate was a 69-page booklet entitled The Ford Motor Company. This publication announced that "The Ford Motor Company wages war on its workers. . . . " It contained pictures of Generalissimo Franco, a gallows, violent strikers, soldiers in combat deployment . . . , a sedan squashed completely flat, and the like. Here are some headings: "Firetrap," "Lies," "Bulldog Henry," "Price of a Life," "Fiery Death," "Thousands Burn," . . . and "Merchants of Death." It bolsters the cause by citing outside authorities: "In September 1977 *Mother Jones*, an American consumer magazine, exposed the horrific example of the irreconcilable conflict between profits and human life." Ford the corporate villain. Greed versus humanity.

Curious . . . I inquired about Counter Information Services. . . . It describes itself as an affiliate of the Transnational Institute. . . . That, in turn, proves to be an affiliate of the Institute for Policy Studies in Washington.

I eventually discovered that IPS had received seed money in a grant from the Ford Foundation, whose money came, of course, from the Ford family.[20]

John Cavanaugh, who has served as Executive Director of IPS since 1998, personifies the networking approach characteristic of IPS. He has served at various times as:

- Founding Fellow and Chair of the Board of Trustees, Transnational Institute,
- Co-founder and advisory board member, Campaign for America's Future,
- Co-founder and Director, International Forum on Globalization,
- Director and Vice President, International Labor Rights Fund,
- Director, Interhemispheric Resource Center,
- Director, Trans National Research and Action Center,
- Director, Fund for Constitutional Government,
- Advisory board member, CorpWatch,
- Co-chair, Civil Society Program of the United Nations Development Program,
- Executive committee member, Alliance for Responsible Trade,
- Executive committee member, Citizens Trade Campaign,
- Director, Chesapeake Climate Action Network, and
- Member of the Citizens Committee for Nader/LaDuke.

In addition to those listed above, IPS is connected through one or another of its projects, activities, or spin-offs to other anti-corporate activists such as NACLA, which invented the methodology of anti-corporate activism in the 1970s, the Interfaith Center on Corporate Responsibility (ICCR), the Council on Economic Priorities (now SAI), and INFACT, the activist group that first formed around the infant formula issue (the campaign to force Nestle to stop promoting infant formula in the Third World) and later moved on to attacking the tobacco companies. Some IPS activities are supported by the Tides Foundation, which, in turn, is supported by the Rubin Foundation, while others are supported by Progressive funders such as the San Francisco

Foundation (which, you will recall, helped to kick-start the surge in fiscal sponsorship arrangements), the Stern Family Fund, the Nathan Cummings Foundation, and, as noted, even the Ford Foundation.

It is interesting to note, by the way, that Train's preceding account appeared in print in November 1980, after the election of Ronald Reagan as President but before his administration actually took office. Indeed, as early as 1978, observers were beginning to note the shift in language away from the rubric of liberalism and toward that of progressivism and the emergence of new activist foundations and groups on the Left.[21] So the mechanisms for rebirth of politics on the Left were being established even before the ultimate demise of liberalism, albeit within the same general era.

In fact, at least as early as 1980, one can see many of the outlines of today's anti-corporate Progressive agenda. Perhaps the clearest example of this is provided by the Corporate Democracy Act, introduced in Congress by Representative Benjamin S. Rosenthal (D-NY) in April 1980.[22] Comprising seven sections, or "Titles," the Corporate Democracy Act presaged a substantial portion of the agenda being advanced today by the AFL-CIO, Institutional Shareholder Services, various social-responsibility advocates and investors, and others in the Progressive community. An example is the emphasis on boards of directors. Title I of the CDA would have required that a majority of all directors be "independent," which is to say, that they had not been employed either by the company itself or by any organization providing it services for a period of at least five years and did not own stock in the company. The Act also would have assigned to directors a series of investigative responsibilities within the company in areas such as employee well-being, consumer protection, environmental protection, community relations, and shareholder rights. And it would have established in every company a Public Policy Committee with a majority of independent directors and responsibility for "those public or political positions taken by the company that may have a significant impact on employees, consumers, suppliers, individual communities and the physical environment." In addition, Title I provided that shareholders could nominate candidates to serve on the board, would be entitled to cumulative voting (which would allow a minority of shareholders to pool their votes and elect one or more directors), and would need to approve by referendum any transaction that increased or decreased assets or shares of stock by 10% or more.[23] In modified form, most of these, as well as other elements of the legislation, have been the subject of shareholder votes at numerous corporations in the last few years.

But most interesting of all, especially in light of our argument here about the discovery and eventual adoption by the Left of the power elite analytical framework, was Title V of the CDA, which directly attacked the structure of interlocking directorates that lay at the heart of that analysis. Under the provisions of this Title, any director or officer serving more than two corporations would have been subject to a civil penalty of up to $10,000 *per day*.[24] Message: Don't go there!

To promote their proposed legislation, advocates organized a group known as Americans Concerned About Corporate Power, and sponsored a "Big Business Day" on April 17, 1980. Modeled after the highly successful Earth Day, which focuses attention on environmental issues when it rolls around each year, the event was designed as a recurring pressure point against corporations. Mark Green, at the time director of Ralph Nader's Public Citizen Congress Watch (and in 2001 the unsuccessful challenger to Michael Bloomberg in the New York City mayoral election), who headed up the effort, summarized the activists' plans for their Day.[25]

In hundreds of communities across the nation there will be teach-ins and debates, alternatives-to-big-business fairs, . . . 'trials' of corrupt companies, nominations for a "Corporate Hall of Shame," symbolic bread lines at banks that red-line communities, and a compilation of models of corporate social responsibility.

Among those serving as directors, sponsors, or members of the advisory board of Big Business Day were Ralph Nader, Gar Alperovitz, Ira Arlook, Julian Bond, Heather Booth, Marc Caplan, Barry Commoner, Jim Hightower, and Stanley Sheinbaum, each of whom also appears on the roster of founders of the aforementioned Campaign for America's Future as well. Others on the board included several labor leaders (including additional CAF founders), Congressman Rosenthal, CEP founder Alice Tepper Marlin, and IPS founder Richard Barnet.[26]

Fastforward to the 1990s—actually 1996. Big Business Day is a thing of the distant past. It simply did not have the "legs" of Earth Day. But the anti-corporate thematic is alive and well—could even be said to have taken on new life—and IPS is still around, as are many of its affiliates, the lines of connection by then blurred or blurring. Organized labor, long distrustful of the political Left, is moving back in that direction under the umbrella of progressivism and the leadership of John Sweeney, and new Progressive activist groups are springing up daily. Time, perhaps, for another try.

That try came on July 17, 1996, when 130 labor leaders, academics, activists, and others announced formation of the Campaign for America's Future (CAF) and its companion think tank, the Institute for America's Future (IAF).[27] The effort was spearheaded by IPS Fellow Robert Borosage, who had represented IPS two decades earlier in its lawsuit against the Nixon Administration and later served as the Institute's Executive Director. Significantly for the narrative here, one of the scholars listed among the organization's founders was Professor G. William Domhoff of the University of California at Santa Cruz—the very scholar whose work had helped to establish an understanding of the workings of the power elite. His inclusion in this group is a clear indicator of the awareness and influence of his research among the very activists who were in the process of implementing an effective counterelite model.

In the years since its founding, CAF/IAF has played a second-tier role in bringing together on an infrequent but regular basis those with an interest in progressive social and political reform. Unlike IPS, it is not heavily institutionalized, but also unlike IPS, it is somewhat insulated from allegations of ideological extremism. This combination has allowed CAF/IAF to act as a sort of clearinghouse for the consideration and dissemination of selected policy alternatives, particularly those that bridge the interests of organized labor, which accounts for many of its founders and advisors, and advocates of other causes. But the real significance of CAF/IAF as an institution is its evident design and service as a networking node where these different interests intersect. Among those present at its creation and/or listed today as advisors are:

- Peter Barnes, founder of Working Assets;
- Heather Booth, founder of the Midwest Academy, a center for training community activists with the ideas of Saul Alinsky, a long-time Democratic activist and Executive Director of US Action;
- Hodding Carter, currently President and CEO of the John S. and James L. Knight Foundation;
- John Cavanagh, Executive Director of IPS;
- Jeff Cohen, Executive Director of the media watchdog group Fairness and Accuracy in Reporting;
- Ken Cook, founder of the Environmental Working Group;
- Barbara Ehrenreich, widely quoted pro-labor writer;
- Jeff Faux, Executive Director of the Economic Policy Institute, a labor-based Washington think tank;
- Richard Flacks, a prominent antiwar activist of the Vietnam era and now a sociologist on the faculty of University of California Santa Barbara;
- Todd Gitlin, a former president of the Students for a Democratic Society (SDS) who played an important role in developing the anti-corporate campaign, now a sociologist at Columbia University;
- Tom Hayden, another SDS president, who drafted the pivotal *Port Huron Statement* and now serves as a state senator in California;
- Jim Hightower, former Agriculture Commissioner of Texas and now a Progressive media personality;
- Patricia Ireland, National Organization for Women;
- Jesse L. Jackson, civil rights activist;
- Robert Kuttner, co-founder and editor of *The American Prospect* (see below);
- Thea Lee, international economist at the AFL-CIO and a rising star of the labor movement;
- Steve Max, former SDS member, more recently of the Midwest Academy;
- Harold Meyerson, currently political editor of the alternative newspaper, *LA Weekly*;
- Ron Pollock, Executive Director of the Families USA Foundation;
- Robert Reich, Secretary of Labor in the Clinton administration, and a co-founder of *The American Prospect*;
- Mark Ritchie, President of the Institute for Agriculture and Trade Policy;

- Jack Sheinkman, President of Americans for Democratic Action (and formerly president of the Amalgamated Clothing and Textile Workers Union);
- John Sweeney, President of the AFL-CIO;
- Richard Trumka, Secretary-Treasurer of the AFL-CIO;
- Katherine and Philippe Villers, co-founders of the Families USA Foundation;
- The presidents of the following unions: Communications Workers of America; United Steelworkers of America; American Postal Workers Union; International Association of Machinists; National Education Association; United Food and Commercial Workers; International Union of Electronic Workers (since merged into the Communications Workers); American Federation of State, County and Municipal Employees; United Mine Workers of America; Service Employees International Union; and the United Auto Workers; and
- Scholars from leading universities such as Georgetown, University of California, Berkeley, Columbia, Northwestern, University of Virginia, New York University, Brandeis, University of Texas, MIT, and Harvard.

In effect, CAF represented the coming together of a veritable Who's Who of labor leaders, early anti-corporate activists, left-leaning academics and media personalities, and a range of activist individuals and groups. To this day, it stands out as a wide-ranging coalition of some of the most influential voices of Progressivism, a number of whom have played roles in our narrative to this point or will shortly do so. Indeed, in addition to making the point about the development and increasing influence of policy think tanks on the Left, CAF illustrates quite nicely the integration of such activities with university-based academic research that is yet another replicated component of the power elite structure laid out by Mills, Domhoff, and Dye.

A rather different kind of think tank is United for a Fair Economy (UFE). Established in 1994 by a group of community organizers, UFE sees its mission as one of "movement support," specifically educating adults on economic issues of concern to the Progressive Left through the mechanism of "popular education," which it defines as follows[28]:

> Popular education is a non-traditional method of education. Primarily aimed toward adults, it is more democratic and cooperative than traditional classroom-type education methods, which are based on lectures and writings by experts. Popular education is also openly political, and popular educators see the learners as potentially powerful people who can change the social conditions that surround them. With popular education, ordinary people define their own problems and apply the lessons of past political successes and failures to their own situation.
>
> The popular education process begins by thinking and talking with a group of others about the events that have occurred in their own lives. With the guidance of a popular educator, participants identify ways to solve the problems confronting them.

Popular education is a concept developed by the Highlander Center, a residential educational center in the Tennessee mountains established in 1932. The Highlander Center has trained leaders of the labor movement of the 1930s, the civil rights movement of the 1950s, and the Appalachian people's rights movement of the 1970s as well as other grassroots and community organizers in its philosophy of participatory and consensual decision making.[29] Susan Williams of the Highlander Center sits on the UFE board of directors.

Although it does not appear to have direct ties to IPS, UFE is a frequent partner with the Institute in various projects and activities. For example, UFE and IPS jointly publish every April a report on executive compensation and its effects under the title *Executive Excess*, and in 2001 jointly researched and produced a special report on the privatization of traditionally public functions such as health care, welfare services, water, and public housing.[30] As that report summarized the relationship between the two organizations, "For UFE and IPS, this is another in a long history of collaborative efforts. We are committed to education and mobilization to strengthen and diversify the U.S. movement against corporate-led globalization."[31] Further reflecting that collaboration, both are partners in the Ecumenical Program on Central America and the Caribbean (EPICA), a faith-based initiative for community organizing and "critical" social analysis that includes other activist groups such as Global Exchange, Friends of the Earth, Public Citizen, a number of religious groups, and the Highlander Center. Both are affiliated with or support the Grassroots Policy Project, a Highlander-type educational initiative for community organizers founded in 1993 by former IPS Director (and later Preamble Center director) Richard Healey.[32] Both are members of the Fair Taxes for All Coalition, a group established to oppose Republican tax cuts, and also of the coalition calling for a boycott of World Bank Bonds. Finally, both are funded by the Samuel Rubin Foundation.

Some of UFE's most interesting activity occurs through a subsidiary organization known as Responsible Wealth (RW), which helps to close a loop in the present analysis. Responsible Wealth was formed in December 1997 to encourage wealthy individuals to contribute to Progressive causes—specifically those that support the group's agenda for redistribution of wealth through changes in tax policy, a living-wage movement, and corporate social responsibility—to show them how to do that, and generally to support their giving through educational and informational efforts. Within six months, the group already had 300 members. In effect, Responsible Wealth is doing very much today what Joshua Mailman and the Doughnuts were doing twenty-plus years ago—organizing and pooling individual wealth as a force for social change. But RW is even more instrumental, as befits an organization coming of age nearly a generation later. Like the social responsibility investment funds and like Institutional Shareholder Services, RW has an agenda of corporate policy actions that it advances through shareholder resolutions, in this case resolutions introduced by individual RW members who hold corporate shares in their own names. In 2003, for example, the RW agenda included (among others) the following resolutions:

- AT&T—pension equity for all employees,
- Bristol-Myers Squib—executive compensation review,
- Citigroup—link CEO pay to reducing predatory lending,
- Coca-Cola—executive compensation review,
- Disney—executive compensation review,
- ExxonMobil—report on corporate taxes,
- Fidelity Magellan Fund—disclosure of proxy votes,
- General Electric—executive compensation review, and
- Pepsico—report on corporate taxes.[33]

Clearly, these initiatives are generally similar to those advanced by other Progressive investment advisors and interests and by organized labor. So whether by design or by coincidence, RW-sponsored initiatives represent yet another drawing together of the web of social-change advocacy.

GETTING THE WORD OUT

We have already mentioned some of the media connections being developed by Progressive activists, or at least by IPS. Viewed more broadly, we can see pro-movement media outlets like *Mother Jones* or *In These Times* as one component of a two-part strategy for getting the word out and shaping media perspectives. The elements of this strategy include creating or redirecting Progressive media outlets and countering perceived anti-Progressive media bias. Let us look briefly at each of these in turn.

There are today a large number of pro-movement media, although none has widespread circulation or especially high visibility. The list includes print magazines with long histories, among them *The Nation*, *UTNE Reader* (with partial funding, you will recall, from Joshua Mailman), and even *The Progressive*, which traces back to the original Progressive Movement of a century ago. It includes alternative newspapers like *LA Weekly* and the flagship paper of its parent company, *Village Voice*. It includes online distribution hubs like the Independent Media Center (www.indymedia.org), an outgrowth of the 1999 anti-globalization demonstrations in Seattle that has since expanded to include a wide range of social change-related content, and AlterNet (www.alternet.org), a project of the Independent Media Institute (IMI), launched in 1998, which searches out and distributes content primarily from relatively more "mainstream" or established alternative and Progressive publications like those listed previously. Don Hazen, the executive director of IMI, is a former publisher of *Mother Jones*; San Francisco-based IMI receives support from the Tides Foundation among other sources and in 2002 received a grant of $200,000 from the Nathan Cummings Foundation.

Online, one of the more interesting sites is Corporate Watch (www. corpwatch.org), founded by Joshua Karliner in 1996 as the Transnational Resource and Action Center and renamed CorpWatch in 2001. CorpWatch, which was active for a period in the campaign against Nike but today is focused more broadly on anti-corporate action (e.g., opposing the growing partnership between corporations and the United Nations), is a project of the Tides Center with a staff of seven. Among the members of CorpWatch's Advisory Board are two familiar names, John Cavanagh and Joshua Mailman. Among its affiliates is the Multinationals Resource Center (MRC), which publishes yet another pro-movement magazine, *Multinational Monitor*. MRC is a component of Essential Information, an entity founded by Ralph Nader in 1982 to advance his various causes, many of which are now reflected in the Progressive Movement.[34]

In print, perhaps the most significant Progressive publication is *The American Prospect* (TAP), which was established in 1990 by Paul Starr, Robert Kuttner, and Robert Reich. Available online as well as in print, TAP maintains a stable of contributing writers, including some, like James Fallows and Lester Thurow, whose names would be familiar to many. Reich, of course, is a former Secretary of Labor, and Kuttner is a long-time author, analyst, and advocate of Progressive causes. Both Reich and Kuttner were co-founders of the Campaign for America, and both are quite active in a variety of movement organizations. Both Kuttner and Reich, for example, serve on the boards of the Economic Policy Institute and the Institute for Taxation and Economic Policy (a policy think tank funded by the Arca Foundation, the Ben and Jerry Foundation, the Joyce Foundation, the Open Society Institute, the Public Welfare Foundation, the Schumann Foundation, the Stern Family Fund, the Tides Foundation, and Working Assets, among other Progressive philanthropies). Kuttner is a member of the board of directors of the Florence Fund, which is effectively a subsidiary of the Schumann Foundation, whose president is media personality Bill Moyers. The Schumann Foundation has been the principal source of support in recent years for *The American Prospect*, although there has been a competition for that support from a Florence Fund project, the online magazine *TomPaine.com*, whose editor-in-chief, Moyers' son John, also sits on the Florence Fund board.[35]

TAP has established an online subsidiary, originally called the Electronic Policy Network and later renamed the Moving Ideas Network, to serve as a clearinghouse for policy ideas of interest to the Progressive Left. This network has more than 100 members, including a significant number of Progressive think tanks—Campaign for America's Future, Center for Economic and Policy Research, Center on Budget and Policy Priorities, Economic Policy Institute, Interhemispheric Resource Center—and Progressive funders such as the Annie E. Casey Foundation, the Century Foundation, and the Open Society Institute.[36] The Moving Ideas Network, then, is a mechanism for the exchange of ideas among think tanks and funding agencies on the Progressive Left— precisely the sort of interaction that was central to the power-elite model.

The second component of the Progressive Left's media strategy focuses on ensuring fairness in mainstream media treatment of the Progressive agenda and its advocates. The model here, too, comes directly from the Right. When the conservatives began their campaign to gain control of the U.S. political system—the campaign that ultimately produced the Reagan Revolution—one of their earliest steps was establishment of "watchdog" organizations whose function was to identify and combat what they perceived as a left-leaning bias in the media. The issue had proven obsessive for the Nixon administration, which went so far as to compile lists of its political enemies that included prominent journalists such as Daniel Shorr, and even played a minor role in the Watergate Scandal in that the so-called "plumbers" who burgled the Democratic offices in that building were first brought together to ferret out troubling leaks of information to the media. Then, in 1972, journalist Edith Efron published a book, *The News Twisters*, that purported to prove the existence of such bias.[37] In reality, however, the analysis in the Efron book was fatally flawed, which led many scholars and other readers to reject its findings. This, in turn, led to establishment by Robert and Linda Lichter, two conservative media scholars, in Washington in 1985 of the Center for Media and Public Affairs. The Center, which conducts extensive content analyses of media coverage and issues a variety of reports and newsletters, has since evolved into a respected source of media analysis.

But data are one thing, advocacy another. So in 1972, Reed Irvine and other conservatives founded Accuracy in Media (AIM), a group whose function was to point out to the media their ideological biases as perceived from the Right. AIM is still active, issuing newsletters, broadsides, and reports with regularity. And AIM is the model for a countervailing Progressive-Left organization devoted to media monitoring and criticism, Fairness and Accuracy in Reporting (FAIR), established by Jeff Cohen in 1986. FAIR sees its mission in its name, but defines that mission from the perspective of the movement that gave it life.[38]

> We work to invigorate the First Amendment by advocating for greater diversity in the press and by scrutinizing media practices that marginalize public interest, minority and dissenting viewpoints. As an anti-censorship organization, we expose neglected news stories and defend working journalists when they are muzzled. As a progressive group, FAIR believes that structural reform is ultimately needed to break up the dominant media conglomerates, establish independent public broadcasting and promote strong non-profit sources of information.

The group's approach is perhaps best, or at least most succinctly, summed up by the T-shirts it was selling on its web site in 2003, which bore the legend "Don't Trust the Corporate Media."[39]

While FAIR has produced a great volume of reports, not to mention radio programs, newsletters, and the like, one of its most interesting products was an introspective study on pro-movement media it completed in 1995. That study described the leading media of the Right and the role of conservative foundations in supporting them and then offered comparisons with the leading media of the Progressive Left and their level of philanthropic support. The comparisons were not favorable. For example, the study's author, Beth Schulman, identified a total of $2.75 million in grants to magazines of the Right during the period 1990–93, most of that for general support of the publications. This support came from the same conservative foundations identified in chapter 1 as major funders of the Right—the Harry and Lynde Bradley Foundation, John M. Olin Foundation, Sarah Scaife Foundation, Smith Richardson Foundation, and others. In contrast, during this same period, left-leaning media, including *The Nation*, *The Progressive*, *In These Times*, and *Mother Jones*, received a total of $269,000, most of which was targeted at specific projects as opposed to general support. Among the donors were the Arca Foundation, the Schumann Foundation, and the Stern Family Fund.[40] A grant made by the Schumann Foundation to support publication of *The American Prospect* in May 1999, several years after the FAIR report was published—$5.5 million initially and eventually $8.5 million before the TAP tap was closed—stands as the only major exception to this observation.[41] But the real point of the study in the present context, and of the establishment and mission of FAIR itself, is that here we find direct evidence of the engineering of the Progressive Left resurgence using the analysis, strategies, and tactics of the Right-wing revolution that occasioned it.

LIFE IN A PARALLEL UNIVERSE

Indeed, that is but one example of the larger lesson of this chapter—that the Left has been actively rebuilding itself by using the Right's Stuff. Over the last quarter century or so, the Progressive Movement has constructed (or remodeled, as in the case of the Pew Charitable Trusts) a network of foundations to raise money, which has been used in turn to support a growing network of think tanks that develop and generate policy ideas and proposals that are then supported and advanced through a network of pro-movement media, both print and electronic. This networking may not yet be fully developed, but it is quite evidently under way.

Yet there are differences between the networking on the Left and on the Right or, more to the point, in the center of the spectrum where the real power resides. This is true in obvious ways. For example, where the Right and the center accept corporate ownership and influence as legitimate aspects of politics and the economy, and thus have access to corporate and pro-corporate resources, the Left is, by choice, design, and rhetoric, destined to be underfunded in all these enterprises—at least unless and until its advocates gain control of sufficient proxies to turn corporate behavior in the desired direction. But it is also true in less obvious ways. In the center of the spectrum, the institutions of pluralism—electoral politics, public opinion, lobbying, and the like—come into play, if not (per the power elite model) to determine outcomes, at the very least to legitimize and, within limits, help shape them. But at this point in the history of the Progressive Left, the votes are not there, either at the ballot box or, for most issues, on Capitol Hill, and the public is not persuaded of the merits of Progressive ideology (any more than they have been of the merits of conservative ideology per se). As a result, outreach from the Left takes rather different forms than that from the Right. With the exception of environmentalists, who sometimes have proven effective lobbyists, the legislative process remains, at least for the moment, out of reach, and the electoral process out of sight.[42] Through the selection of the Progressive label and the effective packaging of policies and rhetoric, the public is being brought within reach, but absent the corporate scandals of recent years it is not clear how much of this progress would have occurred.

All of this means that the game of advancing and legitimizing the Progressive agenda falls not to the traditional avenues of political action that have so captivated the pluralists but to an alternative mechanism for outreach—the advocacy organization. In various forms—membership organizations, virtual online organizations, issue-specific coalitions, and the like—advocacy groups form the core, not of the Progressive Left itself, but of its mobilization and education efforts and its promotion of alternative values, and of changes to politics, the economy, and society at large. These groups have proliferated over the last twenty-plus years, some grounded in labor, some in community organizing, some in environmental or other policy communities, and some in ideologies of various stripes. Although we cannot hope to do them all justice, in the next chapter we examine a few examples of such groups and begin to explore the nature, extent, and significance of the interconnections among them.

ENDNOTES

1. Except where otherwise indicated, information about the Pew Charitable Trusts is based on that found online at www.pewtrusts.com, April 28, 2003.
2. Joel R. Gardner, *Sustaining the Legacy: A History of the Pew Charitable Trusts* (Philadelphia: Pew Charitable Trusts, 2001), pp. 3–24, passim. Found online at www.pewtrusts .com, April 28, 2003.
3. Ibid., p. 35.
4. Ibid., p. 13.
5. Gardner, op. cit., passim.
6. Ibid., p. 36.
7. The text of the speech was found on the Pew Charitable Trusts web site, April 28, 2003, at http://www.pewtrusts.com/pubs/pubs_item.cfm?image=img5&content_item_id=963&content_type_id=19&page=p3.
8. Gardner, op. cit., p. 41.
9. Allison Barlow, David Dyssegaard Kallick and Rhonda Shary, "Who Does Research and Policy Analysis to Support Progressive Organizing?" found online June 25, 1999, at www.preamble.org/resact/report.html.
10. Among them: "Institute for Policy Studies," May 1977; "Campaign for Economic Democracy: Part I, The New Left in Politics," September 1980; and "Campaign for Economic Democracy:

Part II, The Institute for Policy Studies Network," April 1981. All published in Washington, DC, by the Heritage Foundation.

11. Cliff Kincaid, "The IPS and the Media: Unholy Alliance," *Human Events* (April 9, 1983), pp. 311–318.

12. Published in Ottawa, IL, by Green Hill Publishers, 1987.

13. Data for each organization are based on their respective IRS Forms 990 for 2001.

14. *Institute for Policy Studies et al. v. John N. Mitchell et al.*, Stipulated Settlement of Issues and Dismissal, Civil Action No. 74–316, United States District Court for the District of Columbia, October 3, 1979.

15. Sidney Blumenthal, "The Left Stuff: IPS and the Long Road Back," *The Washington Post*, July 30, 1986, p. D1.

16. Neal R. Peirce and Jerry Hagstrom, "Watch Out, New Right, Here Come the 'Young Progressives,'" *National Journal*, 10:52 (December 30, 1978), pp. 2071ff.

17. Greg Mitchell, "Blowing the Whistle: For people who whistle while they work, the government is playing a new tune," *The Washington Post Magazine*, August 12, 1979, p. 12.

18. As listed in Fund for Constitutional Government, IRS Form 990 for 2000.

19. Peirce and Hagstrom, op. cit.

20. John Train, "The Source," *Forbes*, November 24, 1980, p. 50.

21. See, for example, Peirce and Hagstrom, op. cit.

22. "Rosenthal: Corporate Democracy Bill Needed to Check Big Business," *American Banker* (April 21, 1980), p. 2.

23. Eugene McAllister and William T. Poole, "The Corporate Democracy Act and Big Business Day: Rhetoric vs. Reality," *Heritage Foundation Reports* 113 (March 11, 1980).

24. Ibid.

25. Ibid.

26. Ibid.

27. From the organizational history found online at www.ourfuture.org/about/activities.asp, August 27, 1998.

28. Definition found online at http://www.faireconomy.org/econ/index.html, May 13, 2003.

29. Information about this center was found at http://www.hrec.org/, May 13, 2003.

30. Mike Prokosch and Karen Dolan, *Our Communities Are Not For Sale*. Washington, DC: Institute for Policy Studies and United for a Fair Economy, 2001.

31. Ibid., p. 2.

32. See http://www.grassrootspolicy.org/staff.htm, found online May 13, 2003.

33. Listing found at http://www.responsiblewealth.org/shareholder/index.html, January 24, 2003. The list was accompanied by explanations of each position.

34. Information about this entity was found online at www.corpwatch.org, May 13, 2003.

35. For some of the details of this complex relationship, see Donna L. Goodison, "Just what are the prospects for *The American Prospect?*," *Boston Business Journal*, June 14, 2002; Christopher Caldwell, "TAPs for a magazine," *Weekly Standard*, October 17, 2002; and Liz Cox, "Kuttner's Turbulence," *Columbia Journalism Review*, January/February 2003.

36. Membership list found at http://movingideas.org/members/members_all.html, May 13, 2003.

37. Edith Efron, *The News Twisters* (New York: Nash Publishing, 1971).

38. The description was found on the groups website at http://www.fair.org/whats-fair.html, May 13, 2003.

39. Found at http://www.merchantamerica.com/fair/index.php?ba=view_category&category=535, May 13, 2003.

40. Beth Schulman, "Foundations for a movement: how the right wing subsidizes its press," *Extra!*, March/April 1995, published by Fairness and Accuracy in Media, and found online, October 17, 2002, at www.fair.org/extra/9503/right-press-subsidy.html.

41. Goodison, op. cit.

42. In the latter regard, it is worth noting an attempt by a coalition of groups including both Global Exchange and the Institute for Policy Studies, to address this voting vacuum in the wake of the Florida presidential election scandal of 2000. Democracy Summer 2001 was a program designed to educate 200 young people in the workings of the electoral system and in reforms that would make it, in the view of the sponsors, more participatory in character. Description found online at www.ips-dc.org/demsum/about.htm, May 24, 2001.

8

Us!

As a social system we seek the establishment of a democracy of individual participation, governed by two central aims: that the individual share in those social decisions determining the quality and direction of his life; that society be organized to encourage independence in men and provide the media for their common participation.

In a participatory democracy, the political life would be based on several root principles:

- that decision-making of basic social consequence be carried on by public groupings. . . .
- that politics has the function of bringing people out of isolation and into community. . . .

The economic sphere would have as its basis the principles:

- that work should involve incentives worthier than money or survival. . . .
- that the economic experience is so personally decisive that the individual must share in its full determination;
- that the economy itself is of such social importance that its major resources and means of production should be open to democratic participation and subject to democratic social regulation.

—The Port Huron Statement, Students for a Democratic Society, 1962

Ever since Tom Hayden wrote those words more than 40 years ago, "participatory democracy" has been a core value of the American Left.[1] Like the term progressivism itself, participatory democracy is a delightfully ambiguous phrase, one that can be interpreted more or less uniquely by any number of individuals, yet one that, at the same time, binds them together with a sense of moral purpose, common cause, and deep historical roots.[2] Its commitment to participatory democracy helps to define the very essence of the Progressive Left.

But participatory democracy, as understood by its proponents, is not the same as electoral democracy. The key to electoral democracy is the voice—and especially the vote—of the individual. The key to participatory democracy is the voice—and the collective, shared action—of the community. Where traditional, small-d democrats see the institutions of pluralism aggregating and articulating individual preferences, participatory democrats see communities forging and acting on consensus. It is a fundamental difference in understanding of the nature and meaning of democracy, and it produces two very different models of "democratic" action. Electoral democrats express and advance their views through candidacies, platforms, election campaigns, political action committees, fund-raising, and the like. Participatory democrats choose a different means of expression—direct action through means such as mass demonstrations, boycotts, and anti-corporate campaigns. Electoral democrats focus a great deal of energy on the language of means—representation, access. Participatory democrats focus more on ends—justice, accountability, social responsibility. In part, of course, these differences arise from the fact that the electoral democrats are living in the house, and the participatory democrats have their noses pressed to the windows. But there is, in fact, a fundamental difference in worldview between the two groups, one that, if it endures in the event of a Progressive capture of the instruments of power, is likely to produce a different kind of democratic political system.

For a movement built on this collectivist notion of democracy, the critical point of interface between leaders and followers, between the movement and the polity, is not the voting booth. Rather, it is the advocacy organization. Prosocial advocacy, socially organized, is the democratic face of the Progressive Left, just as political parties and interest groups are the democratic face of the pluralist and elitist Center and Right. And the language around which such advocacy is constructed is powerful indeed. One need look no further than the names of Progressive advocacy groups to see the point: Jobs with *Justice*, Environmental *Defense*, Human *Rights* Watch, *Fairness* and Accuracy in Reporting. If cash flow is the beating heart of the Progressive Movement, advocacy is its soul.

Although there are many lenses one might use to examine Progressive advocacy—ideological, programmatic, and so forth—for our purposes it seems most sensible to focus on two aspects of the phenomenon, the form this activity commonly takes, and the types of organizations that engage in it.

PROGRESSIVE ADVOCACY

In general, as noted, the Progressive Left has not taken form as an electoral movement. As with any rule, there are exceptions. In the 2004 presidential cycle, for example, some number of former liberals—the most moderate voices in the new movement—coalesced within the Democratic Party around Moveon.org, a web-based political action committee that showed early strength in generating support for the candidacy of former Vermont Governor Howard Dean.[3] In addition, a coalition of labor unions (most notably the Service Employees International Union, the same union represented on the board of the Tides Foundation), environmental and women's organizations, and several former members of the Clinton administration formed a group in 2003 to support the Democratic challenge to President Bush. International financier George Soros (Open Society Institute) pledged $10 million to the effort, half a dozen other Progressive philanthropists added $12 million, and organized labor pledged $8 million.[4] And not surprisingly, organized labor, the most traditional of the Progressive Movement's components, has continued to raise and distribute millions of dollars to congressional and presidential candidates, almost all of them Democrats. Even old-line activists like Robert Borosage of the Campaign for America's Future, which, of course, has very strong ties to organized labor, still harbor an interest in ballot-based power.[5] And in a 2003 book, G. William Domhoff, whose ideas on the power elite have helped shape the Progrossive Movement itself, advocated working within the Democratic Party.[6] But for the most part, the assumption on the Left appears to be either that progressivism is a minority movement that cannot win in the electoral arena or that the electoral system is structured in ways that disadvantage the demographic communities that make up and are served by the Progressive Left and is, therefore, inherently undemocratic. A third, and perhaps less cynical, view is that the Left simply has not yet gotten around to focusing on electoral politics. Here, too, there are advocates for reverse engineering the success of the Right. Writing in *The Nation*, a Progressive-Left publication, for example, Katrina Vanden Heuvel has offered this[7]:

> How, then, might progressives proceed? Let us begin by taking a leaf from the conservative playbook. The right has built an imposing array of institutions to develop ideas and educate conservatives on how to argue their case. In contrast, progressives . . . have done little to enlist and educate current and future leaders to an agenda and a message that will consolidate a progressive majority. Progressives remain stronger on the ground than they are in the public debate.

These may be different aspects of the same argument, or they may be three fundamentally different arguments. But either way, all point toward a more public form of democratic expression than the isolation of the voting booth.

This expression can take a number of forms—demonstrations, boycotts, mass e-mailings, and the like. But it is most effective, and for that reason more commonplace, when many of these tactics are combined in the form of campaigns like those described in chapter 6. These campaigns tend to be built around two rhetorical elements—a cause to be for and an anti-social enemy symbolic of that cause to be against. The cause, or topical object of the campaign, typically is wrapped in a flag of social justice and human rights, while the enemy is almost invariably an industry or a specific company. Examples abound and are growing in number: harvesting old-growth timber (Home Depot, Kimberly Clark, Mitsubishi), displacement of indigenous populations (Occidental Petroleum, Freeport McMoRan, and other companies in the extraction industries), harming breeding grounds for whales (Mitsubishi and the Government of Mexico), human rights in Burma/Myanmar (Texaco, Unocal, PepsiCo, and others with business interests in the country) and Nigeria (Shell, Mobil, and other oil companies), distribution of infant formula in the Third World (Nestle), tobacco sales (Philip Morris), reduction of polyvinyl chloride (PVC) use (Mattel, Baxter International), opposition to offshore oil development in Alaska (BP Amoco), and the opposition to economic globalization, which pits a broad coalition of Progressive-Left advocacy groups against the sum of all their fears, the community of multinational corporations. To understand the dynamics of these efforts, let us take a closer look at two campaigns that are still under way at this writing.

Our first example is Campaign Exxon/Mobil, an effort to force the giant oil company to establish policies and take actions to reduce global warming. According to this group, the company's offenses include[8]:

1. Continuing to publish ads and repeat rhetorical claims that in global warming science, "nothing is clear," despite overwhelming scientific evidence and consensus that the world is already warming due to human influence.
2. Funding multi-million-dollar propaganda campaigns orchestrated by front groups like the Global Climate Coalition. Using tactics perfected by the tobacco companies, these campaigns confuse the public and policymakers about global warming and sap political will to address it.
3. ExxonMobil is aggressively pushing for more global oil consumption, despite the risks. The company targets developing countries, promising that the way to improve quality of life is to burn more and more oil. ExxonMobil doesn't offer sustainable energy solutions.
4. ExxonMobil is working in the U.S. and abroad to kill the Kyoto Protocol to reduce greenhouse gas emissions, an historic agreement that unifies humanity to solve a common problem. The company lobbied the U.S. Senate to stop the treaty cold. The company also urges developing nations to resist attempts to reduce their use of fossil fuels, while at the same time, it argues that industrialized nations should reject any agreement that doesn't require developing nations to cut their emissions.

Interestingly in light of our analysis here, Campaign ExxonMobil describes itself as a shareholders' campaign, and much of the argument in its materials is framed in terms of shareholder value. In its own words, the campaign was "founded by faith and environmental groups, and works with institutional investors, corporate governance activists and financial analysts to highlight the financial risks of ExxonMobil's current position."[9] In 2001, ISS founder Robert

A. G. Monks climbed on this bandwagon when he introduced a shareholder resolution calling on the ExxonMobil board to separate the positions of chairman and CEO and, in the process, to sanction and restrict the decision making of CEO Lee Raymond.[10] Then, Monks, CERES, and Campaign ExxonMobil jointly sponsored a study by London-based Claros Consulting that criticized the company's environmental policies and their impact on global warming. The report was released three weeks before the 2002 annual meeting of Exxon-Mobil shareholders, and its release occasioned endorsements by both ISS and CalPERS of the Monks proposal.[11] The resolution failed in 2002, and a similar effort was defeated again at the company's 2003 annual meeting, but it remains a goal of the campaign.[12]

On the board of Campaign ExxonMobil are representatives of the Social Investment Forum, the Natural Resources Defense Council, and CERES (Coalition of Environmentally Responsible Economies, see later) as well as the Baptist and Presbyterian Churches and the Catholic Capuchin Order. But the coalition behind Campaign Exxon/Mobil is far broader and in many ways more interesting. For run out of the same office in Austin, Texas, is another entity, Empowering Democracy, that includes familiar names such as the AFL-CIO, Co-op America, Global Exchange, INFACT, Interfaith Center for Corporate Responsibility, Rainforest Action Network, CorpWatch, Friends of the Earth, and USPIRG as well as CERES and others. Included here as well is the firm Corporate Campaign, Inc., the home of Ray Rogers, who, in the 1970s, helped to invent the concept of the corporate, or anti-corporate, campaign.

Empowering Democracy has been established as an educational base for training anti-corporate campaigners. This is accomplished through annual conferences, which have been held to date in Dallas and New York City. The group defines its mission as follows[13]:

Problem: Corporate power and influence are increasing to the point of subverting democracy. Although the newly spreading, corporate pressure campaign movement is proving it can be effective, we have no infrastructure or process to help the movement mature, or to train others in effective corporate campaign strategies and tactics. We're not taking advantage of available skills and intelligence by joint strategizing and collective power by working together.

Solution: Establish an Annual Conference for Corporate Campaigners. We will share skills and teach others the basic strategies and tactics which organizations and activists can use in corporate accountability campaigns, and lay a foundation for an infrastructure for the corporate campaign movement, while each year increasing presence and influence at a single company's annual meeting.

Targets listed by Empowering Democracy include the likes of Dow, Dupont, Citigroup, and ChevronTexaco as well as ExxonMobil.

Topics at the 2002 conference, held in New York, included items such as power-structure analysis, ways to influence corporate CEOs and Directors,

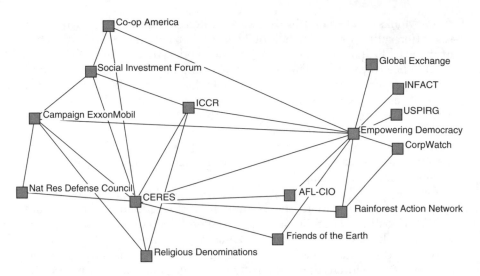

FIG. 8.1. Selected coalition members, Campaign ExxonMobil, and Empowering Democracy.

Internet activism, coalition-building, international coordination, shareholders and governance, researching corporate vulnerabilities, working through local governments to pressure companies, boycotts, legal strategies, organizing days of action, and using the media.[14] Collectively, of course, these areas constitute a substantial portion of the skill set of the anti-corporate campaign.

As shown in Fig. 8.1, which illustrates portions of the membership structures of these two coalitions, there are a number of interesting relationships represented in these conjoined undertakings. For example, Co-op America, a member of Empowering Democracy, is the parent organization of the Social Investment Forum, which co-founded Campaign ExxonMobil. Empowering Democracy is a far broader coalition, with a much more aggressively anti-corporate agenda, but CERES (which as we will see later was created by the Social Investment Forum and which has a number of corporate partners) is a member of both. Denominational membership in Campaign ExxonMobil is direct, whereas in Empowering Democracy it is maintained through CERES and the Interfaith Center for Corporate Responsibility as well as through Campaign ExxonMobil's own membership in Empowering Democracy. And so forth. But when we step out one degree of separation, as indicated in Fig. 8.2, the connections become more interesting still.

This figure adds a single actor to those represented in Fig. 8.1—the Tides Foundation. The connections here are not memberships, as in Fig. 8.1, but recent funding of activist groups by Tides as represented earlier in Table 3.1. Among the members of these two coalitions, Tides has provided support to Co-op America, ICCR, Natural Resources Defense Council, Friends of the Earth, Rainforest Action Network, CorpWatch, Global Exchange, INFACT,

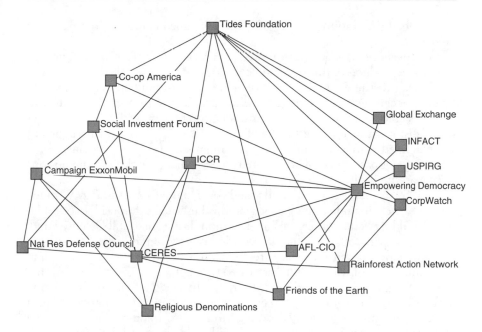

FIG. 8.2.   Tides Foundation connections to coalition members.

and USPIRG. With the exception of CorpWatch, a Tides Center project on whose board Tides is represented, the Foundation is not the sole, nor even the principal, supporter of the group in question. But the connections between so many diverse activist organizations and Tides is not coincidental. In fact, Campaign ExxonMobil and Empowering Democracy are emblematic of the style of activism that Tides actively encourages. Were we to add Working Assets to the figure, we would see a similar, albeit less pronounced, pattern of support.

Our second example is provided by the international campaign against the production and sale of genetically modified, or GM, foods. This campaign is rooted in concerns among Progressives, and especially environmentalists, about the potential dangers of a revolutionary end-of-century technology, bioengineering, and its application to food crops intended for human consumption.

For practical purposes, genetic engineering of plants got its start in the mid-1980s when teams of researchers at Monsanto and other companies began inserting a gene from *Bacillus thuringiensis* (Bt), a bacterium and known toxin, into tobacco plants in an effort to provide natural controls against insect infestations. In a very brief period, successful efforts became commonplace, and new products, engineered to target pests attacking a variety of plants, were developed for market. The biological revolution was under way, bringing the promise of massively higher crop yields and pest-resistant strains that could help to feed the starving masses of lesser developed countries in Africa and elsewhere.[15]

But this success was quickly followed by criticism in the form of an argument that, if the products of this new biotechnology were too widely deployed, they would lead to the evolutionary development of resistant insects and would actually accentuate rather than solve the problem of hunger. Added to this was the ecological notion that the introduction of genetically altered species would disrupt and destroy established ecosystems.[16] Eventually this argument was extended to include human beings as members of such ecosystems, which is to say, foods based on GM crops could pose a threat (of unknown dimension) to human life itself.

By 1989 this set of concerns had found voice in the Biotechnology Working Group, which included, among others, the Pesticide Action Network, National Wildlife Federation, Consumers Union, Environmental Defense Fund, and the lobbying office of the United Methodist Church. These groups not only saw genetic engineering as threatening in its own right—an intrusion in the natural way of things—but distrusted the motives of the companies that were seeking to advance and profit from it.[17] In 1999, a group of French and American farmers backed by Greenpeace filed a class action lawsuit against the company alleging that it had acted to restrain trade by controlling the markets for GM corn and soybean seeds and had threatened the economic viability of the farmers' business by not adequately testing GM seeds for human and environmental safety. In the words of the complaint[18]:

> Monsanto's unlawful conduct in aggregating the power to control all aspects of the production of corn and soy appear to be motivated by its desire to control the basic means of production of the global food supply.

This litigation was typical of the use of the courts in anti-corporate campaigns—intended less to achieve a particular outcome than to create a bully pulpit from which to give voice to a cause—in this instance, to air complaints about GM foods and to build pressure on U.S. regulators to crack down on the industry.[19]

By 2000, GM crops and foods were under tremendous pressure in Europe, where markets were closed to these products, and where consumers were convinced they were unsafe—referring to them as "Frankenfoods." In that year, a coalition was formed in the United States in an effort to replicate both these views and the resultant policy outcomes in the American marketplace. Genetically Engineered Food Alert (GEFA) numbers among its members the state-level affiliates of USPIRG, Institute for Agriculture and Trade Policy, Friends of the Earth, and Pesticide Action Network. Consumers Union, though not a member, has been a close ally. The coalition began with an attack on Campbell Soup Company, and was focused more recently on Kraft Foods; Monsanto is also on GEFA's radar.[20] In January 2001, the Consumers Federation of America, headed by longtime activist Carol Tucker Foreman, with a grant from the Rockefeller Foundation, produced a report critical of the government for what was claimed to be its lax regulation of GM food production.[21] And in March, the North Dakota legislature considered, though it did not pass, a bill establishing a moratorium on the planting of GM crops in that state.[22] By this time, Monsanto had emerged as controlling much of the market for agricultural biotechnology products and as the primary corporate target of anti-GM activists. In Europe events even reached a point of violence, with arsonists destroying a Monsanto seed storage facility.[23]

At about this time, the Pew Charitable Trusts began an attempt to broker a settlement of the issue through the Pew Initiative on Food and Biotechnology, for which purpose it brought together Monsanto with various of its critics to explore legislative and regulatory options. But in May 2003 these talks came to naught.[24] And the next month, when the Department of Agriculture, the State Department, and the U.S. Agency for International Development convened a conference in Sacramento, California, with ministers from 180 nations to discuss reducing world hunger, in part by promoting the exporting of GM crops and foods, delegates were met by demonstrators from the Pesticide Action Network, Public Citizen, and, for the first time, organized labor in the person of legendary United Farm Workers Union leader Dolores Huerta. In Huerta's words, which echoed the Greenpeace-backed 1999 lawsuit against Monsanto[25]:

> Genetically modified foods have never been tested by the EPA and FDA. Nobody knows what they will do in people or the environment . . . This isn't about feeding people throughout the world. It's about Monsanto or other large corporations making profits from selling [GM] food . . . . It's all about control of the world's food supply by large corporations, not about solving hunger.

For its part, Monsanto may wish it never became involved in this line of business. Even as it came to dominate the market for GM crops, it encountered massive waves of negative publicity, saw its profits slump and its share price tumble by half, and in May 2003 named its third CEO in as many years.[26] Nevertheless, and despite the remarkable success of a parallel effort in the European Union, the campaign against GM crops and foods in the United States has yet to gain significant ground.

That said, the anti-GM foods campaign has certainly placed the issue in play and kept it before the American public, so it must be regarded more as a work in progress than as a failed effort. Similarly, the campaign against ExxonMobil has yet to produce the desired shareholder vote, but it is one of several such shareholder-based efforts that are nearing or have achieved their objectives. And some of the other campaigns noted previously in fact have obtained their stated ends—Mitsubishi did not develop its salt works in Baja California, Home Depot did change its purchasing and stocking practices, and many companies have ceased doing business in or with Burma/Myanmar, although at this writing the military regime that was the ultimate target of that campaign remained firmly in power.

As noted earlier and illustrated by both extended examples, these campaigns have in common their framing on the high ground of moral purpose and their conduct in the trenches of anti-corporate ideology, strategy, and tactics. They are in all ways compatible with both the agenda of the Progressive Left and its needs with respect to movement building. They bring together in common purpose an array of activists who then bond in ways that go far beyond the extant issue of the day. And they are the mainstays of Progressive Left advocacy.

PROGRESSIVE ADVOCATES

The Progressive Left is made up of literally hundreds, if not thousands, of activist and advocacy organizations that vary widely with respect to their size, membership characteristics, agendas, and styles of action, to name but a few of the relevant dimensions. Although we have already mentioned a number of these organizations in the course of these pages, it is not possible to list them all here, let alone to say anything meaningful about each one. So let us reserve that task for Appendix A, which includes a selective and briefly annotated listing of Progressive activist groups, and focus here on just three exemplars: Global Exchange, the Rainforest Action Network, and CERES.

Global Exchange

Global Exchange, founded in 1988, is a combination travel agency and human rights organization. The original concept behind the group was to provide opportunities for North Americans to travel to areas of the world that exemplified problems in human rights, environmental practices, and other social ills. These opportunities, in turn, would create and motivate a cadre of concerned individuals who then would become politically active in efforts to address the related issues. Over the years, Global Exchange has conducted what it terms "reality tours" to destinations such as Cuba, Haiti, Indonesia, Mexico (including Chiapas), and Palestine. These tours remain an important part of the Global Exchange mission—the group spent $2.9 million of its $4.7 million annual budget in 2001 on these activities.[27] But over the years, the mission itself has expanded to encompass a significant role in a number of advocacy campaigns and direct actions.

In recent years, Global Exchange has become an important participant in a series of anti-corporate campaigns. Most prominent among these have been the Nike campaign—detailed earlier—in which Global Exchange Co-Director Medea Benjamin played a pivotal role when she shifted support from the Fair Labor Association to the Workers Rights Consortium once the company had accepted the code of conduct and compliance regime advanced by the former—and the broad campaign against globalization that has been marked by a series of demonstrations against the International Monetary Fund, World Bank, and World Trade Organization. Global Exchange was a highly visible participant in the so-called Battle of Seattle in 1999 and remains a leading voice in opposition to a variety of regional free-trade agreements.

A central element of Global Exchange activism today is what the group describes as "campaigns to pressure for greater economic rights as an integral part of human rights, including monitoring and responding to global economic institutions and pushing for greater corporate accountability among multi-national corporations."[28] Global Exchange has worked closely with labor and human rights organizations in developing the anti-sweatshop campaign, especially on university campuses, and in that context has participated in the development of corporate codes of conduct designed especially for educational institutions.[29] The idea behind the emphasis on campus-based efforts is at least twofold: (1) recruit student activists by providing an easy, convenient, and morally unequivocal mechanism for their activism; and (2) use the substantial market in university logo wear as a point of leverage for influencing manufacturers to adopt Global Exchange-sanctioned codes.

Global Exchange is supported in part by the Tides Foundation, the Boehm Foundation, and other Progressive funders. It is a frequent participant in coalitions on labor and human rights issues and those opposing globalization. Its positions on trade agreements and regimes, which it generally opposes, typically are cast in human rights terms. A November 1999 Global Exchange report on the World Trade Organization, for example, characterized that body as having "dangerously eroded citizens' interests in favor of commercial interests." The group went on to say[30]:

> Trade does not constitute simply a commercial transaction; trade is also a political exchange that affects workers' rights, the environment and communities' well being. The WTO's refusal to acknowledge this has inevitably led to the erosion of laws meant to protect the environment, public health, living standards, and the protection of human rights.

In April 2001 Global Exchange took on the proposed FTAA agreement in a similar report headlined "The Free Trade Area of the Americas Places Corporate Rights Above Human Rights."[31] Evident in this rhetoric is the essence of the Progressive Left's view of economic life and the idea that most clearly frames the cultural dimension of its war on the corporation—that economic activity must be judged primarily not on its own terms, as a traditional capitalist might argue, but rather as a social and ecological phenomenon.

Rainforest Action Network (RAN)

RAN is a prototypical Progressive advocacy organization focusing on the environment. Where better known groups such as Friends of the Earth and the Sierra Club began as traditional mainstream interest groups and evolved in recent years into Progressive activist organizations, RAN was created from the get-go with an aggressive and fundamentally anti-corporate persona. Founded in 1985, RAN has taken as its objectives the protection of rainforests, old growth forests, and the indigenous peoples who live in them. Its chosen methodology for pursuing this agenda is the anti-corporate campaign. Beginning in 1987 with a campaign to force Burger King to stop clearing forest lands in various countries to produce inexpensive beef for its restaurants, the group's list of targets has expanded to include Mitsubishi, Home Depot, Freeport-McMoRan, Occidental Petroleum, MacMillan Bloedel, Georgia Pacific, Kimberly Clark, Texaco, and Conoco. RAN's current campaign targets at this writing include:

- Boise Cascade—an effort to force the company to stop logging old-growth forests that has included contacts with 500 of its customers,[32]
- Citigroup—which RAN accuses of providing the financing for other companies to ravage the environment, although this campaign was the subject of a truce and discussions between the parties at the time of this writing,[33] and
- Ford Motor Company—which RAN accuses of having, but not using, the technological capability to reduce gasoline consumption and reduce emissions.[34]

In addition, RAN engages in what it terms a Campaign for a Sane Economy that targets the international activities of the financial services industry—in effect, a specialized component of the broader Progressive attack on the World Bank and other global financial institutions. The RAN campaign against Citigroup has been implemented within this broader framework. Here is a sample of the rhetoric of this campaign[35]:

Mega banks fund the operations of the fossil fuel, logging, and mining industries with impunity, refusing to acknowledge their complicity in the destruction of pristine ecosystems and vulnerable human communities the world over. Like a shadowy cartel of drug pushers, these banks keep the industrialized world hooked on an unsustainable and ultimately self-destructive economic model. If we care about the planet, we must hold the entire corporate finance sector responsible for their investments. The social, economic, and ecological costs of investments in fossil fuels, in particular, have become too high. Global warming, already upon us in its early stages, is the ecological limit to the fossil fuel industry. Society must transition out of our current extractive economy and into a restorative, sustainable economy. The only question is: Will we achieve this transition in time to save the world's forests, protect cultural and biological biodiversity, and prevent climate destabilization?

One of the most interesting aspects of RAN is the style of its protests, which tend to include dramatic actions such as suspending banners from the upper floors of skyscrapers, or suspending demonstrators from trees, bridges, or power platforms. For this hazardous work, RAN activists receive training from a closely allied group, the Ruckus Society, which was created in 1995 by Howard Cannon of Greenpeace and Mike Roselle of RAN for this very purpose. The Ruckus Society's mission is to "encourage the proliferation of skilled, non-violent direct-action activists worldwide."[36]

RAN has received support from many Progressive foundations, among them the W. Alton Jones Foundation, San Francisco Foundation, Turner Foundation, Threshold Foundation, and Tides Foundation; the World Resources Institute, which has developed an extensive strategic handbook for attacking companies in the financial services industry; Working Assets; and many individual donors (including Joshua Mailman).

Coalition for Environmentally Responsible Economies (CERES)

CERES, a group we have already encountered earlier in this chapter as well as in chapter 5, was created in 1988 at the initiative of the Social Investment Forum, a coalition of public pension funds and social responsibility investment firms, which was interested in forming a coalition with leading environmental organizations. The following year, the group released a set of 10 environmental standards for corporations, which came to be known as the CERES Principles, and began challenging corporations to adopt them. Sunoco was the first major corporation to do so (in 1993). At this writing, approximately 50 companies, including 13 in the Fortune 500, have signed on to this code of conduct, and the code itself has become something of a benchmark for corporate environmental responsibility.[37] The 10 points include:

- Protection of the biosphere
- Sustainable use of natural resources
- Reduction and disposal of wastes
- Energy conservation
- Risk reduction
- Safe products and services
- Environmental restoration
- Informing the public
- Management commitment
- Audits and reports[38]

With respect to the last of these standards, CERES encourages all companies to publish annual reviews of their environmental performance, an initiative that was broadened in 1991 when the United Nations Environmental Programme joined with CERES to promulgate the Global Reporting Initiative for multinationals, which covers various aspects of "sustainability" affected by their operations. Companies that formally endorse the CERES Principles per se are subject to a formal 5-year review of their performance by representatives of the coalition, which has broadened since its inception to include religious groups, labor groups, and social activists.[39]

The CERES board of directors includes, among others, representatives of the AFL-CIO, the Calvert Group, Coop America, Friends of the Earth, the

Sierra Club, Social Investment Forum (itself a project of Coop America), and Walden Asset Management. In 2001, the group operated on a budget of just over $2.5 million and received grants from sources such as the Energy Foundation, Ford Foundation, Bill and Melinda Gates Foundation, Charles Stewart Mott Foundation, Domini Social Investments, and Trillium Asset Management.[40]

COALITIONS: THE INTERLOCKING DIRECTORATES OF THE PROGRESSIVE MOVEMENT

As one considers the argument of this book at the broadest level—that the activists of the Progressive Left have (a) analyzed and understood, (b) set out to systematically undermine, and (c) at least partially replicated the power elite model set forth by Mills and later scholars, one obvious point of contention is this: How can a movement that is ideologically opposed to elitism and that is not in direct control of elite-level financial resources, be said to constitute a counter-elite in its own right?

Part of the answer to that question, as we will see in the pages ahead, is to conceptualize the power elite model not in terms of a fixed set of players but rather in terms of an essential set of roles and relationships. And the most central relationships in most formulations of the power elite model—and certainly in the most taxonomic manifestation of the model as developed by Thomas Dye—is the presence of substantial interlocking among members of the elite, primarily corporate, foundation, university, and think-tank directors. There is, arguably, a noticeable measure of such interlocking on the Progressive Left, as personified, for example, by individuals such as Joshua Mailman and John Cavanaugh. But it may be more useful to view this alternative structure on the Left through a slightly different lens. With respect at least to advocacy groups, and by extension to the agencies that fund them, there is, as we can see, a high degree of interlocking. But it takes the form less of shared directors than of innumerable programmatic coalitions where the same groups continually cooperate with one another. In that regard, both Global Exchange and RAN are typical of individual advocacy organizations in their high rates of coalition membership, while CERES is a perfect model of the type of coalition that so often brings them together.

ENDNOTES

1. Hayden attributes the term to Arnold Kaufman, a University of Michigan philosophy professor who taught him and other SDS members, and who spoke at the meeting where the *Port Huron Statement* was adopted. See Tom Hayden and Richard Flacks, "The Port Huron Statement at 40," *The Nation*, August 5, 2002.

2. On this point see James Miller, *Democracy Is in the Streets: From Port Huron to the Siege of Chicago* (New York: Simon and Schuster, 1987), pp. 152–154.

3. For an analysis of the Progressives' own view of both MoveOn and the Dean campaign, and of the role of the Internet in movement building more generally, see Andrew Boyd, "The Web Rewires the Movement," *The Nation*, August 4, 2003, as found online at www.thenation.com/doc.mhtml?i=20030804&s=boyd, August 9, 2003.

4. Thomas B. Edsall, "Liberals Form Fund to Defeat President: Aim Is to Spend $75 Million for 2004," *Washington Post*, August 8, 2003, p. A3.

5. David Von Drehle, "Among Democrats, The Energy Seems To Be on the Left," *Washington Post*, July 10, 2003, p. A1.

6. G. William Domhoff, *Changing the Powers that Be: How the left can stop Losing and Win* (Lanham, MD: Rowman and Littlefield, 2003).

7. Katrina Vanden Heuvel, "Building to Win," *The Nation*, July 9, 2001.

8. Found online at www.campaignexxonmobil.org/cem_brochure.html, July 10, 2003.

9. Found online at www.campaignexxonmobil.org/advisory_board.html, July 10, 2003.

10. Jim Lobe, "Shareholder Attack on ExxonMobil's Climate Policy Gets Big Boost," *Oneworld.net*, December 19, 2001, found online at http://www.commondreams.org/headlines01/1219-03.htm, December 26, 2001.

11. Shareholder Action Network, "ISS, CalPERS oppose ExxonMobil management on key global warming resolutions," found online at www.shareholderaction.org/news/020522_exmob.cfm, January 10, 2003. The Shareholder Action Network is a project of the Social Investment Forum.

12. "ExxonMobil Defends Record: Shareholders reject 'green' investment, anti-gay bias plans," *Boston Globe*, May 29, 2003, p. E2.

13. Found online at www.empoweringdemocracy.org/about.htm, July 10, 2003.

14. Found online at www.empoweringdemocracy/agenda.html, August 2, 2002.

15. Daniel Charles, *Lords of the Harvest: Biotech, Big Money and the Future of Food* (Cambridge, MA: Perseus Books, 2001), pp. 41–50.

16. Ibid., pp. 51–59.

17. Ibid., pp. 92–93.

18. *Bruce Pickett et al. v. Monsanto Company*, complaint filed December 14, 1999, U.S. District Court for the District of Columbia, p. 4.

19. Scott Kilman, "Monsanto Faces Class-Action Suit Over Genetically Altered Crops," *The Wall Street Journal*, December 15, 1999.

20. Andrew Pollack, "Food Companies Urged to End Use of Biotechnology Products," *The New York Times*, July 19, 2000; and the GEFA web site, found online at www.gefoodalert.org/pages/home.cfm, July 10, 2003.

21. "Report Faults U.S. Regulation of Biotech Foods," Reuters, January 13, 2001.

22. Andrew Pollack, "Farmers Joining State Efforts Against Bioengineered Crops," *The New York Times*, March 24, 2001.

23. Alessandra Rizzo, "Monsanto Seed Depot Set on Fire," Associated Press, April 3, 2001.

24. Justin Gillis, "No Deal on Biotech Food: Industry, Opponents Fail to Agree on Recommendation for Regulation," *The Washington Post*, May 30, 2003, p. E1.

25. Dan Bacher, "Butterflies and Farmworkers: Taking on the USDA and the Riot Cops," *Counterpunch*, July 25, 2003, found online at www.counterpunch.org/bacher06252003.html, on that date.

26. David Barboza, "Monsanto Struggles Even as It Dominates," *The New York Times*, May 31, 2003.

27. Data are drawn from the organizations IRS Form 990 for 2001.

28. Ibid.

29. See, for example, "Codes of Conduct for Universities," found online on June 14, 2000, at www.globalexchange.org/economy/corporations/campus/code.html; the more strategic "Compliance Plan for Implementing University Codes of Conduct," found online June 14, 2000,

at www.globalexchange.org/economy/corporations/campus/tools/complianceplan.html; and the model code found online June 14, 2000, at www.sweatshopwatch.org/swatch/codes/code.html.

30. "The WTO Erodes Human Rights Protections: Three Case Stduies," report published by Global Exchange, November 15, 1999, and found online July 11, 2003 at www.globalexchange.org/campaigns/wto/casestudies.html.

31. Found online July 11, 2003 at www.globalexchange.org/campaigns/ftaa/statement040201.html.

32. "Boise Cascade Target of "National Markets" Campaign: Customer Mailing Targets Old-Growth Logger as "National Disgrace," RAN news release, March 23, 2001.

33. "RAN and Citigroup Call Ceasefire," RAN news release, April 15, 2003.

34. The campaign is described online at http://www.ran.org/ran_campaigns/ford/, as found on July 11, 2003.

35. Found online July 11, 2003, at http://www.ran.org/ran_campaigns/global_finance/.

36. Nick Davis, "Raising a Ruckus: Learning How to Monkey-Wrench at Direct Action Camp," *E/The Environmental Magazine*, November-December 1997.

37. Based on information found at www.ceres.org/about/history.htm, June 24, 2003.

38. These standards were found listed in slightly more detailed form on June 24, 2003, at www.ceres.org/our_work/principles.htm.

39. CERES, *Annual Report* 2001, pp. 2–4.

40. Ibid., pp. 26–27.

9

From Networks
to Netwar

The purpose of creating a network of interconnected and similarly directed actors like that described in the preceding chapters, of course, is to put it to work. And that is precisely what the Progressives have done, at both the tactical and the strategic levels. In the present chapter, we explore the tactical use of this networking to achieve relatively narrowly defined objectives. In the next and concluding chapter, we take a much broader view, suggesting that strategic networking has provided the means to achieve the movement-building end of constructing what amounts to an "out-of-power elite" and has done so in ways that are reframing the role of the corporation in American (and global) society.

POWER IN THE INFORMATION AGE

It is by now a truism that we live in an age in which there is more abundant information available to more people through more and faster delivery systems with fewer boundaries and constraints than at any time in human history. This does not change the essential nature of power—the ability to compel through the force of words or arms compliance with one's wishes—nor its grounding in wealth and the control of relatively scarce resources. But it does mean that wealth itself, the relative criticality of various resources, and, perhaps most importantly, the fundamental nature of scarcity are being redefined. And to the extent that control over information becomes decentralized, power, too, may shift from nation states and other powerful institutions—like corporations—to smaller and less formal, but effectively networked, actors.

The most elegant statement of this transformation, and also, in all likelihood, the most extensive, has been advanced by Berkeley sociologist Manuel Castells in a trilogy, *The Information Age: Economy, Society and Culture*, first published in the mid-1990s.[1] In Castells' view, traditional bases of institutional power are being challenged with increasing effect by social and political movements that take form as social networks. If one paragraph can capture the essence of so comprehensive a work, it might be this one[2]:

> *The new power lies in the codes of information and in the images of representation around which societies organize their institutions, and people build their lives and decide their behavior. The sites of this power are people's minds.* . . . Whoever, or whatever, wins the battle of people's minds will rule, because mighty, rigid apparatuses will not be a match in any reasonable time span, for the minds mobilized around the power of flexible, alternative networks. . . . This is why identities are so important, and ultimately, so powerful in this ever-changing power structure—because they . . . anchor power in some areas of the social structure, and build from there their resistance or their offensives in the informational struggle about the cultural codes constructing behavior and, thus, new institutions.

The point here is that networks that possess the capability to attract not only attention, but loyalty, have the potential to emerge as alternative loci of power and to challenge the established institutions. Central to accomplishing that are at least two elements—a focal identity that compels psychological attachment and a means to communicate with those who feel that attachment. The first can be accomplished through effective labeling, as, for example, in the use of "progressivism" as an umbrella image. The second traditionally has been achieved in some measure through mass media and is, in the view of Castells and others as well, greatly facilitated through emails, listserv, and usenet applications, web logs, web sites, satellite and cellular telephones, and other applications of the new computer and telecommunications technologies.

Earlier in this volume, we made reference to one of the Tides Center projects, the Institute for Global Communication (IGC). IGC is an example of the electronic dimension of networking. IGC is a virtual network, which is to say, it is only minimally an actual physical organization and is much more significantly a communications node organized into four issue-specific subsets—PeaceNet, EcoNet, WomensNet, and AntiRacismNet—each of which should be self-explanatory. These components have developed and changed a bit over time since the system was established in 1985 as an electronic mailing list for anti-war nonprofits, and, for a brief period, IGC also administered LaborNet. These topical networks feature stories, action alerts, and discussion forums as well as newsletters, resource sharing, and other services. IGC also once provided a range of basic computer services for the activist community, including functioning as an Internet service provider, although this aspect of its role has since been supplanted by others.[3] Because IGC is a member of a still larger, global network, the Association for Progressive Communications, it is, in effect, an agent, not merely of national, but of transnational networking.[4] And the latter name itself—under which banner all the related networks and subnets, issues, and actors comfortably congregate—gives testimony to the functionality of progressivism as a unifying identity.

The potential inherent in such networks, of course, may or may not be realized by a given network or by a broader movement of which it may be a component. Or to put that another way, the mere existence of a network— whether virtual or real—does not imply that it will be able to claim or exercise power or that it will do so in any particular manner.

As one might imagine, the questions of which networks might effectively challenge the established social institutions, by what means, and under what circumstances have interested not only the advocates of social change but also the defenders of the status quo, not least among them the U.S. Department of Defense. As early as the 1980s, the Pentagon was showing increased interest in what came to be known as low-intensity conflict (LIC) and operations other than war (OOTW in Pentagon-speak), the latter focused mainly on peace-keeping and humanitarian operations. And, lest we forget, the Internet itself, in its earliest form, was the progeny of a defense agency, the Defense Advanced Research Projects Agency, or DARPA. Known in its earliest incarnation as DARPANET, it grew from a 1960s effort to decentralize and build redundancy into the nation's defense computing capabilities so that they might survive a Soviet nuclear attack. The resulting network architecture was later transferred to the National Science Foundation where, as ARPANET, it was used to link research computers at leading universities across the country. From there it evolved, primarily in the 1990s, into the system we know today as the Internet.

These two interests came together in a series of studies commissioned by the Pentagon and conducted by researchers at the RAND Corporation, a defense and intelligence think tank. Beginning with a focus on what was termed "cyberwar," or either using or attacking computers as instruments (or targets) of high-intensity conflict, this work shifted over time to focus on more subtle forms of networked warfare, or what the researchers leading the RAND team—John Arquilla and David Ronfeldt—termed "netwar." In their words[5]:

> The term "netwar" denotes an emerging mode of conflict ... at societal levels, in-volving measures short of war, in which the protagonists use—indeed, depend on using—network forms of organization, doctrine, strategy, and communication. These protagonists generally consist of dispersed, often small groups who agree to commu-nicate, coordinate, and act in an internetted manner, often without a precise central leadership or headquarters. ...
>
> The netwar spectrum may increasingly include a new generation of ... activists who espouse post-industrial, information-age ideologies that are just now taking shape. In some cases, identities and loyalties may shift from the nation-state to the transnational level of "global civil society."

But netwar, as Arquilla, Ronfeldt, and their colleagues soon came to realize, extended well beyond cyberspace. Real, as well as virtual, activists began to organize themselves into transnational "issue networks" that were positioned to engage not simply in netwar but in what the RAND researchers termed *social* netwar. Here they were drawing on work by political scientist Kathryn Sikkink, who, in a 1993 article in the journal *International Organization*, characterized such networks as comprising organizations, mainly nongovernmental organizations (NGOs), bound by shared values, dense communications, flows of funds and exchanges of services, and working toward common objectives.[6] The strategy here, argued Sikkink, centered on a recognition that establishment actors make decisions in the context of the informational environment in which they operate, which is to say, based on what they know and say and what significant other actors on whose good will they depend know and say. Rather than attempting to change such decisions directly, these NGO-based networks work to alter the environment in which they are being made in such ways that the decisions themselves will change.[7] This is, of course, the very same dynamic that we encountered earlier as the application of power structure analysis in the anti-corporate campaign.

In a later work, Sikkink and co-author Margaret Keck set forth four general uses of these NGO-based social networks, including[8]:

1. *Information politics*, or the ability to quickly and credibly generate politically usable information and move it to where it will have the most impact,
2. *Symbolic politics*, or the ability to call upon symbols, actions, or stories that make sense of a situation for an audience that is frequently far away,
3. *Leverage politics*, or the ability to call upon powerful actors to affect a situation where weaker members of a network are unlikely to have influence, and
4. *Accountability politics*, or the effort to hold powerful actors to their previously stated policies or principles.

Here, too, we see echoes of the methodology of anti-corporate campaigns, where, for example, generating and framing information to advantage, bringing into play powerful organizational or celebrity allies, and advancing strategically positioned codes of conduct have long been standard items in the campaigners' toolbox.

Arquilla and Ronfeldt, the RAND researchers, quickly grasped the significance of these insights but recast them as a prospective social threat—NGO networks, bound, not merely by information technology, but by their collective image, resource, programmatic, and ideological elements, into a new collective force—to wit, social networks capable of challenging national actors with some effect by waging social netwar. As an example they proffered the EZLN insurrection in Chiapas, Mexico, popularly known as the Zapatista movement. It is an example that does have instructional value in the present instance, although we clearly are not focused here on armed insurrection nor even, for that matter, on anti-state action.

In January 1994, approximately 1,000 armed insurgents took control of a city and several towns in the southernmost Mexican state of Chiapas, declared a revolution against the Mexican government, and invited foreign observers to come to the region. The Mexican government, long accustomed to putting down such insurrections, dispatched forces to quell the rebellion, sometimes with a heavy hand, even while downplaying its significance. The EZLN, in turn, called for genuine democracy in Mexico and for socioeconomic reforms including, in effect, abrogation of the North American Free Trade Agreement (NAFTA), which had been aggressively opposed by labor and other activists in the United States, and called on human rights groups to monitor the conflict. Through press conferences and communiqués, and especially through a media-savvy spokesman known as Subcomandante Marcos, the Zapatistas established an identity for themselves, which, contrasted with the government's efforts at suppression, generated considerable sympathy in world opinion.[9] Picking up the narrative from Arquilla and Ronfeldt[10,11]:

> Within days, delegations were flowing into Mexico . . . , where links were established with local NGOs and EZLN representatives. Demonstrations, marches and peace caravans were organized, not only in Mexico but even in front of Mexican consulates in the United States. The NGOs made good use of computerized conferencing, e-mail, fax, and telephone systems, as well as face-to-face meetings, to communicate and coordinate with each other. . . . The fax numbers of Mexican and U.S. officials were often posted in Internet news groups and mailing lists. . . . In addition, the activists worked to assure that the insurrection became, and remained, an international media event . . . [and] that the EZLN and its views were portrayed favorably.
> . . . Many NGO activists sensed they were molding a new model of organization and strategy based on networking that was different from Leninist and other traditional approaches to the creation of social movements.

Just who were these groups that intervened on behalf of the Zapatistas? They included church and religious groups, indigenous rights and human rights advocates, trade and development policy advocates, and many others. Among the more familiar names were Amnesty International, Institute for Agriculture and Trade Policy, IGC's PeaceNet, and Global Exchange. But to begin building an understanding of the network of relationships among these groups, let us look first to a less familiar entity, the Mexico Solidarity Network (MSN).

MSN, a coalition of 88 organizations, was created at a Washington, DC, meeting in April 1998, after the initial conflict in Chiapas had cooled but in the midst of a continuing effort to maintain pressure on the Mexican government. Its National Coordinator, Tom Hansen, also serves as co-director of the Chiapas Media Project. Represented on MSN's board of directors are groups such as Global Exchange, the Committee in Solidarity with the

Central American People (CISCAP), and the Zapatista Support Committee. Interestingly, the North American Congress on Latin America (NACLA)—the group that literally invented the anti-corporate campaign—is also a member of MSN. MSN maintains a staff of six, with offices in Washington, Chicago (shared with the Chiapas Media Project), and San Francisco. Many of the member organizations in MSN are locally based Zapatista or Chiapas support groups, including, for example, Carolina-Chiapas Connection, Chiapas Coalition of Denver, Chiapas Committee of Cleveland, Howard County (MD) Friends of Latin America, Kentucky Interfaith Task Force on Central America, Marin Interfaith Task Force on Central America, Mid Ohio Pastors for Peace, and NY Zapatistas. Most of these, and many other member groups, are faith-based organizations of greater or lesser scope.

A more interesting exercise than simply listing members, and a more illuminating one, is to map some of the interconnections among some of the more significant MSN members. We can do that in stages, and in the process begin to develop an appreciation for the nature of foundation-NGO networks. Let us begin this mapping by looking very selectively at some of the member organizations. This is accomplished in Fig. 9.1.

Also included in Fig. 9.1 is one organization in which the direction of participation is reversed—MSN is itself a member of another coalition, the Latin America Working Group (LAWG). We can see from the figure that several MSN members such as Global Exchange and the Catholic Foreign Missions Society are also members of LAWG, which suggests at least the potential for a significant degree of interlocking between the two organizations and among their respective members. We can weigh this potential more fully by adding to our illustration, again selectively, other members of LAWG. The results of this second exploratory step are shown in Fig. 9.2

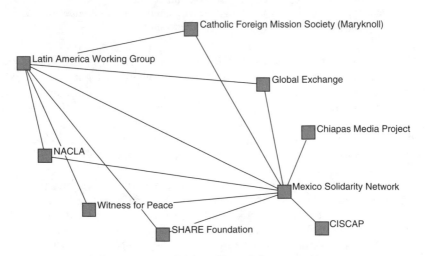

FIG. 9.1.   Mexico Solidarity Network direct connections.

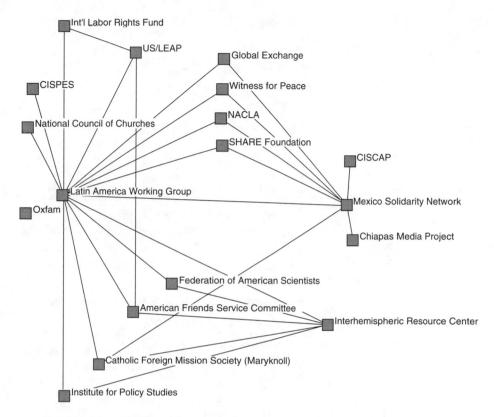

FIG. 9.2. Mexico Solidarity Network plus Latin America Working Group direct connections.

LAWG is a Washington-based coalition of more than 60 organizations that have banded together to influence U.S. policy toward Latin America and the Caribbean by promoting a Progressive agenda of policies with respect to human rights and sustainable development. As the figure shows, LAWG brings into the mix several additional players, among them the Institute for Policy Studies, the National Council of Churches (which partnered with SDS in forming NACLA and in formulating the anti-corporate campaign in the 1970s) and two other major activist religious organizations, the American Friends Service Committee and the Catholic Foreign Missions Society (Maryknoll); and a set of labor-based NGOs. It also brings in yet another node of apparent significance, the Interhemispheric Resource Center (IRC), which is partnered with the Institute for Policy Studies in a joint Foreign Policy in Focus Project. Adding a more complete (but still selective) exploration of this third node produces the even more elaborate network diagram illustrated in Fig. 9.3.

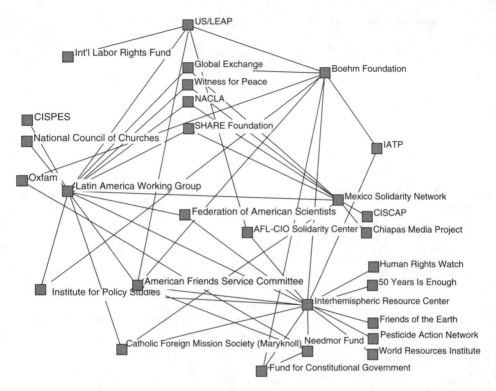

FIG. 9.3. Mexico Solidarity Network and Latin America Working Group plus Interhemispheric Resource Center direct connections.

IRC has some connections of its own to several groups already on the map—literally speaking—but also brings into the mix its connections to the environmental movement, to the anti-globalization movement (through 50 Years is Enough, a leading voice in the campaign against the International Monetary Fund, World Bank, and World Trade Organization), and Human Rights Watch, to name but a few. In some ways more importantly, IRC brings in the first of the foundations whose funding supports NGO activism in Latin America, most notably the Boehm Foundation. Boehm is an example of the type of activist family foundation discussed in chapter 3, as is the Needmor Fund, another supporter of IRC and other networked entities.

We could, of course, extend this particular subnetwork out still further, but, at least in visual terms, we are near the point of diminishing returns, the point at which the complexity of the network overwhelms the brain's ability to interpret the extant patterns. So, rather than create total visual spaghetti, let us simply note that focusing on any one or more of the remaining components already included in our illustration can generate still more interesting links. As examples, Kevin Danaher, founder of Global Exchange, Daisy Pitkin, Executive Director of the Campaign for Labor Rights (not shown), and Mary Zerkel of the American Friends Service Committee all serve as Directors of 50 Years Is Enough; the Tides Foundation and Center receive support from both Needmor and Boehm, and in turn support Global Exchange, Oxfam, and Human Rights Watch; and the Campaign for Labor Rights brings together in coalition, among others, the International Labor Rights Fund, US/LEAP (US Labor Education in the Americas Project), Witness for Peace and CISPES (Committee in Solidarity with the People of El Salvador). Nor should we forget that the Chiapas Media Project, which provides video equipment and support to activists in southern Mexico, has been funded in part by Joshua Mailman, with whose inventiveness we began this line of our narrative many pages ago.

The other important point here is that this already extensive cluster of relationships has developed around a relatively small issue in a very remote corner of the world. So, while it may help to give texture to the argument of Arquilla and Ronfeldt and others that the Zapatista movement represented a watershed in activist methodology, it also should put that argument in perspective. NGO support for the EZLN, even as an exemplar of the new phenomenon of social netwar, was merely the tip of the proverbial iceberg. That the same approach to networked collaboration is evident in the ongoing anti-globalization movement, to pick but one example, should not be in the least surprising, given that groups such as Global Exchange and 50 Years Is Enough have been in its forefront.[12] Similar tactics have been used as well in the campaign to force the resignation of Myanmar's (Burma's) military government, which have centered in large measure on pressuring American and other corporations to cease doing business in or with that country.[13]

SOCIAL NETWAR COMES HOME

While these examples, and the conceptual work by the RAND researchers that gave rise to them, take as their targets nation states, regimes, or quasi-governmental transnational institutions, the boundary between international and domestic applications of social netwar is porous, if it exists at all. More and more, we are seeing evidence of the very same marriage of organization, communication, and doctrine at work within economic or political systems like the European Union and the United States. To make the point, let us draw from what has been, in essence, an extended example we have developed almost from the beginning of this book. Let us look at the network of diverse interests that has come together, some directly and some through intermediaries, to bring just one type of pressure on one class of targets—the network that is using shareholder resolutions and proxy voting to press American corporations to change their governance structures and social policies in ways aligned with the Progressive worldview. In doing so, we will draw from various elements of our argument as it has developed to this point and show how these seemingly disparate actors have been woven together into a coherent and increasingly effective social network.

Figure 9.4 illustrates the key elements of this network.[14] To facilitate discussion, most component groups have been assigned to one of six primary clusters. Beginning in the upper left, these include:

- Social responsibility investment activists—Listed here are the principal firms—Calvert, Domini, etc.—identified in chapter 4 as pursuing a Progressive social agenda through various investment strategies. These investment professionals help to research and evaluate corporate performance.
- Environmental activists—Though they are not individually named in the figure, virtually all the major environmental organizations play a role in this network, primarily through CERES, which, you will recall from chapter 8, was created as a coalition between these activists and their social-responsibility-investment counterparts through the initiative of the Social Investment Forum (SIF; also shown). SIF is itself a project of a lesser-known environmental group, Co-op America. For its part, Friends of the Earth (FoE) has produced a how-to guide for shareholder activism under the title *Confronting Companies Using Shareholder Power: A Handbook on Socially-Oriented Shareholder Activism*. Among the topics covered are the use of shareholder activism as a component of an anticorporate campaign both domestically and internationally, the drafting and defense of shareholder resolutions, solicitation of proxies, and activities both inside and outside the target company's annual meeting.[15] In 2002, FoE convened an international meeting of advocacy and other NEOs in Italy where Michelle Chan-Fishel, coordinator of the group's Green Investment Project, set out a plan to hold private financial institutions like banks and institutional investors responsible for advancing environmental sustainability and social justice initiatives on the part of the corporations they support and control.[16] More generally, environmentalists bring to the effort a specific policy agenda but also lend their considerable public legitimacy to any shareholder resolution they may support.
- Religious activists—Here, too, we have not named individual organizations, in this instance because they would be far too numerous. Working primarily through the Interfaith Center for Corporate Responsibility (ICCR), these groups add an explicit moral dimension to the pressure that is brought on corporations.
- Unions—For the most part, because I have given substantial attention to labor-based attacks on corporations in previous work, we have not focused extensively on unions and the labor movement in this volume. But it would be a mistake to assume for that reason that labor is not well integrated into the new Progressive Left.[17] To the contrary, one

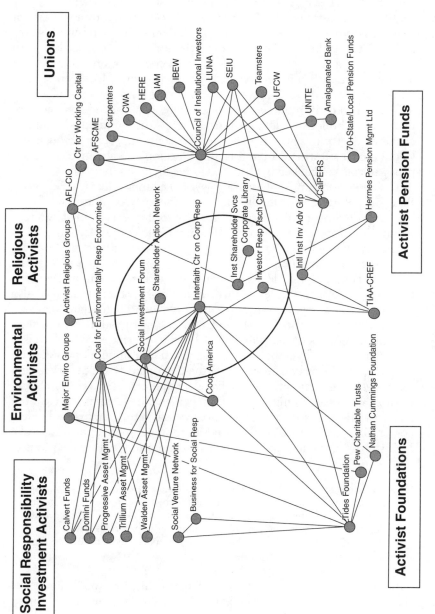

Environmental
Activists

Religious
Activists

Unions

Activist Pension Funds

Activist Foundations

FIG. 9.4. Selected components of the proxy activism network.

Calvert Funds
Domini Funds
Progressive Asset Mgmt
Trillium Asset Mgmt
Walden Asset Mgmt
Social Venture Network
Business for Social Resp

Major Enviro Groups

Activist Religious Groups
AFL-CIO
Coal for Environmentally Resp Economies

Ctr for Working Capital
AFSCME
Carpenters
CWA
HERE
IAM
IBEW
Council of Institutional Investors
LIUNA
SEIU
Teamsters
UFCW
UNITE
Amalgamated Bank
70+State/Local Pension Funds

Social Investment Forum
Shareholder Action Network
Interfaith Ctr on Corp Resp
Inst Shareholder Svcs
Corporate Library
Investor Resp Rsch Ctr
Intl Inst Inv Adv Grp
CalPERS
Hermes Pension Mgmt Ltd

Coop America

TIAA-CREF

Tides Foundation
Pew Charitable Trusts
Nathan Cummings Foundation

171

of John Sweeney's primary objectives during his tenure as president of the AFL-CIO has been to reconstruct the historic bonds between labor and other interests on the Left, and he has succeeded to a substantial degree in doing so. Here, in the arena of shareholder activism, this new and important alliance truly comes to the fore because labor brings to the network at least two resources—a high degree of organization and money—that are lacking elsewhere in the Progressive Movement. In the present instance, these resources combine in the form of labor-influenced or—managed pension funds that collectively, as we have noted, control hundreds of billions of dollars of investments and hundreds of millions of shares of stock, which is to say in this context, votes. Through the Council of Institutional Investors, they develop and advance corporate policy initiatives backed by their collective financial influence.

- Activist Pension Funds—In many ways, these funds—like CalPERS and the other public pension funds—are extensions of the unions themselves. The CalPERS Board of Administrators, for example, is headed by a representative of the United Food and Commercial Workers Union and has a majority of members who are either union representatives per se or were selected with union support.
- Activist Foundations—Here we have listed three familiar names— Cummings, Pew, and Tides—but there are many others that have also encouraged and supported groups or initiatives relating to shareholder activism. For its part, the Tides Foundation has openly advocated policies that would enhance the influence of Progressive shareholder activists. For example, in November 2002, Tides President Drummond Pike and two of his colleagues wrote a letter to the Chairman of the Securities and Exchange Commission calling for broader requirements on the disclosure of proxy votes cast by mutual fund companies. The letter made clear the strategy of using institutional shareholders as leverage against individual corporations and, less directly, of positioning independent arbiters like ISS as prospective legitimizing agents for the proxy-voting decisions of fund managers. It said in part[18]:

Greater disclosure of proxy-voting policies and practices would pressure fund managers and advisers to refrain from unilateral rubberstamping of management's decisions.... Indeed, the proposed rules would not only help investors identify those funds and advisors that carefully examine proxy proposals before voting on them, but also those who emphasize strong corporate governance or high standards of corporate social responsibility.

At the center of the network, at least functionally, is a small number of organizations (one of) whose principal function(s) is to initiate, evaluate, and/or cast proxy votes on shareholder resolutions. These groups—ICCR and ISS are most notable among them—are linked in various ways to the other interests represented in the network and act more or less as their agents. They also function to add a patina of independence and legitimacy to what are often, in fact, highly agenda-driven votes and other actions. And one entity in particular—the Institutional Investors Advisory Group—which comprises *only* CalPERS and TIAA-CREF from the United States, Hermes Pensions Management Ltd. (which is owned and operated by the British Telecom and British Post Office pension system and has a significant stake in ISS), and Pensions Investment Research Consultants (the U.K. equivalent of ISS)— is designed as a mechanism to move the Progressive corporate governance agenda into the international arena, where transnational NGOs can add to the pressure.[19]

If one views Fig. 9.4, not as a static representation but as a dynamic model of action, the relevance of the social netwar analogy becomes immediately apparent. Fill in the blanks. Standing up for [the environment, working people, moral behavior] and the public interest, as validated by the actions or recommendations of [ICCR, ISS, the Corporate Library, the Council of Institutional Investors, etc.], the trustees of [pension fund, foundation, mutual fund] voted against management of the [pick one] corporation, whose existing policy on [corporate diversity, forest use, mineral extraction, genetically modified foods, and so forth] is contrary to the public interest. Supporting this position are the combined and arrayed forces of pro-social activism—whether religious, environmental, human or civil rights, consumer, or otherwise centered. Just as NGOs literally swarmed into Mexico in support of the Zapatistas a decade ago, so do activist NGOs, foundations, and even companies swarm their corporate targets today, employing computer networking, opinion management, and the other instruments of social netwar.

Through a variety of interlocks, this network of interests has functioned with considerable unity of purpose in recent years, influencing proxy votes and pressuring management at diverse companies such as AOL Time Warner, General Electric, Hewlett-Packard, Marriott International, and Sprint to name but a very few. Some of the connections among members are transparent and widely recognized; others are oblique and little known. Some are direct and explicit; others are indirect and subtle. But collectively they have produced an increasingly effective form of leverage on corporate management suites, board rooms, and policies. And they are but one of many theaters of conflict in the building of the Progressive Movement and the attack on the corporation as a social institution.

Here, too, as elsewhere in the broad argument of this book, there is reason to believe that real-time knowledge of advances in information warfare and social netwar, and of the RAND research in particular, existed in the Progressive advocacy community. In this instance one Progressive group, the Federation of American Scientists, has long maintained an online bibliography linking to several related studies.[20] Given the deeply rooted intellectualism of the Progressive Movement and the porous membrane that separates thinkers from doers, it should not be in the least bit surprising to find the latest strategic theorizing at any given point in time reflected in the latest strategic actions of the Progressive Left.

FORM, FUNCTION, AND FOLLOWERS

This is not the place to engage in a detailed discussion of the methodology of network analysis or to conceptualize broadly about the relationship between networks and social movements. Others have already done so with consummate skill, producing a rich literature that is 30 or more years in depth.[21] Nor shall we set out to "prove" that Progressive activists are affirmatively engaged in net-think. On that point, we can take their work product as evidence, but we are also guided by Keck and Sikkink's observation that[22]:

> Social science did not dictate our choice of "network" as the name to be given the phenomenon we are studying. The actors themselves did: over the last two decades, individuals and organizations have consciously formed and named transnational networks, developed and shared networking strategies and techniques, and assessed the advantages and limits of this kind of activity.

But this should not be taken to indicate that the form and functioning of social activism networks is not important. Indeed, it can help us a great deal in understanding how networks are formed through time and issue space, which members are most central to the formation and operation of a network, what the contribution of each component member might be, what types of networks various activist entities choose to join, and so forth. We have already seen implicit answers to some of these questions even in the limited analysis presented here.

We would be remiss, however, were we not to give at least some more direct attention to these generic issues of structure and process. For that, we can take guidance once again from Ronfeldt and his colleagues, who have drawn on the afore-referenced literature to specify three basic classes of networks—chain, star, and all-channel—each of which is represented, seriatim, in Fig. 9.5.[23]

In a chain network, the first type, no participant has direct contact with more than two other participants, and none is necessarily aware of the existence of other network components, let alone their identities. This type of

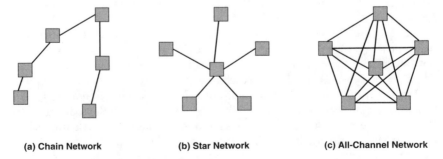

    (a) Chain Network   **(b) Star Network**   **(c) All-Channel Network**

FIG. 9.5.   Classes of networks.

structure may be functional for a smuggling network, intelligence contacts, or perhaps even guerrilla movements, but it appears to be of limited value in movement building, where its potential strengths are in fact weaknesses. Nevertheless, we can see evidence of such a structure in Fig. 9.2, in that the three major nodes of the subnetwork depicted there—MSN, LAWG, and IRC—are connected only in chainlike fashion. It is not difficult to extend this network as a mental exercise by adding still more such nodal links. And when we take the expanded network portrayed in Fig. 9.3 into account, we can see the contribution that a chain structure can make, especially when the links on the chain are themselves nodes in other networks. MSN brings together those interested in Chiapas and Mexico. LAWG convenes, at least metaphorically, those with broader Central American interests as well as labor activists. IRC is a focal point for environmental and globalization activists. There is no programmatic reason for each of these clusters to know or interact directly with one another, yet when they are linked together through a chain of subnetwork nodes, their potential for collective action is broadened, deepened, and further legitimized.

Figure 9.2 is also useful for noting that chain networks need not be simple, single-linkage structures. In addition to the direct membership connection between MSN and LAWG, there are at least five indirect connections through other entities that participate in both subnetworks. Similarly, the direct connection between LAWG, and IRC is supplemented by four joint participants. Neither of these sets of connections alters the basic chain-like nature of the relationships among MSN, LAWG, and IRC, but they do, clearly, strengthen the linkages among the primary nodes.

In a star network, a central actor defines the collective agenda and controls communication among the members and between the members and other actors outside the network. Within their own spheres of interest, the three primary nodes in Figs. 9.1–9.3 function in precisely this way. Each has been created for the express purpose of representing a coalition of interests in speaking or acting on a given issue or set of issues. This central node, which may be real or virtual in character, gains from strength of numbers, and contributes a unity of voice, both of which can magnify the effectiveness of the component organizations in influencing public opinion or decision making.

The third network structure, the all-channel network, represents complete interconnection and collaboration among the participants—every entity is connected to every other entity. This may be possible to achieve in relatively small networks, and the advent and use of the Internet and related technologies has certainly expanded the definition of "small." But in reality, large-scale all-channel networks are unlikely to develop, if only because of the logistical challenges they present and, if developed, are unlikely to function effectively. That said, networks that approximate an all-channel structure in some degree may well be strengthened by the cross-cutting interlocks among members, which can facilitate trust, communication, continuity, and joint action. We can see elements of such a structure in Fig. 9.3, where the participation of funding agencies like the Boehm Foundation and religious organizations like Maryknoll can influence the interplay among various actors, primary and secondary alike. Indeed, if a social movement like that of the Progressive Left is to construct a relatively unified and efficient structure for influencing public perceptions and policies, some measure of all-channel architecture is essential.

ENDNOTES

1. The three volumes include *The Rise of the Network Society* (Oxford, UK: Blackwell Publishers, 1996, 2000), *The Power of Identity* (Oxford, UK: Blackwell Publishers, 1997), and *End of Millennium* (Oxford, UK: Blackwell Publishers, 1998, 2000).
2. Castells, M. *The Power of Identity*, pp. 359–360.
3. Craig Warkentin, *Reshaping World Politics: NGOs, the Internet, and Global Civil Society* (Lanham, MD: Rowman & Littlefield, 2001), pp. 145–147.
4. In fact, IGC and its international connections were singled out for attention in an early Pentagon report on political uses of the Internet. See Charles, Swett, "Strategic Assessment: The Internet," Office of the Assistant Secretary of Defense for Special Operations and Low-Intensity Conflict, July 17, 1995, found online at www.fas.org/cp/swett.html, March 1, 1999.
5. John Arquilla and David Ronfeldt, *The Advent of Netwar* (Santa Monica, CA: RAND Corporation, 1996), pp. 5–6.
6. Kathryn Sikkink, "Human Rights, Principled Issue-Networks, and Sovereignty in Latin America," *International Organization* 47:3 (Summer 1993), pp. 415–417.
7. Ibid., p. 441.
8. Margaret Keck and Kathryn Sikkink, *Activists Beyond Borders: Advocacy Networks in International Politics* (Ithaca, NY: Cornell University Press, 1998), p. 16.
9. David Ronfeldt, John Arquilla, Graham E. Fuller and Melissa Fuller, *The Zapatista Social Netwar in Mexico* (Santa Monica, CA: RAND Corporation, 1998), pp. 1–3.
10. Ibid., pp. 50–51. For an analysis of Chiapas media coverage see Adrienne Russell, "Chiapas and the New News: Internet and Newspaper Coverage of a Broken Ceasefire," *Journalism: Theory, Practice and Criticism*, 2:2 (August 2001), pp. 197–220.
11. Ronfeldt et al., op. cit, p. 52.
12. Paul de Armond, "Netwar in the Emerald City: WTO Protest Strategy and Tactics," in J. Arquilla and D. Ronfeldt, eds., *Networks and Netwars* (Santa Monica, CA: RAND Corporation, 2001), pp. 201–235.
13. Tiffany Danitz and Warren P. Strobel, "Networking Dissent: Cyber Activists Use the Internet to Promote Democracy in Burma," in J. Arquilla and D. Ronfeldt, eds., *Networks and Netwars*, op. cit., pp. 129–169.
14. This figure was first developed by the HR Policy Association, and is reproduced here with permission.
15. Found online at www.foe.org/international/shareholder/, June 17, 2001.
16. "Pressure Groups Traget the Private Banks Behind Corporate Misdeeds," Friends of the Earth news release, U.S. Newswire, January 21, 2003.
17. Indeed, for an application of the social netwar concept to trade union activism, albeit in the international arena, see Steve Walker, "To Picket Just Click It! Social Netwar and Industrial Conflict in a Global Economy," Working Paper, School of Information Management, Leeds Metropolitan University, 2001.
18. Letter from Drummond Pike, Idelisse Malavé and Lauren Webster to the SEC, November 14, 2002, found online, January 27, 2003, at www.sec.gov/rules/proposed/s73602/dpike1.htm.

19. Donkin, Richard, "Powerful support for international guidelines," *Financial Times*, March 19, 1999, p. 4.
20. See http://www.fas.org/irp/wwwinfo.html, found online August 7, 2003.
21. As examples, see David Knoke, *Political Networks: The Structural Perspective* (Cambridge, UK: Cambridge University Press, 1990); and the collection of articles in Mario Diani and Doug McAdam, eds., *Social Movements and Networks: Relational Approaches to Collective Action* (Oxford, UK: Oxford University Press, 2003).
22. Keck and Sikkink, op. cit., p. 4.
23. The figure is based on Ronfeldt et al., *The Zapatista Social Netwar*, Figure 1, p. 12.

10

Biz-War and the
Out-of-Power Elite

I began this essay by suggesting that, by the late 1980s, the American Left found itself in need of reconstruction and that in the years since it has pursued a strategy of reframing its own image, identifying a suitable opponent or enemy, constructing an alternative power structure paralleling the power elite model extant at the time, waging anti-corporate campaigns against numerous targets to advance its agenda, and gaining in the sophistication of its weaponry and in its influence. The idea is not that this is a carefully planned conspiracy of some sort—which I do not believe to be the case—but rather, that it is the collective product of a series of both isolated and integrated decisions made by like-minded activists of some considerable cleverness. The Progressive-Left activist community today is broadly based, highly sophisticated, well financed, highly motivated, and broadly integrated. And this network of philanthropists, foundations, advocates, and nongovernmental organizations is focused on achieving its diverse aims through a common and interactive strategy, the waging of a war of reputation, regulation, litigation, and financial pressure on the corporation, both individually and institutionally. This is today the dominant model of exchange between the activist communities and the corporate community. It is Biz-War.

Biz-War is not an accidental and random phenomenon; it is a purposeful and relatively systematic one, informed and woven together by an understanding of the power elite structure explicated by Professors Mills, Domhoff, and Dye; of the centrality of social networking to the functioning of that structure; of the role of human and financial resources, the power associated with effective agenda generation and control, the legitimizing effects of language and imagery; and the possibility—perhaps remote at first but now nearing achievement—of constructing an alternative structure based on the very same principles, in effect, defeating the establishment with its own tools of power.

Over the last quarter century or so, a collection of intelligent, street-smart, cunning, and capable activists on the Left has come to the very threshold of producing their desired end-product—an Out-of-Power Elite.

This Out-of-Power Elite—let us refer to it as the OPE for the sake of simplicity—does not precisely mimic the structure and dynamics of the original power elite model. The times, the players, the circumstances, and the available resources are different from what they were 30 and more years ago, and, of course, development of the OPE is inevitably constrained by the fact that it has occurred entirely in the shadow of the establishment power structure it seeks to displace. But, as these pages have shown, there are a great many substantial similarities. To explore them, we need only to bring back into focus the elements of the elitist model as characterized by Thomas Dye and as captured in Fig. 1.1 on page 13.

The driving force behind the power elite as seen by Dye was money that originated from wealthy individuals and major corporations, which themselves were interconnected through foundership, ownership, and membership on corporate boards of directors. This money was then distributed directly or through corporate- or family-based foundations to a network of researchers, policy think tanks, and other institutions, where it supported the development of menus of policy options that were compatible with the interests and preferential standing of the funding sources. This menu of choice was then filtered through the media on its way into the policy-deciding institutions of government—executive, legislative, and judicial—where expressly political actors (Presidents, regulators, members of Congress, judges) would choose freely (or at least, politically) among the available options, creating the appearance of free choice but the reality of a restricted range of selection.

The OPE is built along very similar lines. Let us consider some of the key elements:

- Personal wealth. In chapter 2, we took one individual, Joshua Mailman, as an exemplar of activist philanthropy with a Progressive bent. That analysis, as well as Mailman's cameo appearances later in our narrative, showed him to be an exceptionally bright, innovative, talented, and dedicated long-time player in this game—an institution-builder of considerable note. But he is hardly alone. His own activist philanthropy was shaped in part by stories he heard of J. Irwin Miller, who built diesel engine manufacturer Cummins Engine into an industrial powerhouse in the middle of the last century and then turned his attention, and his fortune, to addressing civil rights and other issues.[1] (Among other things, Miller served a term as president of the National Council of Churches in the 1960s, and the Cummins Engine Foundation, which he established, was an early funder of the Institute for Policy Studies.) And Mailman has ample company among old- and new-generation philanthropists, among them names such as Rockefeller, Rubin, Soros, and Stern. What is new here is the number of those we might term the "Progressive rich"; the common acceptance among the wealthy that Progressive philanthropy is a mainstream and even a favored activity; the establishment of specialized institutions, such as Responsible Wealth, to recruit and train Progressive philanthropists; and the systematic pooling of relatively small donors into collectively influential ones.

- Corporate wealth. Not surprisingly, the OPE model diverges from the Power Elite model with respect to the role of corporations. There have been, to be sure, some experiments with Progressive corporate philanthropy. Ben & Jerry's, the Body Shop, and Working Assets come immediately to mind. But these have proven inadequate to the purpose. So the activists have come to rely less on developing pro-social corporate wealth than on turning traditional corporate wealth to pro-social purposes. This is, of course, the central thread of our argument in this book, and we return to it later. For the present, however, suffice it to say that the OPE can be differentiated from its predecessor and conceptual antagonist on the basis of the way in which it seeks to exploit corporate wealth.

- Foundation agenda-setting. Here the Progressive activists have used two strategic approaches that collectively mirror the role of foundations in the power elite formulation. First, they have marshaled and consolidated personal wealth in a series of family foundations—the Stern Family Fund, the Rubin Foundation, the Schumann Foundation, as examples— that closely resemble those of an earlier era (Ford Rockefeller, Pew), and in a set of amalgamating foundations—Threshold and Tides, for instance—that pool and channel donations. (Both Joshua Mailman and, especially, Drummond Pike have been notable innovators here.) Second, they have altered the agendas of older and often substantially larger foundations, working either through new generations of the founding families or through capturing the loyalties of current-generation professional foundation directors and program managers and as a result have turned old money to new purposes. The Pew Charitable Trusts represent a case in point. In addition, they have moved activist philanthropy to a new level by redefining and, in the process, legitimizing the application of fiscal sponsorship as a mechanism by which nonpartisan, but nonetheless clearly political, activism can be supported by tax-exempt philanthropic institutions. Many projects nurtured within the Tides Center, for example, have taken advantage of such a structure.

- Policy planning and agenda development. In the power elite model, university researchers, together with think tanks like the American Enterprise Institute, the Brookings Institution, the Heritage Foundation, and the RAND Corporation, conduct research and formulate options and proposals that eventually help to shape public policy. In the OPE, this role is filled by organizations such as the Institute for Policy Studies, the Economic Policy Institute, the Center for Economic and Policy Research, the World Resources Institute, and the Institute for America's Future as well as by labor policy specialists at Cornell University's School of Industrial and Labor Relations, environmental policy scholars at Dartmouth and Harvard, and many other university researchers around the country.

• Dissemination through the news media. The major news media in the United States are corporate entities but ones in which many content-related decisions are made by journalists, many of whom are—by virtue of a professional code that encourages them to "give voice to the voiceless,"[2] and, in many cases, of their own membership in the Newspaper Guild, a component of the Progressive activist union, the Communications Workers of America—inherently sympathetic to elements of the Progressive-Left agenda. This creates opportunities for the relatively uncritical placement of pro-movement news stories and helps to define and power the media component of the anti-corporate campaign. But of more direct interest in the present, narrower context, is the development of media outlets that are expressly and overtly Progressive—on the business as well as the editorial side. Some of these have been around for many years, while others are more recent in origin. Among them are outlets such as *The Progressive, Mother Jones, The Nation, Multinational Monitor,* and *The American Prospect.* These media, and others like them, can be counted on to publish a steady stream of articles that both interest and support Progressive activists. There are some more limited parallels to both situations among the broadcast media, with National Public Radio and various television "magazine" programs providing targets of opportunity for placing pro-movement stories or viewpoints and Pacifica Radio providing a more institutionalized voice for Progressive causes and actors. There is even the example of Bill Moyers, who has anchored various topical programs on the Public Broadcasting System relating to issues on the Progressive agenda even while serving as President of the Schumann Foundation and as a director of George Soros's activist Open Society Institute. Finally, and not surprisingly in light of the time period during which their movement has developed, the Progressive activists have moved well beyond the traditional establishment in their use of new media, including the full range of interactive computer and Internet applications.

• Legitimizing policy through "independent" government review. This is not an area we have explored thoroughly here, though there is reason to believe that some Progressive-activist organizations try to influence government-sponsored research programs to address issues or questions in which they have a particular interest. For example, in 1998 the Natural Resources Defense Council issued a report naming the 10 "dirtiest"

utilities in the United States. That report was based on a 1996 study conducted by the Environmental Protection Agency and the Department of
Energy.[3] This is not precisely the same use of government commissions
noted by Dye in his analysis. He had in mind, as an example, the use of
so-called nonpartisan commissions to advance solutions to problems, like
the sustaining of the Social Security System, that were urgently in need
of action but for which no winning political coalition could be mustered.
In such instances, the role of the commission was to proffer a solution in
the public interest, and to serve as a lightening rod for the political fall-
out that would surely follow. Here the idea is to use public resources to
advance and legitimize the Progressive agenda. But the Progressives have
also begun to use what we might think of as *quasi*-governmental agencies for similar purposes. The role assigned to Institutional Shareholder
Services as a seemingly independent arbiter of shareholder resolutions,
for example, even as it serves a union clientele and is controlled in part
by an activist pension fund, is a case in point.

If, however, we consider the *role* of commissions in the Dye model
rather than merely their form, we can see a similar functionality in
the great number of coalitions created by the Progressive Left. These
coalitions serve to generate and legitimize policy options and to mask
the participation or influence or responsibility of their individual member organizations . . . precisely the same role assigned to commissions in
the power elite system. Their sheer number, as well as the levels of effort and resources devoted to them, are indicators of their perceived
centrality to advancing the Progressive agenda. These coalitions, with
staff, officers, directors, and advisory board members drawn from their
many constituents, also serve as important points for interlocking among
Progressive organizations and institutions. They provide the functional
equivalent of the interlocking directorates of the Power Elite model.

- Policy decision making. The outcome in this, the ultimate arena of influence, is yet to be determined. The OPE is not, at this point in time,
an electoral movement, nor is it (with the exception of organized labor
and a few very recent initiatives) an aggressive, or even a significant,
contributor to political campaigns. As a result, its influence in the White
House and on the Hill is determined more by its ability to marshal public
sympathy and by the sympathies of individual politicians than by any actual political juice. The same cannot be said, however, of the courts and
the regulatory agencies of government. Indeed, the movement has relied
fairly heavily on litigation (for example, against the tobacco companies) and regulation (especially through the Environmental Protection
Agency, where many like-minded individuals occupy decision-making
positions, and the Securities and Exchange Commission) to advance its
agenda. The reinterpretation of SEC Rule 14a-8, which, you will recall,
substantially facilitated the placing of social policy shareholder resolutions in corporate proxy solicitations, is a particularly organic example

of the latter, while *Kasky v. Nike*, the commercial speech case discussed earlier, for a time played a similar role on the judicial side.

We can illustrate the close parallels—and also the important differences—between the Power Elite and the OPE models of influence by a simple graphic comparison. Figure 10.1, which resembles Fig. 1.1 but has been modified to illustrate the peripheral role assigned to pluralist political institutions such as public opinion and elections, summarizes Dye's characterization of the original power-elite structure. Figure 10.2 summarizes the structure of the OPE as we have characterized it here. Clearly, the two models are similar in many ways.

Both are based on the assumption that power resides in agenda control, which, in turn, can be exercised through the careful and strategic application of wealth. Both use many of the same (or equivalent) sets of key actors—wealthy individuals, foundations, university researchers, policy think tanks, media—to do the heavy lifting of developing, legitimizing, and advancing acceptable policy options. Both rely on networked linkages among various actors facilitated by financial support and by various forms of interlocks. And both treat democratic institutions and processes as peripheral intrusions, even as they afford those institutions and processes great symbolic respect.

Yet they are not identical. We have already noted some of the lesser differences between the two models. Let us now turn to two that are more significant.

The first of these is immediately apparent when we compare the two figures themselves. In the power elite model, the institutions of pluralist democracy—political parties, interest groups, elections, and public opinion—are peripheral to actual decision making. They are eyewash. That is the central point of the power elite model—that it is *elitist*—and the central point of disagreement at the core of the elitist-pluralist debate to which we eluded many pages ago. In the OPE model, these traditional pluralist institutions have no role whatsoever, at least to date. As noted, Progressivism is not primarily organized as an electoral movement. In their stead we find an alternative set of institutions—if that remains the correct word—that are summarized by the activists as constituting "participatory democracy." These include activities related to advocacy and protest, which are regarded by the Progressives as pure expressions of the public will. By advocacy and protest, Progressive activists seek to promote and legitimize their policy agenda as inherently public regarding. And yet, when viewed from 30,000 feet, these activities are every bit as peripheral to the real action of the OPE as are more traditional expressions of democratic will to the power elite formulation. So even as both pay lip service to democracy, the two models use very different understandings of the term.

The second difference, as suggested earlier, pertains to the role of the corporation in the two models. In the Power Elite scheme as characterized by Dye, corporations and the wealth they generate serve as the engines that drive the system, as both the prime movers and the principal beneficiaries of the exercise of power. But their role in the OPE is unavoidably more complex. In this

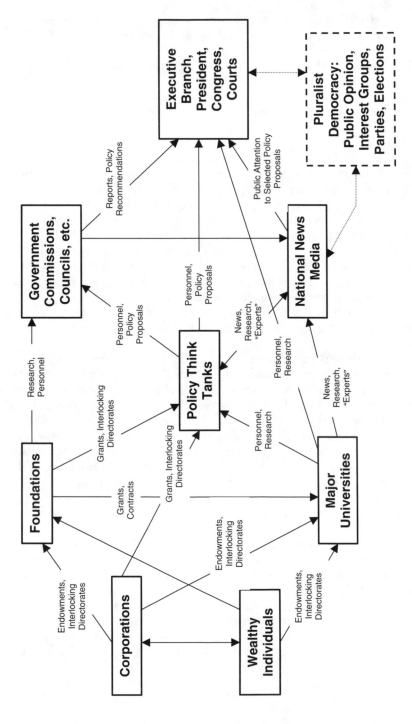

FIG. 10.1. The power elite model modified to incorporate elements of pluralism.

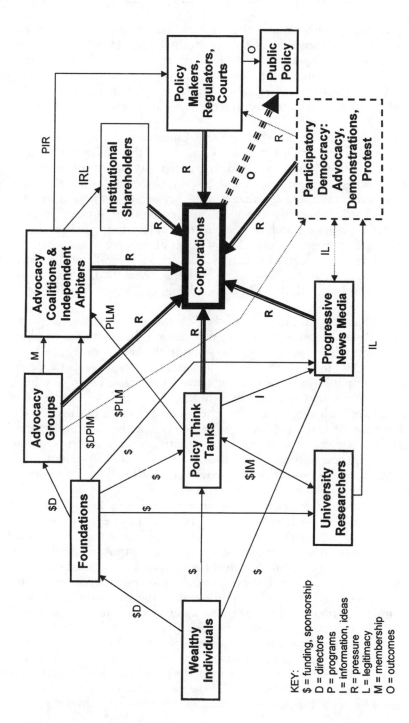

FIG. 10.2.   The out-of-power elite model.

KEY:
$ = funding, sponsorship
D = directors
P = programs
I = information, ideas
R = pressure
L = legitimacy
M = membership
O = outcomes

185

world, corporate wealth remains the source of power, but corporations are no longer the beneficiaries of its exercise. Rather, the objective is to make these institutions more public regarding and less self-interested. Accordingly, much of the history and institution-building we have described in these pages has been directed toward gaining control over corporate, or corporate-generated, resources and redirecting them to new social and political purposes.

This is more than a matter of mere social mechanics; it is, if successful, a fundamental change in the political economy of the United States. For capitalism is built on the assumption that a diversity of self-interested actors, each seeking competitively to serve its own objectives, will collectively produce an economic outcome that benefits society as a whole through a mechanism that is inherently sufficiently self-regulating to protect the public interest. Corporations, and the financial institutions that have developed around them, are the agents and brokers of this collective enterprise when it is practiced on a large scale in a modern industrialized society. By restructuring corporate objectives to weigh the social good more heavily than the private good, the Progressives are thus directly challenging a fundamental tenet of capitalism.

The core ideology and message of the Progressive Left is distinctly and enthusiastically anti-corporate, and its policies and rhetoric alike are thoroughly infused with this perspective. For some on the Left—notably, perhaps, the old pre-1980s Liberals—this may be a matter of strategic or tactical convenience, an opportunity to take advantage of a vulnerable foe in rebuilding one's base, and they may not have thought through, or fully appreciated, the consequences of their success. But for others—the remnants of the Old Left, the SDS generation of the 1960s and 1970s New Left, and some contemporary ideologues—it is much more. Some of these activists are less anti-corporate than they are anti-capitalist, and to the extent that their influence in the Progressive Movement is ascendant, the movement itself will view and pursue such systemic change as a salutary primary outcome.

Reflecting this complexity, the corporation is accorded a dual role—object of vilification and pivotal determinant of success. On the one hand, the corporation is the focal point of most of the rhetorical assault from the Left, rhetoric that seeks to position it as an inherently anti-social institution. And yet, on the other hand, the successful capture of the corporation—at least indirectly through mechanisms such as shareholder resolutions and proxy voting—with its wealth, power, and influence, and the transformation of these resources into a throbbing engine of Progressive social change, is the very essence of the enterprise. It is, after all, the one possible outcome that has the potential to convert the Out-of-Power Elite into the New Power Elite.

At the end of the day, then, where corporations and the wealth they generated were portrayed as being in control of the power elite model, control *of* corporations may be the ultimate test of the OPE. And if that is indeed the case, then we can see Biz-War not only as a *methodology* for achieving power but as the *ideology* toward which that power, once achieved, will be directed. Biz-War is not merely a means to an end, but is itself, like these very words . . .

The End

ENDNOTES

1. George Harris and Daniel Yankelovich, "What good are the rich? Charitable activities of the affluent," *Psychology Today* 23:4 (April 1989), p. 36.
2. From the *Code of Ethics* of the Society of Professional Journalists, found online at http://www.spj.org/ethics_code.asp, July 4, 2003.
3. "Report names power plant polluters," United Press International, July 16, 1998.

Appendix: Annotated Listing of 100 Selected Progressive-Left Organizations

Association of Community Organizations for Reform Now (ACORN)—Formed in 1970 by Wade Rathke, now a union organizer and a director of the Tides Foundation; network of community activists that campaigns on issues such as predatory lending and community investment; has played a central role in the Living Wage movement. *www.acorn.org*

American Federation of Labor–Congress of Industrial Organizations (AFL-CIO)—Umbrella organization of major U.S. unions; adopted corporate campaign approach to building membership under presidency of John Sweeney; through its Center for Working Capital and Office of Investment, plays a key role in the use of proxy voting to influence corporate governance and policies. *www.aflcio.org*

Alliance for Justice—A coalition of environmental, civil rights, women's rights, consumer, and other advocacy organizations established in 1979; maintains programs to educate and support advocacy groups and foundations in efforts to influence public policy. *www.allianceforjustice.org*

American Prospect—Magazine publishes Progressive ideas and viewpoints; established 1990 by Paul Starr, Robert Kuttner, and Robert Reich; received substantial support from the Schumann Foundation; publishes articles that support or lend credence to anti-corporate campaigns. *www.prospect.org*

Amnesty International—Worldwide human rights organization with 1.5 million members in 150 countries; conducts research and engages in advocacy on human rights abuses, freedom of conscience, freedom of expression. *www.amnesty.org*

Applied Research Center—Think tank that supports community organizing; established 1981; issue foci include race, immigration, education, and welfare rights; supported by Tides and other Progressive foundations. *www.arc.org*

Arca Foundation—Established 1952, based on Reynolds Tobacco fortune; emphasizes environmental issues, U.S. foreign policy toward Cuba and Central America, and efforts to curb corporate influence in American politics; in 2001 had net assets of about $75 million and made more than $3 million worth of grants. *www.arcafoundation.org*

Association for Progressive Communications—International network of Progressive organizations across issues such as environment, human rights, and strategic use of communication technologies; established 1990; U.S. affiliate is Institute for Global Communications, which was among its founders; provides online communication and clearinghouse services to advocacy groups. *www.apc.org*

Business for Social Responsibility—Organization created by the Social Venture Network in 1992 to encourage companies to operate in a socially responsible manner with respect to their communities and the environment; provides issue expertise, advisory services, and networking opportunities; funding from Energy, Ford, Joyce, Macarthur, and other Progressive foundations. *www.bsr.org*

CalPERS—The California Public Employees Retirement System is the nation's largest and most influential pension system; governing board is chaired and controlled by representatives of unions; reputation for shareholder and proxy activism in support of the Progressive agenda. *www.calpers.org*

Calvert Group—Largest of the social-responsibility investment management firms; established in 1976 and first socially active in the South Africa divestment movement in 1982; 1986 was first mutual fund to sponsor a social policy shareholder resolution. *www.calvert.org*

Campaign ExxonMobil—Shareholders campaign to change company's policy on global climate change; directors include representatives of CERES, Natural Resources Defense Council, Social Investment Forum, and several religious orders and denominations. *www.campaignexxonmobil.org*

Campaign for America's Future/Institute for America's Future—Advocacy group and think tank founded by 130 SDS alumni, academics, traditional Liberals, union leaders, and others to develop and advance a Progressive agenda; headed by Robert Borosage, former Executive Director of the Institute for Policy Studies. *www.ourfuture.org*

Campaign for Labor Rights—Coalition of union, human rights, and ideological activists focusing on labor issues, primarily in Central America and Asia; includes groups with ties to Latin American Left, anti-globalization movement. *www.campaignforlaborrights.org*

Center for Economic and Policy Research—Think tank established in 1999; research and public education on public policy issues, primarily economic matters such as taxes and trade; Working Assets founder Peter Barnes is a director; funding from Ford, Rockefeller, and C. S. Mott Foundations. *www.cepr.net*

Center for Science in the Public Interest—Research center emphasizing public policies and corporate practices relating to food safety; established 1976; provides data to support campaigns and is frequent participant in Progressive coalitions; early funding from Arca Foundation, support from Public Welfare Foundation, Pew Charitable Trusts, Needmor Fund, others. *www.cspinet.org*

Center on Budget and Policy Priorities—Washington-based think tank emphasizing policies affecting low- and moderate-income people, especially budget and tax-policy matters; established 1981; directors include academics and activists. *www.cbpp.org*

Citizens for Tax Justice—Advocacy group addressing tax-related issues, especially corporate tax avoidance and tax breaks for corporations and wealthy individuals; established 1979; parent of Institute on Taxation and Economic Policy. *www.ctj.org*

Coalition of Environmentally Responsible Economies (CERES)—Coalition of social-responsibility investment firms, major environmental advocacy groups, AFL-CIO; created by Social Investment Forum in 1988; religious organizations and pension funds also participate; promulgated code of environmental conduct for corporations. *www.ceres.org*

Consumer Federation of America—Consumer advocacy group established 1968; coalition of nonprofit organizations; member groups and governance structure are not disclosed; focuses on areas such as financial services, product safety, health care, and food safety. *www.consumerfed.org*

Consumers Union—Consumer group with two parts, one that evaluates products and publishes *Consumer Reports*, and one that engages in advocacy for Progressive causes; total staff of 450; frequent co-participant with Consumer Federation of America in variety of coalitions. *www.consumersunion.org*

Co-op America—Little-known environmental advocacy group established 1982; created subsidiary Social Investment Forum, which in turn created CERES and the Shareholder Action Network; receives support from Tides Foundation. *www.coopamerica.org*

Corporate Campaign, Inc.—Firm established by Ray Rogers, an inventor of the anti-corporate campaign; provides strategic advice and other services to unions and Progressive groups engaged in campaigns; member of Empowering Democracy. *www.corporatecampaign.org*

Corporate Library—Established 1999 by Nell Minow and Robert A. G. Monks, who had jointly founded Institutional Shareholder Services earlier; provides data on corporate governance and ratings of corporate board performance; tracks shareholder resolutions. *www.thecorporatelibrary.org*

CorpWatch—Originally a project of the Transnational Research and Action Center, this online node has provided information and support for anticorporate campaigns against companies such as Nike and Coca Cola; supports campaigns by groups such as Institute for Policy Studies, Rainforest Action Network, National Labor Committee; organized as a project of the Tides Center. *www.corpwatch.org*

Council of Institutional Investors—Established in 1985; members are large union-controlled and public employee pension funds; organization endorses and legitimizes initiatives on corporate governance reform. *www.cii.org*

Data Center—Established by Fred Goff in 1977 as a spin-off from North American Congress on Latin America to provide research on corporations in support of potential campaigns; now provides targeted research and training to social justice advocacy organizations; clients have included ACORN, Alliance for Global Justice, CorpWatch, Project Underground, Ruckus Society, Sierra Club, United for a Fair Economy, many others; support from C. S. Mott Foundation, Open Society Institute, Public Welfare Foundation, others. *www.datacenter.org*

Democratic Socialists of America—The largest socialist organization in the United States and the U.S. affiliate of the Socialist International; formed 1983 from a merger of the Old-Left Democratic Socialist Organizing Committee and the New-Left New American Movement; among prominent Honorary Chairs and Vice Chairs are Barbara Ehrenreich, Dolores Huerta, Gloria Steinem, Cornel West, Steve Max, Harold Meyerson, and Frances Fox Piven. *www.dsausa.org*

Domini Social Investments—Social responsibility investment firm that grew out of the development by Amy Domini and two partners of the Domini Social Equity Fund; publishes the Domini 400 Index, which ranks the financial performance of socially responsible corporations; active in shareholder/proxy campaigns. *www.domini.com*

Earthjustice—A public interest law firm that uses the courts to advance the environmentalist agenda; originally founded (1971) as the Sierra Club Legal Defense Fund; provides legal representation to groups such as Environmental Working Group, Natural Resources Defense Council, and even the AFL-CIO; supported by Tides Foundation, others. *www.earthjustice.org*

Empowering Democracy—Coalition including AFL-CIO, Co-op America, Global Exchange, INFACT, and other Progressive advocacy organizations; purpose is to provide training in techniques of anti-corporate activism; ties to Campaign ExxonMobil; many members supported by Tides and other Progressive foundations. *www.empoweringdemocracy.org*

Environmental Defense—Grassroots environmental organization established in 1967 as the Environmental Defense Fund; focuses on linkage between science and economics as they affect the environment; maintains online "Action Network" that includes Center for Science in the Public Interest, state and local environmental groups. *www.environmentaldefense.org*

Environmental Working Group—Environmental research resource using database and other computer-based methods; research has supported media attack components of campaigns; supported by Pew, Tides, W. Alton Jones and Joyce Foundations, others; Drummond Pike of Tides and David Fenton of Fenton Communications are Directors. *www.ewg.org*

Essential Information—Since 1982 the "mother ship" for organizations with ties to Ralph Nader; publishes books and magazines (including *Multinational Monitor*), sponsors conferences, and provides grants to investigative writers; through Essential Action engages in anti-corporate campaigns; through Multinationals Resource Center provides corporate research information to activists. *www.essentialinformation.org*

Fairness and Accuracy in Reporting—Established in 1986 as a Progressive media watchdog group; supports diversity of content in the media and structural changes in the media industry to decentralize ownership; support from Tides Foundation, others. *www.fair.org*

Federation of American Scientists—Originally founded as the Federation of Atomic Scientists in 1945 to warn of the dangers of nuclear war; now active on a range of issues from arms sales to energy and the environment; expertise in information warfare. *www.fas.org*

Fenton Communications—Public relations firm active in supporting Progressive campaigns; clients have included Environmental Working Group, Greenpeace, Natural Resources Defense Council, Rainforest Action Network, Sierra Club, Council on Economic Priorities, Global Exchange, Open Society Institute, Pew Charitable Trusts, many others (including several labor unions). *www.fenton.com*

50 Years Is Enough—Network of organizations opposed to policies of the World Bank and International Monetary Fund; prominent in anti-globalization movement; steering committee includes Campaign for Labor Rights, Global Exchange, several faith-based organizations. *www.50years.org*

Foundation for National Progress—Established 1975; originally the West Coast affiliate of Institute for Policy Studies; publisher of *Mother Jones* magazine. *www.motherjones.com*

Friends of the Earth—Prominent environmental group founded in 1969; increasing emphasis on corporate accountability, including encouraging shareholder activism, which it coordinates with Social Investment Forum; publishes online handbook for anti-corporate activism; supported by C. S. Mott Foundation, Public Welfare Foundation, Open Society Institute, Working Assets, others. *www.foe.org*

Fund for Constitutional Government—Founded in 1974 to expose corruption in government and other institutions; Alice Tepper Marlin, founder of Council on Economic Priorities, is a director; works through projects including Government Accountability Project (originated by Institute for Policy Studies), Project on Government Oversight, Electronic Privacy Information Center, Investigative Journalism Project, some of which have played roles in various campaigns. *www.epic.org/fcg*

Global Exchange—Founded in 1988 to promote human rights and social justice; initially conceived as travel service providing tours of human rights hot spots to motivate activism; also plays broader advocacy role on sweatshop and anti-globalization issues; was active in supporting Zapatistas; supported by Tides Foundation, others. *www.globalexchange.org*

Greenpeace—International environmental advocacy organization founded in 1971 with an agenda that includes climate change, protecting forests, opposing GM foods and crops, and more; noted for its aggressive tactics; operates in 41 countries. *www.greenpeace.org*

Highlander Research and Education Center—Since 1932 this residential learning center in Tennessee has trained community, labor, civil rights, and other activists, as well as journalists and academics, in facilitating Progressive social change and overcoming oppression; Tides Foundation and AFL-CIO are represented on board of directors. *www.hrec.org*

Human Rights Watch—Established 1978 (as Helsinki Watch) to investigate and expose human rights abuses; awards Hellman/Hammett Grants to writers who have been victims of human rights abuses; supported by Open Society Institute, Rausing Trust, Ford, Rockefeller. *www.hrw.org*

Independent Media Institute—Publisher of AlterNet.org, established 1998 as an online magazine and clearinghouse for news of, and of interest to, the Progressive Movement; Executive Director is former publisher of *Mother Jones*; supported by Tides Foundation. *www.independentmedia.org*

Industrial Areas Foundation—Established in Chicago 1940 by prominent community organizer and early anti-corporate activist Saul Alinsky and others; now operates a network of affiliated community-based organizations; local affiliates are typically coalitions of faith-based organizations focused on housing, tenants' rights, living wage, and employment issues.

INFACT—Established 1977 with a boycott of Nestle for marketing infant formula in the Third World; other campaigns have attacked General Electric, Dow Chemical, Kraft Foods, HCA, and the tobacco industry; support from Tides Foundation, others. *www.infact.org*

Institute for Agriculture and Trade Policy—Founded in 1986, this organization engages in research, monitoring of corporate activity, coalition building, and networking on policies relating to food and agriculture, trade and globalization, multilateral institutions, and the environment; Tides Foundation is a major donor. *www.iatp.org*

Institute for Global Communications—Tides Center project affiliated with the Association for Progressive Communication; established in 1987 to provide computer and other communication services to the Progressive Movement; currently operates PeaceNet, EcoNet, WomensNet, and AntiRacismNet online information services. *www.igc.org*

Institute for Policy Studies—Established in 1963 with solidly Old-Left roots, the oldest and most influential think tank of the Progressive Left; over the years has spawned large number of media, policy, and advocacy organizations; early focal point of anti-corporate strategy development; extensive networking; Harry Belafonte and Barbara Ehrenreich are prominent directors. *www.ips-dc.org*

Institute on Taxation and Economic Policy—Research and education group focusing on taxation and spending policy; founded in 1980; project of Citizens for Tax Justice; supported by a wide range of Progressive foundations (Arca, Public Welfare, Open Society Institute, Stern, etc.) and by Working Assets; among directors are Robert Kuttner and Robert Reich of *The American Prospect* and a representative of the Service Employees International Union. *www.itepnet.org*

Institutional Shareholder Services—Highly influential firm providing proxy-voting advice to many institutional shareholders; increasingly advocates Progressive positions on governance and social policy issues; division advises and votes proxies for union-based pension funds; founded 1985 by shareholder activist Robert A. G. Monks, who later co-founded Corporate Library. *www.issproxy.com*

Interfaith Center for Corporate Responsibility—Founded by the National Council of Churches shortly after publication of the NACLA guide to researching corporate targets; coalition of 275 faith-based organizations, pension funds, and foundations; tracks corporate behavior and advances shareholder resolutions on governance and social policy; members and affiliates include Institutional Shareholder Services, Amnesty International, Nathan Cummings Foundation, and several social responsibility investment firms. *www.iccr.org*

Interhemispheric Resource Center—Founded in 1979; works to ensure that U.S. foreign policy reflects a commitment to Progressive social change; directors include representatives of Boehm Foundation, Institute for Policy Studies, the Maryknolls, Fund for Constitutional Government, and the Needmor Fund; support from Arca, Ford, S. R. Mott, Rockefeller, and Rubin Foundations. *www.irc-online.net*

International Institutional Investors Advisory Group—Coalition of four major public pension and proxy advisory entities (CalPERS and TIAA-CREF from the United States, two from the United Kingdom including part owner of Institutional Shareholder Services); established in 1999 with objective of internationalizing the movement to reform corporate governance through proxy voting.

International Labor Rights Fund—Established in 1986 by a coalition of labor, human rights, and religious groups to protect workers' rights in the global economy; Bishop Jesse De Witt of the United Methodist Church (founding president of the National Interfaith Committee for Worker Justice) is president, John Cavanaugh of Institute for Policy Studies is a vice president; works closely with labor unions in United States and internationally. *www.laborrights.org*

In These Times—Began as a socialist newspaper in 1977; taken over 1978 by the Institute for Policy Studies and now published by the Institute for Public Affairs in Chicago; established Progressive media voice; focus on corporate malfeasance and government wrongdoing and on covering news of the Progressive Movement. *www.inthesetimes.com*

Investor Responsibility Research Center—Founded in 1972 to support shareholder initiatives on social policy issues; Ford, Carnegie, and Rockefeller Foundations provided initial seed money; provides proxy-voting analyses on social policy and governance issues. *www.irrc.org*

Jobs With Justice—Established in 1987 at the initiative of the Communications Workers of America, this umbrella coalition unites labor unions with faith-based activists in local chapters across the country; 50 Years Is Enough and many unions are members; plays an active role in supporting union-based campaigns and in the process served as a principal conduit for exposure of other activists to campaign strategy and tactics. *www.jwj.org*

Media Access Project—A public interest law firm established in 1978 and specializing in telecommunications policy issues; has focused on Fairness Doctrine, media diversity, broadcasters' obligations to the public, media ownership. *www.mediaaccess.org*

Midwest Academy—Founded by former SDS activist Heather Booth as a training school for community activists; curriculum reflects philosophy of Saul Alinsky; publishes *Organizing for Social Change*, a manual for direct action. *www.midwestacademy.com*

Moving Ideas Network—Originally founded as Electronic Policy Network, this online exchange point is an arm of *The American Prospect*; presents news of 130 Progressive research and advocacy organizations; members include ACORN, Annie E. Casey Foundation, Campaign for America's Future, Center for Economic and Policy Research, Citizens for Tax Justice, Interhemispheric Resource Center, Open Society Institute, TomPaine.com, United for a Fair Economy, many others. *www.movingideas.org*

Multinational Monitor—Anti-corporate magazine published by Essential Information; articles focus on individual corporations, but also on corporations as institutions and legal entities; established circa 1980. *www. multinationalmonitor.org*

Nathan Cummings Foundation—Named for the founder of what is now Sara Lee Corporation, on whose fortune the foundation was built; major contributor to Progressive organizations on issues of environment, health, and social justice; among recipients have been Environmental Defense, Sierra Club, Center for Science in the Public Interest, Institute on Taxation and Economic Policy, Government Accountability Project, Jobs with Justice, National Interfaith Committee for Worker Justice, and the Tides Center. *www.nathancummings.net*

National Council of Churches—Established in 1950; 36 Protestant, Anglican, and Orthodox member denominations; has long adopted a Progressive social policy agenda and played a critical early role in creating North American Congress on Latin America and Interfaith Center for Corporate Responsibility. *www.nccusa2.org*

National Interfaith Committee for Worker Justice—Established in 1995 by Kim Bobo of the Midwest Academy to provide a mechanism for involving local faith-based organizations in support of union organizing efforts; Bishop Jesse de Witt of United Methodist Church, founding president, is also president of International Labor Rights Fund. *www.nicwj.org*

National Labor Committee—Labor-based organization founded in 1981 to oppose U.S. interventionist policies in Central America; now addresses trade policies, human rights, and labor conditions in the Western Hemisphere; headed by Charles Kernaghan, whose resume includes "Making Kathie Lee Cry"; corporate targets have included Disney, GAP, Liz Claiborne. *www.nlcnet.org*

National Lawyers Guild—Association of lawyers, law students, and legal workers that seeks to replace a system of law based on property rights with one based on human rights; founded in 1937, component of Old Left; active in civil rights movement and Vietnam War resistance movement. *www.nlg.org*

National Network of Grantmakers—A network of foundations that fund Progressive programs advancing social and economic justice; helps to organize philanthropy that will produce an equitable distribution of wealth and power; members include foundations such as Arca, C. S Mott, Joyce, Nathan Cummings, Needmor, Open Society Institute, Public Welfare, Rubin, Stern, Threshold, and Tides, as well as Working Assets. *www.nng.org*

Natural Resources Defense Council—Established in 1970; one of the most prominent grassroots environmental advocacy groups; member of numerous Progressive coalitions, including CERES; initiatives combine legal and scientific dimensions; support from Tides, Public Welfare Foundation, others. *www.nrdc.org*

North American Congress on Latin America—Established in 1966 by National Council of Churches, SDS, others; published first how-to manual for campaigns against corporations in 1970; through conferences and publications stimulates activism on North–South issues in the Americas. *www.nacla.org*

Open Society Institute—International organization with substantial U.S. component that channels the philanthropic efforts and advances the policy agenda of financier George Soros; in the United States this agenda is closely aligned with the Progressive Movement and this group is emerging as a significant funding source for advocacy. *www.soros.org*

Oxfam—International human rights organization with a U.S. affiliate; also active on issues of global poverty; sample issues of interest have been trade policies and the costs of medicine in the Third World; participation in coalitions is central to defined mission. *www.oxfam.org*

Pesticide Action Network—Environmental group that works to replace pesticide use with ecologically sound and socially just alternatives; opposes multinational corporations that use pesticides; funded by Public Welfare Foundation, Tides Foundation, and Rockefeller Brothers Fund, among others, and by U.S. EPA. *www.panna.org*

Pew Charitable Trusts—Founded on the Sun Oil fortune, this foundation has adopted a Progressive agenda in recent years; operates several programs through fiscal sponsors, notably Tides Foundation; grant commitments have ranged from $160 million to $250 million over the last decade. Programs on environment, civic engagement among others. *www.pewtrusts.org*

Progressive Asset Management—Oakland-based social responsibility brokerage firm that maintains a network of likeminded brokers elsewhere; established in 1987; makes investment recommendations based on social screens (e.g., environmental performance, workplace policies) of companies. Active on social-policy shareholder resolutions. *www.progressive-asset.com*

Project Underground—An environmental group that links human rights and indigenous peoples' rights to the effects of extraction-based industries such as petroleum and mining; established 1996; supported by Tides Foundation,

Public Welfare Foundation; Institute for Policy Studies represented on board of directors. *www.moles.org*

Public Citizen—Founded as a consumer advocacy group by Ralph Nader in 1971; has challenged automobile, airline industries among others; active on environmental, telecommunications, product safety issues; frequent participant in Progressive coalitions (e.g., led coalition against free trade treaties); operates own foundation to support work. *www.publiccitizen.org*

Public Welfare Foundation—Established in 1948; grant programs include criminal justice, environment, health, community and economic development, human rights, others; recent recipients have included Data Center, Friends of the Earth, Natural Resources Defense Council, Project Underground, 50 Years Is Enough, Alliance for Justice, Coalition for Justice in the Maquiladoras, Economic Policy Institute, National Interfaith Committee for Worker Justice, others. *www.publicwelfare.org*

Rainforest Action Network—Environmental advocacy group established in 1985; best known for high-profile direct action; emphasis on preserving old-growth forest (e.g., Boise Cascade), though this can be interpreted broadly (e.g., Ford, because its vehicles damage the rainforest); supported by Tides Foundation among others. *www.ran.org*

Responsible Wealth—Project of United for a Fair Economy established in 1997; purpose is to recruit and train individual or family Progressive philanthropists; encourages members to engage in shareholder actions. *www.responsiblewealth.org*

Rubin (Samuel) Foundation—Based on the fortune generated by Faberge Perfumes; one of the earliest funders of the contemporary Left; mission is to advance peace, justice, and the equitable reallocation of the wrold's resources; provided seed funding for Institute for Policy Studies; other grantees include Interhemispheric Resource Center, International Labor Rights Fund, Tides Center (to support what is now CorpWatch), and United for a Fair Economy. *www.samuelrubinfoundation.org*

Ruckus Society—Founded 1995 by alumni of Greenpeace and the Rainforest Action Network to provide advanced training in direct action to experienced activists; conducts camps and other training sessions with instruction on scaling buildings and towers, banner construction, and the like; Anita Roddick of The Body Shop serves as a director. *www.ruckus.org*

Schumann (Florence and John) Foundation—Established 1961 and recently headed by journalist Bill Moyers; focus on effective government, environment, and media; through the Florence Fund, operates TomPaine.com public affairs web site.

Shareholder Action Network—Project of the Social Investment Forum; purpose is to organize individuals to invest in companies that adopt Progressive social policies; provides clearinghouse for shareholder action information; encourages members to introduce and support shareholder resolutions and to support campaigns like that at ExxonMobil (initiated by its parent organization); ties to CERES, Co-op America, Interfaith Center for Corporate Responsibility, ACORN, Amnesty International, Rainforest Action Network, many others. *www.shareholderaction.org*

Sierra Club—Prominent and influential grassroots environmental research and advocacy group with 700,000 members, founded in 1892; in 1990s changed style of action from mainstream politics to Progressive activism; important as a legitimizing member of numerous coalitions; major support from a range of Progressive foundations. *www.sierraclub.org*

Social Accountability International—Founded in 1969 as the Council on Economic Priorities to identify investment opportunities in companies not profiting from the Vietnam War and the armaments trade; evolved first into research service providing critical reports on companies, then, with issuance of SA8000 code of conduct, into compliance monitoring organization; changed to present name in 2001; international labor federations represented on board. *www.sa-intl.org*

Social Investment Forum—Organization created by Co-op America; essentially the trade association of the social-responsibility investment sector; more than 500 investment professionals and institutions (e.g., Calvert, Domini) are members; initiated Shareholder Action Network to advocate specific issues and resolutions; created CERES to provide links with labor and environmental movement. *www.socialinvest.org*

Social Venture Network—Founded in 1987 to develop and advance new models of socially responsible business; maintains information clearinghouse and conducts forums and networking opportunities; members are companies like Ben & Jerry's, Domini Social Investments; Joshua Mailman and Drummond Pike are both emeritus and ex officio members of the board; Co-op America also represented on board; spawned Business for Social Responsibility. *www.svn.org*

Stern Family Fund—Based on the fortune of Sears heir Philip Stern, who provided early funding for the Institute for Policy Studies; supports policy-oriented government and corporate accountability projects; awards seed grants to support new public interest organizations and projects, strategic opportunity grants to assist organizations at critical times; board of four includes two members tied to Public Citizen. *www.sternfund.org*

Threshold Foundation—Home of the Doughnuts; established by Joshua Mailman and others in 1982 as the prototypical mechanism for pooling modest wealth from numerous families into a meaningful sum to support Progressive action; later affiliated with Tides Foundation, which now operates it; grants to wide range of advocacy groups such as Institute for Policy

Studies, International Labor Rights Fund, Government Accountability Project, United for a Fair Economy, Friends of the Earth, CorpWatch, Ruckus Society. *www.doughnuts.net*

Tides Foundation and Tides Center—Though not the biggest, the most wide-ranging and strategic of the Progressive foundations; Center provides fiscal sponsorship for numerous projects, including CorpWatch; Foundation supports literally hundreds of advocacy and other Progressive groups, as well as a range of more traditional charitable causes; Foundation board includes Wade Rathke, founder of ACORN and now a Vice President of Service Employees International Union. *www.tides.org*

Transnational Institute—Founded in 1973 as the international program of the Institute for Policy Studies, with which it remains affiliated; based in Amsterdam; major support from Samuel Rubin Foundation; like IPS, a think tank for Progressive scholars and researchers. *www.tni.org*

Trillium Asset Management—Social investment firm established in 1982; manages investment portfolios for individuals and institutions; files average of 12 shareholder resolutions annually on issues such as animal rights, environment, employment, human rights, and sexual orientation; awards 5% of pre-tax profits in grants to organizations. *www.trilliuminvest.com*

United for a Fair Economy—Established to raise awareness that "concentrated wealth and power undermine the economy, corrupt democracy, deepen the racial divide, and tear communities apart"; intended to provide movement support through educational campaigns that incorporate some ideas developed by the Highlander Center, which has a spot on its board along with several activists; example is Responsible Wealth, a UFE project. *www.ufenet.org*

United Students Against Sweatshops—Group was created in conjunction with the Nike campaign and the effort to shift manufacturers from the Apparel Industry Partnership to the Workers Rights Consortium, which was more directly controlled by unions and Progressive advocacy organizations; USAS has several seats on the WRC board of directors; close ties to unions; members on 200 campuses. *www.people.fas.harvard.edu/~fragola/usas*

US Public Interest Research Group—Another organization with Ralph Nader roots, this is the national advocacy operation of the state-level PIRGs; established 1983; active primarily on environmental and consumer issues, which it defines broadly and which includes a corporate reform agenda. Support from Tides and others. *www.uspirg.org*

Working Assets—Established in 1985 to pursue a business model in which a portion of the cash flow from utility and service businesses such as long distance telephone service, credit cards, and electricity generation would be channeled to Progressive advocacy groups and other nonprofits; close ties to Tides Foundation, which helps allocate the contributions among groups nominated by subscribers. *www.workingassets.com*

World Resources Institute—Environmental policy think tank whose board brings together directors from diverse agencies such as the Natural Resources Defense Council, Dow Chemical, and Edelman Worldwide (public relations firm); most notable in context for publishing *Leverage for the Environment: A Guide to the Private Financial Services Industry,* that set out a highly sophisticated strategy for pressuring pension funds, mutual fund companies, banks, and others to advance Progressive positions on the environment. *www.wri.org*

Index